THE TWERP

OTHER BOOKS BY DALE MCMILLAN

A Long Way from Clearwater
At Home in Clearwater Volume I
At Home in Clearwater Volume II

THE TWERP

DALE MCMILLAN

LIBRARY OF CONGRESS CONTROL NUMBER:		2010909099
ISBN:	HARDCOVER	978-1-4535-2505-0
	SOFTCOVER	978-1-4535-2504-3
	EBOOK	978-1-4535-2506-7

This book was printed in the United States of America.

To order additional copies of this book, contact:
Xlibris Corporation
1-888-795-4274
www.Xlibris.com
Orders@Xlibris.com
82936

Dedicated To My Wife, Janell—my encourager—my friend. This is the story of her Fredricks throughout her thirty year teaching and Library career mixed in with some that I have known.

Acknowledgements

With much gratitude, I thank those who have encouraged me during the writing of this book. The list is long and I will miss some, but several stand out. My wife has been often at my side. My brother Paul McMillan has read the book several times and can almost quote it line for line. His enthusiasm has been a great encouragement.

Thanks to my son Paul McMillan, and son-in-law Graeme Seibel for their editorial help. Many thanks to Laura Rice and Pete Saddler who reviewed the book and offered encouragement. Pete suggested the name, which fit perfectly. Thanks to all of you who made this a fun project.

Prologue

The town of Pressley is one of those quaint little Central Texas towns where those who are "The Salt of the Earth" live, work, and raise their families. Many live for Friday Night High School Football. However, things are not always the way they appear on the surface. Two powerful families, through intermarriage and political connections ruled with an iron hand. Using coercion and corrupt politics, they stymied growth and economic development, which kept the good people of the town in an almost subservient status. They also set wages, manipulated building permits and denied loans to certain individuals.

Then, along came Fredrick.

Chapter 1

From any angle, Fredrick Lane Overall was an ugly baby—wrinkled, ears too big for the attached body, nose way out of proportion for his thin face, and scrunched up eyes. When his daddy first saw him through the nursery window, he exclaimed, "Lord! He can't be mine!"

His father carried that view all through Fredrick's childhood. He was a sickly child, prone to severe cases of bronchitis and even pneumonia as a toddler. For his dad, a high school football coach, part time farmer, and an ex starting lineman for the Texas A&M Aggies,—Fredrick was a *bitter disappointment* . . . Two older brothers, James and Mark, who were strapping young men and following their father's footsteps, did not help endear Fredrick to his dad. He was one of those surprise babies—born ten years after his closest brother and fourteen years after his older sister, the oldest child. Fredrick or Freddy as he was nicknamed was a child that only a mother could love, and love him she did. She was thirty-nine when he was born and his dad forty. When his mother began to show her pregnancy, an assistant coach once asked Luther Overall if they were expecting. He answered, "Not really, but it's gonna happen anyhow."

Velma, Freddy's sister, came to visit her mother and see her new brother in the hospital. She found him in the room cradled in her mother's arms. She took one look at him and commented, "Well, that's one we didn't need."

Unfortunately, all of the family except Freddy's mother, Mary, shared this view. She saw in her young Freddy a vibrant but sensitive individual with a deep probing look, which at a very early age seemed to absorb, analyze, and quantify. Fredrick always strived to understand even the minutest detail. Mary Overall observed all of this in her son and in her heart senses, *"This is a very special and gifted little boy."* In later years, his mother's intuition will prove to be accurate, but there were many dark rivers to cross before this dream becomes reality . . .

Freddy kept a knot on his head as soon as he started walking, which did not occur until he was almost two. His mother decided the knot was a result of the fact that he was very near sighted. Mary carted him off to an ophthalmologist, who outfitted him with thick glasses.

Freddy's daddy, Luther, always explained that his poor vision was because his mother ran over an opossum when she was carrying him. She stopped the car and went back to see if she could help the poor thing only to find that car had gone across the animal causing its eyes to bug out. Luther surmised that the shock from seeing that caused Freddy to have bad eyesight. All of the family accepted this as fact except Freddy and his mother.

At age three, with thick oversized glasses, his unruly red hair with a cow lick already developing, Freddy Overall was, it seemed, a disaster in the making. An obvious tendency to freckle, big ears, along with his frail stature, did not enhance his looks. However, Freddy Overall had one ace in the hole; he was extremely bright. He was counting at three, and after he got his glasses, he taught himself to read at four. His mother Mary, realized early on that Freddy was intellectually gifted, but she simply hid these things in her heart thinking, *"It will surface in due time."* She diligently tried in every possible way to help him develop his mind. All three of Mary's older children adored and worshiped their father but viewed Mom more or less as their servant. Velma the oldest was very athletic and her dad worked with her constantly to develop her skills. Mark and James were also chips off the old block and were constantly involved in sports. The reality of the matter was that Mary had never had a child of her own until Freddy came along.

The family lived on the old Overall family home farm left to Luther by his parents. Luther was an only child and spoiled growing up. His father was a Texas A&M graduate at a time when a college education was a rarity. He had amassed a good size, 1300 acre farm about three miles from the Central Texas town of Pressley, the county seat of Walcik County. After graduating from college, Arthur Overall, Luther's father, came to Pressley as a high School Mathematics teacher. He eventually became Pressley's School Superintendent. He retired from that position when Luther graduated from college so he could become Pressley's High School football coach. The school district at that time did not allow two people to work for the district if one was in administration, or if they had a relative who served on the school board.

Luther was a successful coach. His second year at Pressley he won the state 3A championship. That secured his position and endeared him to the town, which was already "football crazy."

Velma was a star basketball and volleyball player, and she would have been an excellent linebacker if she had only been a boy. At ten and twelve Mark and James were each showing all of the potential of following in their father's footsteps. "Frail Freddy", as he became known in the family, was a bitter disappointment and embarrassment.

Freddy's preschool days were grand. He and his mother roamed the farm learning about and enjoying the beauties of nature. He could identify all species of trees on the farm before starting school and he knew every species of bird. He and his mother spent many hours picnicking and fishing in the meandering creek that ran across the Overall farm. Freddy Overall loved the farm and everything about it.

Two tenant families lived on and actually did all of the farming. One black family had a little girl the same age as Freddy. Her name was Eva May. Eva's mother kept house for Mary Overall and always brought her when she came to work. Eva and Freddy became best friends, and Rosalie, her mother, and Mary also became close friends. They often sat and drank coffee together. These were facts that Mary did not share with Luther since he was extremely prejudiced. Eva Mae was only half-black. Both her parents were half-white and half-black, but to the town of Pressley they were black. The other tenant family was Latin American and spoke very little English. Freddy learned to speak Spanish before he started to school from the children of this family. By his first year in school, he spoke fluent Spanish.

Mary Overall was a very attractive woman. She had been one of the "popular kids" growing up in Pressley—drum major in the band, and voted most popular girl in the senior class. All through high school she also had the distinct honor of being Luther Overall's, the star football player's, girlfriend. She was a petite girl, but with her German ancestry her figure was *tremendously* endowed making her the envy of all the girls and the object of lust for all the teenage boys, however since Luther had a lock on her she was off limits to anyone else. It was a fore drawn conclusion that Luther would kick your butt if you got near her. Mary had never questioned her love for Luther until Freddy came along, but now trouble was brewing in the Overall camp.

Luther was somewhat overbearing and did not consider Mary an intellectual, which was a gross mistake. About all Luther typically knew was football. He lived and breathed football. Mary on the other side of the coin, taught first grade for several years before Freddy was born and she was an avid reader. She had much more interest in the farming operation and really ran that business. Under her tutelage, it had shown a good profit for several years. Luther took no interest in family finances—Mary handled all of the family business, did the taxes, paid the bills and managed investments. Since Luther's lack of interest in Freddy was a "burr under her saddle," she had started quietly investing a good portion of the farm income into an account in her and Freddy's name. Mary simply chalked that up to her pay for managing the farm. Mary and Luther's problems came to a head when Freddy started to school. The night before the first day of school, Freddy told his mother that he wanted to go by himself. Luther overheard this and stated emphatically, "No, your mother is going with you."

Mary asked, "Why? Why do I need to go with him if he wishes to go alone?"

Luther was stunned, "Well, you need to tell them about him," pointing toward Freddy.

Mary's "dander" was up. "Tell them what, Luther?"

"Well, he's—you know."

"No I don't know. Do you want to explain it to me?"

"Well, he's you know—different."

"Different? How? Luther?"

"Well, he is just different. You need to explain it to them."

"You are going to have to explain it to me, Luther."

"Damit, Mary, you know what I mean."

"No I don't know what you mean. Do you mean he probably won't play football? Is that what you mean?"

"Well yeah, that's part of it."

"Has it ever occurred to you there are things other than football?"

"Well yeah, but it just ain't normal. You know what I mean, Mary."

Freddy was listening to this argument and he became somewhat amused. He had already figured out that his mother was more intelligent than his father was and he was enjoying watching him sweat. It was no surprise to him that his father thought him a big disappointment as a son. Mary, over the tender years, instilled in him that he was unique and that his day would come. She had quietly cautioned that his unusual mind would cause problems with jealously and for him not to flaunt his abilities—that people would resent this.

Luther looked around and saw his young son looking at him and he was embarrassed that he had made the comments in front of him. He turned to Mary and exploded, "Aw Hell, let him go by himself if he wants to," and stomped out.

Mary and Freddy just smiled at one another. Mary walked over and hugged him but no words were exchanged between them. The next morning, Freddy got up, dressed himself, ate a good breakfast, and Mary drove him to school. She dropped him off at the front door where he hugged his mother and went running into the building with his new book bag. Since he had already been to school and seen his room, he made his way down the hall, walked in and sat down at his assigned seat. The room was full of parents with their first graders clinging to their hands begging moms and dads not to leave them. Freddy opened his book bag, pulled out a new Robert Newton Peck "Soup" book and started to read. Several parents smiled at the strange looking little boy sitting at his desk pretending to read and pointed that out to the teacher. She too, thought this amusing.

*   *   *

At the end of the first two weeks of school, Mary got a call to set up an appointment with the principal and Freddy's teacher to discuss a problem. Mary asked, "What kind of problem?"

Mr Griffin, the principal was non-committal and he would only divulge that they thought Freddy might need some special help. Mary was astute enough to ask the principal to have Luther present for the conference. "Just call him and have him set the time. I will be there," she instructed. The conference was set for 2:30 the next afternoon.

Luther arrived at 2 pm and he and the principal agreed the move Freddy to a special education class before Mary arrived. Mary entered the building at 2:25 and Luther was ready to leave. When she walked in, Luther informed her, "Everything is worked out."

Mary looked stunned and replied, "I thought the conference was at 2:30?"

"Well it was, but I have to get back to practice."

"Well, it is not worked out, Luther because I have not been involved and I will be involved in this decision. Do you understand me?"

Luther started to puff up, but the bite in Mary's voice stunned him, so he backed off.

The young teacher walked into the office about this time and knew immediately that a battle was shaping up. She was a first year teacher and terrified. Principal Griffin, seeing that things were about to get out of hand admonished, "Perhaps we should all sit down and discuss the issues more calmly."

Mary sharply responded, caustically, "I think that is a very good idea . . ."

Mr. Griffin, began, "Mrs. Overall, we want to provide what is best for this child here at our school. Based on Miss Green's observations, we feel it best, and Mr. Overall concurs with our conclusions, that Fredrick should be placed in a 'Special Needs Class'."

"And just what has brought you to this astute observation, Mr. Griffin. May I see the test results?"

"Well, we haven't done any actual testing at this point Mrs. Overall. Miss Green has simply been observing his behavior."

"Has he been disruptive?"

"Oh no, he is very well behaved," Miss Green responded.

"Well, just what have you observed?"

"Well, he doesn't participate with the other children at anything we do. He doesn't play with them at recess and he doesn't seem interested in anything that going on in the classroom. It is just like he is in a world all his own. He just sits with a book in his hand, pretending to read."

"Has it ever occurred to you that he just might be bored to tears, Miss Green?"

"Well, no?"

"Where is Freddy?"

"He is in the room with a teacher's aide."

"Get him in here."

No one in the room liked the tone of Mary's voice. Mr. Griffin stepped to the door and asked his secretary to have Freddy brought to the conference room. The conference room was very quiet with no one speaking while they were waiting for Freddy to make his appearance. Shortly thereafter, he walked in. He did not speak but simply smiled at his mom. He did not even acknowledge that his father was in the room.

Mary asked, "Mr. Griffin, do you have a third or fourth grade book handy?"

He stepped to his office and came back with a fourth grade social studies book. He started to hand it to Mary and she simply said, "Open it to a page, any page, and hand it to Fredrick."

When Freddy took the book, Mary instructed, "Read for us Fredrick."

Freddy looked at the book and frowned. He then began, "A hab—habi—habitat is an area oc—occu—occupied by many sp—spece—species. A home is a place within a habitat where a par—partic—particular animal species can protect itself and its young from the weather and pre—pred—predators. Homes include nests built by birds and wasps, and burrows dug by moles." He looked at his mother and said, "I'm sorry Mama. Some of those words I have never seen before."

She replied, "That is okay, Son. You did fine."

Everyone in the room except Mary was sitting on the edge of their seat with their mouth open in awe. Mary then went to the blackboard and wrote three double-digit math problems on the board. She asked Freddy to solve them.

He added all three correctly.

Mary turned to Mr. Griffin and remarked, "You do have a problem—I am sure you can fix it. Call me when you have a solution. Come, Freddy."

With that, Freddy and Mary left. Mary was afraid she would say something she would regret. It was the right move because she was about ready to lash out at the stupidity of the teacher for not recognizing her son's ability. Mr. Griffin was a reasonably good principal and he recognized this fact immediately and did not try to stop her. Luther knew he was in deep trouble at home and dreaded having to face Mary.

Mr. Griffin looked at Miss Green and remarked, "I do not believe we have read this one correctly."

He then turned to Luther and asked, "Mr. Overall, why didn't you tell me this child could read?"

Luther stammered, "Well, I, I didn't know he could read like that!"

Mr. Griffin sat reflectively for a moment and then remarked, "I am going to have to think this one through. I do not believe I have ever seen a first grader that bright in all my years of teaching. We are not equipped for this. There is no mechanism in the system for this."

With that, the meeting broke up.

*   *   *

Luther went to football practice with his team, but he was very distracted and harsh with his players. Even the assistant coaches gave him a wide berth. At the end of practice, he told the team to do 40 laps around the football field, but the assistant cut it to 5. Luther had already gone by the time they finished five laps. He went straight home to face Mary. She was packing her clothes when he arrived. She already had Freddy's packed.

Rushing in, Luther gasped, "Mary, what are you doing?"

"I'm packing."

"Why, Mary? Why?"

"Luther, for years you have been overbearing and abusive. I could accept that when it was simply me involved, but the fact that you would agree to allow Freddy to be placed in a special education class with no testing is more than I can accept."

"But Mary, I didn't know that he was that smart. I hadn't heard him read."

"Did it ever occur to you that I am a first grade teacher?—that I have some knowledge of children's abilities? Yet, you went right ahead and tentatively agreed to Special Education without even considering my opinion."

"Now Mary, you know that I am sometimes impulsive. I did not mean to bypass you in this decision. I am sorry that I was so inconsiderate."

"This was more than inconsiderate Luther. This was total dis-regard."

"Mary please don't leave me. I promise to do better. Please give us time to sort this out. I'd be lost without you. Please don't leave me. I'll sleep on the couch till we have time to work through this."

Mary was very angry. Luther was getting a glimpse of a Mary that he did not know existed. She stood glaring at him for a few moments and saw him for what he was—a simple, spoiled child who never grew up. He was always the center of attention, even in his adult life as a successful coach. His whole world was centered on himself. His children's successes in sports were simply an extension of his personality, and they were "following in his footsteps".

"Luther, I am not sure I even want to try. I am afraid we have reached the point of no return."

The shock and reality of the moment hit Luther full in the face and he gushed, "Oh no, Mary. I love you—I always have, ever since we were kids."

"I'm not sure you even know the meaning of the word. You have never respected me as an equal, I have always been submissive to your every whim. Even to your taking away from me what I could never get back when I was fourteen."

Luther's defenses went on high alert. "Now look Mary. You wanted that as much as I did. You are not being fair."

Mary had struggled with this question most of her adult life, and now the issue had come boiling to the surface all jumbled up with Luther's lack of interest in their young son. She saw in him the self-centeredness that had overshadowed their marriage from the beginning. As she stood looking at him, her emotions were a mixture of love, hate, pity and contempt.

"Perhaps so, Luther. I have asked myself that many times. I sometimes wonder. I was so young, so immature. Too young for that to happen. I've tried to blame my parents for not being more protective. They pushed me at you, you know." She smiled slightly and continued, "They thought you were a good catch. They trusted you, Luther. You were Luther Overall, the superintendent's son. One of the leading young people in the church—the football star. I was just a nobody—my Daddy was a poor dirt farmer and my mother clerked in the dry goods store so we could eat. I wish I could blame someone, but I still have to look at myself in the mirror."

"But Mary, that was a long time ago. I always intended to marry you from our first date."

"Oh, and that makes it all OK? Well, what about Marcy, and Artie and Allyson, and goodness knows how many others."

Luther turned ashen. He had never dreamed that Mary was aware of his indiscretions.

The two stood looking at one another for a long moment. They both realized their marriage was in deep trouble—the issues were many and the hurts deep. Luther had the good sense to back off. He looked at Mary and realized just how deeply he loved her and the thought of losing her tied him in knots.

He quietly begged, "Mary, please don't leave like this. I will do whatever it takes to save our marriage. Please at least give me a chance to try to change."

Mary stood looking at him for a very long and pregnant moment before she answered. She loved her home, the farm, the friendship she shared with Rosalie and she realized that she also had three other children who would feel the effects of her decision to leave. Reluctantly she replied, "Luther, I will stay for now, but don't touch me. I do not think I could stand that right now. At this moment I feel like I hate you and I have to sort this out."

"Luther was crying. Mary wanted to run to him and comfort him but she kept her emotions in check. Luther finally got his composure back and answered, "That is fair enough. I will give you some space, but Mary, please remember one thing; I love you—I always have and I always will. I give you my word I will do whatever necessary to restore our marriage. I will go to counseling or whatever it takes."

Luther turned and left. He was weeping and crushed. Velma was standing in the hall listening to the exchange between her mother and father. She had always been a "daddy's girl" and really had no consideration for her mother. Velma was a strong athletic girl and a student at Texas A&M on a basketball scholarship. She was about to leave to go back to school for the new semester.

Velma walked up behind her mother in the bedroom where her mother was replacing her clothes in the dresser. She screamed, "Why do you have to be such a bitch, upsetting Daddy over that idiot kid???"

Mary swung around and with one sweeping motion slapped Velma across the face with a blow that sent her back against the wall, crashing into a lamp causing it to fall and explode into a million pieces. Standing over Velma, Mary said, "You are about to find out just what a bitch your mother can be young lady," She turned and continued unpacking.

Velma got up whimpering. She threw her clothes in her car and left to return to school, carrying a hefty welt from Mary's handprint across her face. A new Mary Overall had just been born . . .

Chapter 2

Mr. Griffin decided he needed to have Freddy tested. He called the counselor and suggested that she line up an IQ test with a professional. Feeling that he was going to need all of the backing he could get, he suggested that the district pay a professional counselor to administer the test. The school counselor, Sarah Adams, arranged for a psychologist at Baylor University in Waco to test Freddy. Mary agreed to take him, but Mr. Griffin insisted that the school counselor should go along, so early one morning Mary, Freddy, and Mrs. Adams headed for Waco. Mary drove and she and Mrs. Adams sat in the front seat with Freddy and his stack of books in the back seat.

They were driving along with Mrs. Adams and Mary chatting amicably while Freddy was reading in the back seat. All at once, Freddy looked up from his book and asked, "Mama, what is incest?"

Mary swerved and almost lost control of the car. She gasped, "Freddy, what are you reading? Where did you get that book?"

"It was on daddy's desk."

"Give me that book!"

He handed the book to Mary. She rolled the window down, glanced at the book, and then tossed it out the window.

Freddy commented, "Mama, you are going to jail for littering."

"It will be worth it, Son."

Freddy commented under his breath but loud enough for both women to hear, "I guess I'm not supposed to know that word. Oh well, I've got a dictionary."

Mrs. Adams glanced at Mary. Her knuckles were white where she was gripping the steering wheel."

Shortly thereafter, they heard faintly from the back seat, "Sexual int—inter—intercourse between persons so closely related that they are forbidden by law to marry. Oh my, I better not ask about that."

Again, Mrs. Adams glanced at Mary. She could hardly stifle a laugh, but she felt sorry for Mary and tried hard to think of something to say to comfort her. About all she could come up with was, "Mrs. Overall, you have my sympathy."

Mary just shook her head and murmured, "Oh Lord, what am I going to do?"

This response was more of a groan from an anguished heart and a sincere cry out to God. Mary secretly felt that she was being punished for her actions as a teenager and the guilt she felt was overwhelming. They rode in silence for the next ten miles and then Fredrick asked, "Mama, you are not mad at me are you?"

"Why, no dear! Why would I be mad at you?"

"Because I took daddy's book."

"No, I'm mad at daddy for having the book in the first place."

There was silence for a few more miles and then Mary and Mrs. Adams heard a faint, "I wonder if she knows about his magazines?"

Mary screamed, "What magazines?"

Fredrick, in a fake German accent' quoted Shultz from Hogan's Heros, "I know nuthin."

Mrs. Adams could take it no more. She burst into laughter. "Mary, he is jerking your chain."

Mary finally saw the humor in the situation and burst into laughter.

"Young man, I am going to box your ears. You are toying with me."

Mrs. Adams began to get a glimpse of this young man's personality and realized for the first time just how bright he really was. From that day forward, she was on his team.

*   *   *

The Baylor psychology professor told some of his colleagues that an elementary counselor from Pressley was bringing a student that they think is a boy genius for testing. He laughing commented, "All of these little schools think they have a genius on their hands." He had agreed to meet with Mrs. Adams at 9 AM. He was almost an hour late.

Professor Clark came in with a rather condescending attitude and his first comment was, "So, we have a genius on our hands do we?"

This flashed Mary and she responded, "Whatever that means."

This raised his eyebrows. "What makes you think this child is so smart?"

Mrs. Adams was intimidated but Mary was not. "Why don't you just test him and decide for yourself?"

This flashed him and he responded, "Well, that is what we intend to do."

Mary did not back down, "Well good! That is why we are here. I presume you will go about this in a professional manner and not with preconceived notions."

This really flashed him. "Of course we will be professional."

Freddy was just sitting with his arms crossed while this exchange occurred, looking at the professor through his thick glasses, and studying him. Professor Clark looked at Freddy and Freddy looked directly into his eyes and smiled as if to say, "You don't scare me one bit."

One thing Mary had done was to instill into her young son a quiet confidence that he was able to reason through any circumstance. His look was a direct challenge to the professor. Mrs. Adams simply sat in awe of this child.

Professor Clark tested, and he retested and he tested again. Freddy met each challenge. Except for motor skills, he was off the chart, and his motor skills were not that far out of line. His mechanical aptitude was amazing. His verbal and reasoning skills were far out of range.

With hat in hand, Professor Clark came in and admitted, "We cannot measure this child's abilities. He is off the charts."

Mrs. Adams asked, "What can we do? We do not know how to place him."

The dumbfounded professor simply shook his head and replied, "I don't know what to tell you."

Mary spoke up and commented, "Well I do."

"And just what is that Mrs. Overall?"

"Turn him loose and let him learn."

*   *   *

Mary and Sarah were somewhat giddy on the return trip to Presley. Freddy appeared to be uninterested in the events of the day. He seldom changed expression, which gave the outward appearance of his being dense. The two women's conversation was mostly about what to do with Freddy. Sarah wanted to take his test scores and place him as high up as possible. Mary on the other hand did not think this was a good idea.

She responded to that suggestion, "Mrs. Adams. Freddy must learn some social skills, and he has the right to be a child, at least for a little while.

Sarah agreed but added, "But how in the world does a teacher keep him challenged?"

Mary's answer was chilling. "They won't. It will be too much trouble. I taught school for several years before Freddy was born. I know that many teachers are burned out, some are having trouble at home that consumes their energies, others simply don't care, some are just plain lazy and the ones who really care and try soon become overloaded. Some are working on advanced degrees to move up and that takes up their time. Young ones are courting or looking for someone, thinking the world is passing them by if they don't have a mate in their life. It is an imperfect world, Sarah. Smart kids learn, the less fortunate pick up enough to get by, the really bright, generally go unchallenged. A child is fortunate if they go through twelve years of school and they have one or two teachers who challenge them to be the best that they can be. It is going to be a rocky road for Freddy, but I have watched him for six years now and mark my word, he is the one who will do the challenging and it is going to cause all kinds of problems. No one is going to want him in their class."

Sarah was quiet for several moments as a plan formulated in her mind. A third grade teacher, Mrs. Butler, was about six months pregnant. Her doctor had already told her she needed to go on bed rest for the remainder of her pregnancy. Sarah Adams had a plan.

*   *   *

Mrs. Adams was in Mr. Griffin's office early the next morning. She was excited and hyper. Summarizing results of the intelligence test, she ended her summary with, "Mr. Griffin, we have no idea how smart this child is."

She related the incident in the car over the word incest, describing how Mary took the book and threw it out the window. Mr. Griffin burst into laughter over this. She then related how Freddy had pretended to read the definition to himself, but loud enough so they would hear. She ended her dissertation with, "Not only is he bright—he has a sense of humor and a devious streak in him that is going to make our life interesting. I do not mean he is bad, he is just fun loving."

Mr. Griffin sat reflectively for a few moments and then commented, "Mrs. Adams, I do not know a lot about gifted children and I must lean on you and your judgment. Is this not unusual for a very bright child to have this kind of sense of humor?"

Sarah thought for a moment before she answered, "I can't really answer that question. I think it depends somewhat on the child's environment. Mary Overall has done a marvelous job with him. Mr. Griffin, she is very bright herself."

Mr. Griffin responded, "I do not know Mrs. Overall very well. She taught in another district for a while. I know Coach Overall. My son is on his football team. He certainly doesn't have much of a sense of humor."

Mrs. Adams only smiled and did not comment. She gathered from Mr. Griffin's tone of voice that he was not one of Coach Overall's fans.

"So, where do we go from here, Mrs. Adams? Just what do we do with Fredrick?"

"Mr. Griffin, I want Fredrick to have every opportunity to learn and develop his wonderful mind. Mrs. Overall does not think we should advance him too far ahead of his age group since she thinks that it is most important that he learn social skills. Keeping him challenged is going to be a tremendously difficult task for any teacher.

"I suggest that we put him in the third grade and place him in Mrs. Butler's Class."

Mr. Griffin almost came unglued. "But Mrs. Adams, Mrs. Butler is six months pregnant! She has already told me that the Dr. wants her to go on bed rest. I am going to have to bring in a substitute."

Mrs. Adams smiled, "I know."

The two educators sat across the desk from one another, with Mr. Griffin perplexed and Mrs. Adams smiling.

"Oh, you have a suggestion?"

"Yes."

"Who?"

"Mrs. Overall."

"I'm not sure Luther will agree."

"I do not think he is in any position to disagree."

A smile broke out on Mr. Griffin's face. A silver lining to a very dark cloud on his horizon was just peeping over the edges. "You two have discussed this?"

"No way."

"Do you think she will take the job?"

"I would stake my reputation on it."

Mr. Griffin arose from behind his desk and remarked, "Let's go see if Mrs. Butler is here yet and break the news to her that she is getting a new student."

The two walked down the hall to Mrs. Butler's room. She was there and already looking miserable. After greetings, Mr. Griffin began, "Mrs. Butler, we came to tell you that you are getting a new student."

Looking from Mr. Griffin and then at Mrs. Adams, Mrs. Butler didn't even have to ask. "Fredrick Overall. You are placing Fredrick Overall in my class. Why? Mr. Griffin I have already told you I am going to be forced to go home and go on bed rest. Why? Why would you place him in a class that is going to have a long term substitute?"

"We have a plan."

"Who?"

"Well, I haven't talked to her yet, so I can't say just yet."

"Oh. Well she had better get here soon. My feet were as big as watermelons when I got home yesterday."

"Maybe tomorrow."

Kids were beginning to come in, so Mr. Griffin and Mrs. Adams left. On the way back to the office, Mr. Griffin asked Mrs. Adams to retrieve Fredrick from his classroom and take him to Mrs. Butler's class. He went directly to his office and called Mary.

Mary answered, "Hello, Overall residence."

"Mrs. Overall, this is Arnold Griffin. We are planning to place Fredrick in the third grade with your approval of course."

"Yes, Mr. Griffin, Mrs. Adams and I discussed that yesterday."

"We are placing him in Mrs. Butler's class."

"Mrs. Butler's class! Isn't she going on maternity leave?"

"Yes?"

"Why are you placing him in a class that is going to have a long term substitute?"

Arnold Griffin could almost feel the heat in Mary's response.

"Mainly because I am hoping that I can persuade you to take that job."

There was a brief silence on the other end of the phone.

"Mrs. Overall, are you still there?"

"I am. When do I start?"

"Can you come in today?"

"Yes, I will dress and be there within the hour."

"Do you need to discuss this with Luther?"

"No!"

"Are you sure?"

"Yes!"

"OK, I will see you in a little while. I do not wish to cause problems."

"That is my worry."

"Thank you, I will be expecting you soon."

Arnold Griffin felt chilled by this interview. He feared he had just made a powerful enemy. Luther had been head Football coach for almost 20 years. In reality, he had been head football, basketball and baseball coach. The superintendent was slated to retire within the next few years and since Luther was going to summer school and working on his Master's in Administrative Education, it was a fore-drawn conclusion that he was slated to take over as school superintendent. This was more or less a reward by the school district in appreciation for his success as a coach. It gave the advantage of gaining the elevated salary for the last few years before retirement. That would sweeten one's pension. Mr. Griffin toyed with the idea of trying to forewarn Luther, but decided it might be easier to get forgiveness rather than permission, if Luther was opposed to this move.

*   *   *

Mrs. Adams went to the first grade classroom and informed Miss Green that Fredrick was transferring to Mrs. Butler's classroom. Miss Green wondered about this move, but did not ask. She was most happy to have him out of her class.

Fredrick and Mrs. Adams then went to Mrs. Butler's classroom. When they walked in, Fredrick looked around, focusing briefly on every person in the room. One smarty kid asked, "What's that little *twerp* doing in here?

Fredrick promptly put his book bag down, whipped out his dictionary and looked up "twerp".

He read aloud, "Twerp: a silly, insig—insignif—insignificant, or con—contem—contemptible person."

Closing his dictionary, he looked up and smiled at the kid who had made the comment. The rest of the class burst into laughter.

Mrs. Butler could not stifle a laugh. The smarty kid felt chastised. Mrs. Adams smiled at Mrs. Butler and commented, "Don't worry. He can match wits with the best of them."

Poor Mrs. Butler did not know where to start with Fredrick. She simply asked him to take a couple of math work sheets and work on them. She explained the instructions on the sheets and asked, "Fredrick, can you multiply and divide?"

"Yes, ma'am."

"Do you know how to do word problems?"

Fredrick looked confused and answered, "Depends on the words."

She asked, "Well, a problem like, a man has five pigs and he takes away two. How many pigs does he have left?"

"Depends on where he takes them. If he just takes them to another pen, he still has five. If he takes them to town and sells then he has three."

"That was not a good example. If a man has five apples and he eats two. How many does he have left?"

"He has five. Three in his hand and two in his stomach."

Mrs. Butler was getting a headache. Fredrick had not cracked a smile and he was just staring at her stomach and she surmised, correctly, that he was thinking that she had been eating way too many apples.

Thus began Fredrick's introduction to third grade, but this was about to change. Mama was on her way in to take over and Fredrick was going to be challenged.

*   *   *

Mary Overall came to school and spent the day with Mrs. Butler. Mary had not taught for the past seven years, so she asked another third grade teacher to mentor her. She readily agreed. A warm friendship between these two teachers began. Mrs. Butler was a good and conscientious teacher. She had very detailed lesson plans for an entire month. Mary was most grateful. At the end of the day, Mrs. Butler passed the baton and the class belonged to Mary.

*   *   *

Before the day was over, Luther learned through Pressley gossip that his wife accepted the teaching job. He was livid that she had not consulted him before taking the job, but then the cold hard facts hit him full in the face. Mary would now have her own income and that made him an un-necessary factor in their marriage. James Butler, Mrs. Butler's husband was a middle school physical education coach. He had told Luther that his wife was going to become a stay at home mom after their baby was born. Although Mary was only a long-term substitute, Luther knew, from his conversation with James, this was her inroad back into the teaching profession and that she would be under contract the next year. By the end of the day and time for football practice, he was a 'bowl of jello'. Luther did indeed love Mary—just slightly less than he loved himself and he had great fear that she was slipping away from him. He felt powerless to stop the slow erosion of their relationship and now a huge gaping gully seemed to have formed right down the middle. In his mind, he blamed that "idiot kid" as he always thought of Fredrick.

Luther knew he must lay aside his problems at home and concentrate on the upcoming game. The district championship more than likely hinged on Friday night's game. His closest friend, his assistant coach who knew some of the issues troubling Luther, came into his office and closed the door. As a good friend, he stood 'toe to toe' with Luther and admonished, "Luther, I know you have problems at home, but you also have a responsibility to the kids you are coaching. You are going to have to put your problems behind you and concentrate on this game."

The two friends stood staring into each other's eyes for a pregnant moment. Luther knew Bill Hinds was a good friend who was expressing a concern not only for the team, but also for him. "Bill, I know you are right, but I am afraid I am losing Mary. I don't want that. We were happy B. F."

"B. F.?"

"Yeah, 'Before Fredrick'!"

Bill smiled, but he felt empathy for his friend. He could plainly see a gargantuan problem that needed fixing, but probably would not be. A father with a son that he did not understand and a wife who understood the son and not the father. Bill shook his head. "Lew, you have a unique son. He is a nerd and you know about nerds don't you?"

"Naw! What about 'em?"

"Well, they get laughed at all through school. While us 'jocks' are beating our brains out on the football field, they are studying and making good grades. They go off to college and excel, get the best jobs, make the most money, marry the prettiest women and have the smartest kids, and we wind up working for them."

Luther stood for a moment letting Bill's words sink in. His mind immediately went to his own high school days and Morris Elliott. Morris had been one of those nerdy kids with thick horn rimmed glasses that everyone laughed at. He was now Dr. Morris Elliott, back in Pressley, head of the Hospital board and president of the school board. He and Bill stood smiling for a couple of moments. Both men knew who Bill's model nerd was.

"Maybe you are right Bill. I'm just not that far sighted though. I tend to let my problems bury me. Let's go play football."

The two friends walked out of the office and went to the practice field arriving with the team ready to work out, and work out they did. Luther felt a huge load lifted from his shoulders and he was back to being Coach again.

This was the second year that Pressley had black students on their football team. None made the starting lineup the first year, but this year Luther had two that he could not keep down. He was still very prejudiced, but during scrimmage that afternoon a black tight end went out for a pass, caught it, and with one spin and a stiff arm he blew through Luther's starting defense like they were stick men and ran 75 yards. Luther looked at Bill Dunn and remarked, "Lands sake Bill—the faster that boy runs, the whiter he gets."

This began the quelling of Luther's prejudice against black players because that same young man performed similar feats four times during the Friday night game chalking up 122 yards rushing. He not only scored his own yardage, but he also freed up the defense allowing other runners to score as well. The game turned out to be a rout of their toughest opponent.

*   *   *

Freddy spent a quiet day his first day in third grade. He completed all of the important work sheets the class had finished the first two weeks of school. Most kids in the class were obviously resentful that a first grader was promoted to their class, but mostly Freddy was little more than a curiosity to them. Recess and PE were difficult because he obviously did not fit in. Other than the usual jeers and catcall one would expect in Freddy's situation, he had a reasonable normal day. Mary apprised Fredrick what would happen and cautioned him to give the appearance that it did not bother him. She and her son talked often about a "poker" face and he understood the term well and mastered it to a fine art. This 'bugged' the kids, because it was as though Fredrick knew something that they did not. It seemed to give him the upper hand. Teachers were more upset than the students were and they resented Mary. People do not like others who are different. They do not understand them so this translates into an intense dislike.

*   *   *

Luther came home from practice, went in and congratulated Mary on her new job. To say that Mary was shocked would be a gross under-statement. She was expecting a serious confrontation and was again prepared to leave if it came to that. Life normalized in the Overall household. Mary learned that she simply was not geared to not share her husband's bed and she moved out of Velma's room and back into her own bedroom with Luther.

*   *   *

Third grade work was no problem for Fredrick, and Mary struggled to keep him from getting bored. She kept a set of Compton's Encyclopedias in her classroom that she brought from home. When Fredrick was not working on schoolwork, she would assign him various topics to study. He set a high standard for the rest of the class, which did not endear him to other students. "He just ain't normal" was heard often around the school. These conversations would have been devastating to most kids, but for Fredrick it became a badge of honor. By the end of Freddy's first year of school, he had read the entire set of encyclopedias. He knew where Madagascar was, what species of animals were indigenous to Siberia and lots of useful stuff.

Pressley's schools integrated two years prior to Fredrick and Eva Mae's arrival, and Freddy's friendship with Eva was a scandal and the source of much teasing for both. Being the astute observer of human nature that she was, Mary forewarned both Eva and Freddy of what to expect. One would not have known that Eva Mae was part black unless you knew her parents. Since Eva was half-black, she was considered black by most people in Pressley; often called a "high yeller nigger" by the white trash that enjoyed having someone to look down on.

*   *   *

At the end of the first six weeks of school, Mary was in the workroom one afternoon using the copy machine. The PE coach stuck his head in the door and announced, "Mrs. Overall, Fredrick is going to fail PE this six weeks."

Mary turned and looked at him and calmly asked, "Mr. Dunn, just why is Fredrick going to fail PE? Is he un-cooperative?"

"Oh no, he tries hard. He simply cannot do anything the other students can do."

"Well, what if he was blind and couldn't do what the other students can do. Would you fail him if he tried?"

"Why, no. That's different."

"Explain to me how it's different."

"Well, it's just different."

"Mr. Dunn, you had better have a darn good reason to fail Fredrick unless you can prove that he has not done the best he could have done."

Ed Dunn left in a huff. Mary just shook her head and commented under her breath but loud enough for everyone in the room to hear, "Coaches, they are not worth a dam for anything off the ball field—well maybe one thing, but we'll not go there."

The workroom exploded into laughter. Pressley is a small town and Mary's comments reached Luther before school was out for the day. He was strutting like a peacock.

Freddy did not fail Physical Education.

*   *   *

One evening at dinner, Luther and Mark were discussing football, which was a common occurrence. Luther was really trying to reach Fredrick and be the kind of father that he needed, but all Luther knew was sports. He had no concept of why one would not be interested in sports.

He turned to Fredrick and commented, "Freddy, we have got to find a sport for you. Maybe baseball? Come baseball season, why don't you give little league a try?"

Fredrick gave his dad one of those looks that so very much unsettled and irritated him before answering, "Well, I am somewhat interested in the game. It is interesting to me that a person stands up at a marker with a stick in his hand and tries to hit a round object tossed in his direction with the stick. Now, should he make contact with the air born object when he swings the stick, then another person out in the field tries to retrieve that object and toss it to another person at another marker before the person who hit the object can run and reach that marker. Now the interesting thing to me is that the mind of the person in the field has to process the information from the sound of the stick striking the object and observe the trajectory the object assumes when struck. He or she then has to take that information and predict what location he is to assume in order to retrieve the struck object and throw it in a timely manner. Don't you find that interesting?"

Of course, Fredrick was toying with his dad, but Luther never knew it. He just sat deflated and beaten. On other occasions, Luther tried to interest Fredrick in shooting baskets. Luther erected a basketball goal over the driveway just as soon as Velma showed an interest in basketball and it was still in place attached to the garage. It became readily apparent to Luther that it did not make Freddy one particle of difference if the ball came near the goal or not. After several attempts at finding a sport for Freddy, Luther simply threw up his hands in surrender and gave up.

What Freddy lacked in sports interest, was filled with an interest in mechanical devices. He mowed with the riding lawn mower from the time he was five years old. He "barked" a few trees at first, but he finally got the hang of driving the mower. He tinkered with something mechanical constantly. He kept his bike torn apart more than it was together. Anything that stopped working on the Overall farm was analyzed by Freddy before it was laid aside.

*   *   *

When he was nine years old, Freddy entered sixth grade. Mary already had him working complex algebra and introduced him to geometry by this time. Since he read incessantly, he was miles ahead of his class in history and social studies as well. Mary bought him a Comodore 64 computer when they first came out and he could write fairly complex programs to make calculations, sort and alphabetize by the time he entered Junior High School. He turned in a complete math assignment that he had completed with the computer, allowing it to do all of his calculations for him. His math teacher sat down and cried because she did not know how to grade his work. She finally told him he would just have to do it over and do it by hand. He stood looking intently at her for a very long moment, took his paper, sat down, copied the answers on a sheet of notebook paper, and handed them back to her. She looked at the answers and then back at him.

She asked, "But how did you arrive at the answer?"

Fredrick answered, "I programmed my computer to solve the problems for me."

"Well that won't do. You are going to have to solve them yourself."

Freddy came close to being impertinent. With his hand on his chin, he commented under his breath, "Now I am smart enough to tell my computer how to make these calculations, but that is not good enough. She wants me to calculate them myself. Why didn't I think of that? What a concept!"

Freddy sat down and in about five minutes, he worked 10 algebra problems showing all of his work. Miss Smyth knocked off ten points for the work being late and gave him a grade of 90. He just smiled at her, turned and walked out of the room. Miss Smyth felt very small and ashamed.

*   *   *

About this time, Freddy went into a growth spurt and it seemed that almost overnight he shot up in height. In fact, Mary and Luther became alarmed because suddenly it seemed that his spine was crooked. Standing behind him with his clothes off one evening as he was getting out of the shower, Luther noticed that he had a sharp curve to the right side in his spine. Luther called Mary and had her take a look. She panicked. "He has to see a doctor tomorrow!" By the time Dr. Elliot's office opened the next morning, Mary was on the phone.

Dr. Elliot took one look and ordered an X-ray. He told Mary, "I have a very good friend at Baylor Medical School in Dallas that I want to look at these X-rays. He is an Orthopedic Surgeon and a good one. I really do not know what to make of this. He seems very healthy, so I would not get too worried just yet.

Two days later, Luther and Mary were back in Dr. Elliot's office for the results. Dr. Elliot came in smiling. "Luther and Mary, I have very good news. Dr. Hamner says that Fredrick is just going through a growth spurt and that one side is outgrowing the other. He says not to worry—this is something he sees all the time with kids that are slow bloomers as far as stature is concerned. Obviously, little Freddy's brain has outgrown everything else. He is a very bright young man."

Luther exploded, Hell! He can't even grow like a normal kid. He has to do it his own way."

This outburst flashed Mary, but Dr. Elliot was amused. Over the next several weeks, Dr. Elliot's predictions came true. Freddy's spine straightened out and he continued to grow. Almost overnight he was no longer that scrawny, out of proportioned bungling little boy, but rapidly catching up with his peers. He was still freckled and had his unruly red hair, but his looks were improving almost daily.

Sixth grade was difficult socially for Freddy. He learned just how cruel kids could be and that some would crush another just for a laugh from their friends. Freddy, being the odd ball was generally the object of their attacks. Teachers were not much help because they thought he should not be in junior high at age nine. Mary insisted that this was the place for him. Luther did not agree, but in his wisdom had decided to stay out of the fray. The middle school principal knew how Luther felt and he too raised objection, but Mary won out. Socially, Mary was also an outcast.

Mary and Freddy became more and more reclusive. They stopped attending ball games after Mark and James graduated from High School, and Freddy attended no school functions. Both of the older boys were playing football at Texas A&M and in ROTC. Luther had season tickets, but Mary never went with him. All three of the older siblings had been very mean spirited toward Fredrick and there was a rift between them and their mother. Mary's only friend was Rosalie, and Eva Mae was Freddy's. This too became a scandal in Pressley and drove a serious wedge between the Overalls and the town. Luther's greatest concern was that it was going to wreck his chances at becoming superintendent. The Turner and Gipson families both fed the animosity toward the Overalls. These two families hated Luther because of his popularity as a successful coach.

During their growing up years, all three of the older Overall kids were unhappy that they lived three miles out of town on the farm. They had no interest in anything that related to farm life and constantly badgered their parents to move into town. Luther would have agreed, but Mary would not give in. She loved the farm. Freddy on the other hand shared his mother's love for the peace and tranquility that the farm afforded. He knew every animal den; the location of every bird nest and what locations on the creek were the best fishing spots. He could name all of the wild flowers that grew so prolifically in the spring. There was only one thing that he disliked about the farm and that was hog killing time. On those days, he would shut himself up in his room and not come out. He loved everything else, especially the tractors and farm machinery. When he was barely old enough to reach the clutch, he badgered Eva Mae's daddy to let him plow.

Duke went to Mary and got her permission before he would allow Freddy on the tractor and Mary reluctantly agreed with one stipulation. He was never to use the rear-mounted Bush Hog Mower. A young man Mary knew apparently went to sleep while mowing a large field. The tractor drifted out of the field, and a lone pine tree caught the tractor between the wheel and the frame. The impact threw the young man off of the tractor and the mower ran over him. The tractor continued to travel around and around the tree until it ran out of gas. Each round it made around the tree, the mower passed over the young man. This incident traumatized Mary and she insisted that none of her kids could use a tractor with a rear-mounted mower.

Freddy's favorite tractor was an old Farmall Super M with a two-bottom breaking plows. He would plow all day long with that tractor. What most did not realize was that plowing was Freddy's thinking time. On the long rows with the hum of the tractor engine, Freddy had plenty of time to allow his mind to work on any kind of problem he might dream up. He rehashed books he had read, he tried to figure out math problems, he would recall history and try to come up with scenarios' of how history might have been changed if victories had been reversed.

One of Freddy's favorite subjects for meditation was the Bible. The disconnect between the God of the Old Testament and the God of the New Testament troubled him, but he was afraid to discuss this with anyone, so he just brooded over it. Once in Sunday school class, Freddy raised the issue with a teacher who became so upset and rattled that Freddy decided this was off limits, however it was a cauldron just waiting to boil over.

That pot erupted during the summer between sixth and seventh grade when Freddy was 10 years old. The Baptist Church was having a one-week summer revival, complete with a visiting evangelist, and his choice song leader. Various people in the community signed a roster to provide meals for the evangelist, song leader and the church's pastor. Mary signed up for lunch on Thursday. Mark and James were both home for the summer—they were present and Luther came home for the meal. Rosalie helped Mary cook the meal and it was superb. The meal conversation went along fine with everyone (except Fredrick) joining in, cracking jokes, and telling stories until just before dessert time. The visiting evangelist was watching Fredrick all during the meal He remembered him as the young man who always brought a book and read all during his sermon.

Just before Mary arose to bring out the dessert plates, the evangelist, Brother Lyles turned to Fredrick and asked, "Young man do you know Jesus?"

The pastor almost fell off his chair ~he had forgotten to warn this young man about Fredrick. He wanted to intervene before things got out of hand but was powerless to do so. Fredrick did not turn and look directly at Brother Lyles He simply looked at him out of the corner of his eyes and did not speak for a very long, extended moment. Luther, Mary, Mark, and James froze and became tongue-tied.

When Fredrick did finally answer he asked, "Do you mean Jesus Garcia who comes to help us pick corn every year? Everybody knows Jesus. He's a neat guy. Always has lots of funny stories; of course some of them I can't tell here."

Brother Lyles stammered, "Oh—Oh no, son! I mean the real Jesus. The one that died for our sins."

Again, Fredrick was quiet for a long moment. Luther, Mary and the boys were anxiously waiting Fredrick's response. Finally, he answered, "Well, I can't say that I have ever seen him. I have studied a lot about him during my short life. I suppose I would have to say that I am simply trying to apply Phillipians 2: 12 in my approach to him."

Stunned, Brother Lyles asked, "Phillipians 2:12?" He could not remember the passage—his mind simply went blank.

"Yep."

"What does it say, son?"

"*Therefore, my dear friends, as you have always obeyed—not only in my presence, but now much more in my absence—continue to work out your salvation with fear and trembling.*

"You see, I am still working on my belief with fear and trembling. I have read the Bible through a couple of times and I'm not real sure that God told those Israelites to do all of those bad things that they did. You know, I just learned that the Canaanites were probably the people who gave us the alphabet. Now why would God tell the Israelites to go in and kill all of them after he had revealed the alphabet to those people? I believe that those old guys thought that up themselves and blamed it on God. In addition, why did God tolerate that? Well, all the people he had back then were just a half a step away from being barbarians and it was just the best he could do at the time. It is just like a coach. If he doesn't have a great quarterback, he uses the best he has." Under his breath, he added, "Even if he is black."

This was a shot at his daddy. Eve Mae's brother was the promising quarterback for the upcoming football season.

"What do you think?" Brother Lyles.

Brother Lyles simply sat for a moment with his mouth open. He finally answered, "We—well son, If the Bible says it, I believe it. I don't question God's word."

Fredrick turned and stared at him for an uncomfortable moment for everyone around the table, and then he commented, "Well, I believe that what is in the Bible is what God wanted us to know. I'm just not convinced that we always understand it the way he wanted us to.

"You know Brother Lyles, it is hard for a child to understand why God would give us the Ten Commandments and then turn around and tell folks to break them, but you know, I am just a kid and I don't know much."

The poor minister was duly chastened and had no response. That ended the discussion. Mary saw a break in the conversation and quickly brought out the pie and cake, and Luther was able to shift the conversation away from Fredrick. He was omitted from conversation for the rest of the meal and he excused himself and went to his room.

Just after Freddy left the table Brother Lyles commented, "You have a very unusual son there. I have noticed that he brings a book to Church and reads while I am preaching."

Mark spoke up, "Oh, don't worry. He is hearing you, and can probably repeat every word you said and quote everything he read out of the book at the same time. He ain't normal."

Mark's statement was 'food for thought' for all the guests and essentially ended the dinner conversation. Brother Lyles, the pastor and the music leader, Mr. Jones, left shortly after lunch to everyone's relief—host and guests alike.

After the guests left, Mary went to Fredrick's room and out of curiosity, Luther followed. Fredrick was sitting with his feet propped up on his desk reading. Mary looked at him, "Jesus Garcia?—Fredrick, that wasn't nice."

Fredrick put down his book and looked at his mom and dad with that far away look that was always so unsettling to everyone in conversation with him, and replied, "It wasn't nice for him to ask me a very personal question in front of a room full of people. He did that because he thinks I have not been listening to him. If he had an issue with that, he should have addressed it to me in private rather than try to embarrass me in front of my family. Do you agree?"

Mary looked at her son. She knew he was not mean spirited but generally very compassionate. She also knew he had chastened a guest in their home, which she did not like, but for the life of her, she could not feel remorse for this action. Gently she replied, "Yes, Fredrick. I agree."

Mary and Luther turned and left Freddy's room. Luther looked at Mary, smiled and remarked, "I hope I have sense enough not to try to match wits with that kid. He would tear me up."

Mary thought, "Maybe, just maybe there is hope for Fredrick and his dad."

*   *   *

Fredrick progressed through Junior high, a very rocky road for him, but one that he was able to navigate by sheer will and determination. Junior high kids are tough on everyone who does not conform to their view of the norm and Fredrick did not even approach the norm. He was teased, badgered and bullied. His only salvation was that the "jocks" knew they would be facing coach Overall when they left junior high and entered high school. He had a reputation of being 'bad'. Because of 'Coach's' reputation and the reputations of Velma, James, and Mark who were all star athletes, one 'wise acre' once referred to Freddy as 'The mutant'. The name stuck and from that day forward, that became Freddy's name with all of the kids. This was most hurtful for Freddy and tore at his self-esteem more than anything he had experienced. He was aware of his Daddy's statement when he first saw him, "Lord he can't be mine." Velma, James, and Mark all thought this was hilarious and mentioned it often. Mary had a constant battle to keep him encouraged and fighting off depression.

*   *   *

A crisis arose in eighth grade. Freddy rode the bus home from school each day. The same bus picked up the elementary students. Eva Mae rode this bus also, and she and Freddy always sat together. They had been doing this for some time without notice, but suddenly one day, all of the kids seemed to pick up on the fact that Eva and Freddy liked one another and the jeering began. Freddy tried to protest against the name-calling but he was shouted down. He and Eva always got off the bus at the same location, in front of the Overall home. They both exited the bus crying; the first time anyone had ever seen Freddy cry. Eva ran home and Freddy went into his house, straight to his room and shut the door. About forty-five minutes later Mary came in and started looking for Freddy. He was normally outside tinkering with something, and there was generally a trail of dishes left from afternoon snacks, but not today. She went to his room and found him lying across the bed staring at the wall.

"What's wrong, Son?"

"Nothing."

"Freddy, you are talking to your mother. Don't lie to me."

Freddy sat up. Mary could tell he had been crying and this alarmed her. Freddy did not cry. At least no one ever saw him cry.

He gushed, "I hate them. I hate them all. I would like to shoot them all."

"Freddy! Goodness sakes! Don't talk like that. You know you don't mean that."

"Yes I do!"

Mary sat down beside him on the bed. "What happened, Son?"

For the next thirty minutes, Freddy poured out an anguished heart that had been building all year. He related how much the 'mutant' name hurt. His greatest pain was the fact that Eva had been hurt by the jeers and name calling."

Mary did not take his pain lightly, and she felt powerless to offer any real help. With a stroke of genius, she told him she would be back in a couple of minutes. Mary went to the phone and called Dr. Elliot's office. She explained to the nurse that she had a crisis situation on her hands and asked if she could possibly speak with Dr. Elliot. Shortly thereafter Dr. Elliot came on the phone, "Mary, this is Dr. Elliot."

"Oh thank Goodness. Dr. Elliot, is there any possible way you could see Freddy for a few moments. He has had a devastating experience on the bus today and is an emotional basket case. If anyone could get through to him right now, I believe it is you. I know you are not a psychiatrist, but I believe you could help him."

"Mary, bring him in and come to the back door of the clinic. Just tap on the door. I will be waiting for you."

Mary went back to Freddy's room and said, "Come with me. We are going to see Dr. Elliot."

"Why? I'm not sick."

"Because I think Dr. Elliot will understand more than anyone else. You see, he was an unusual young man also when he was growing up. I think you need to talk to him."

Reluctantly, he got up and followed his mother to the car. She stopped briefly at the kitchen desk and left Luther a note explaining that they would be home later and that she would pick up Kentucky Fried Chicken on the way home. Neither mother nor son spoke on the way into town. Mary did not know what to say. Freddy was in no mood to talk.

Dr. Elliot was waiting and opened the door immediately when Mary knocked.

Smiling he said, "Come in."

They went into Dr. Elliot's private office.

Mary asked before they were all seated, "Freddy, would you like to talk to Dr, Elliot alone, or do you want me to be present?"

"Well, since you are the one that wanted me to talk to him, maybe you should be present."

Dr. Elliot sensed anger in Freddy's voice.

He turned to Mary. "Perhaps you should begin by telling me what this is all about."

Mary turned to Freddy, "Do you want to fill Dr. Elliot in on what happened?"

"Well, what happened was that all of those idiots on the bus started calling Eva and I names because we were sitting together." Looking at Dr. Elliot he explained, "Eva and I are friends. She lives behind us. We have been friends all our life."

Dr. Elliot asked, "Eva is Duke and Rosalie's daughter?"

"Yes Sir."

Dr. Elliot did not just jump right in and start counseling, he thought for a long moment and then asked Freddy, "Tell me Fredrick, what did you feel while this teasing or ridicule or whatever one wants to call it—what thoughts were running through your mind?"

Freddy did not respond immediately, but sat pondering the question. "That is difficult to explain. I guess if I were to choose a single word to describe my feelings it would be *inadequate* . . . I felt inadequate to respond. Inadequate to defend Eva. Inadequate to defend myself. I don't like to feel inadequate to defend myself. I also wished at the time that I had a machine gun to mow them all down and that scares me. It scares me that I could hate that intensely!"

Now it was Dr. Elliot's turn to ponder. Mary was a 'bowl of jello'—shaking like a leaf inside.

Finally Dr, Elliot smiled at Freddy and replied, "In all my years of practicing medicine and dealing with people, I do not think I have ever heard anyone express their true feeling better than you have just done. Fredrick, I doubt that you really hated the kids who were calling you names. I suspect that if it had just been you and Eva had not been involved, it would have gone off your back like water off a duck. However, when those we care about are hurt, that creates a new dimension for that hurt. It amplifies and intensifies it. Am I correct?"

"Yes. You are correct. I hurt for Eva. Being part black must be hard enough in a white man's society. She is a good person. I might marry her one of these days."

Mary's heart was in her throat.

Dr. Adams glanced at Mary. She was pale as a sheet and he feared that she might faint, but he had to concentrate on Freddy.

"Well, I think you have a few years left before you make that decision and I am sure that when the time comes you will make the right choice, but back to the issue at hand, how do you plan to handle the problem?"

Freddy did not answer immediately but sat in introspection. "I don't know. I really don't know how to handle the problem. I can't run away from it. I am still thinking about it."

Mary had not said anything but she jumped in. "Well, I am going to give the bus driver a piece of my mind for not stopping this abuse."

Freddy's eyebrows went up as he glanced at his mother. Dr. Elliot caught this look. He knew immediately that Freddy did not approve.

"What do you think of that idea, Fredrick?" Dr Elliot asked.

"I don't like it. It will just cause more problems."

There was a long and extended pause in the conversation. Dr. Elliot did not know exactly where he was heading, but he tossed the ball back to Freddy and asked, "Well Freddy, I can see that your mind has been working. Have you come up with any ideas?"

Freddy sat reflectively before he answered. Mary had seen this intensive look before and she knew the wheels were turning.

"Well, I might just give them something to talk about."

Mary turned cold all over. She did not know what to expect, but she figured it was not good. She gushed, "Freddy, you watch your step."

Dr. Elliot smiled. He had accomplished what he sat out to do, and that was to bring Freddy out of his depression. His manner had changed as they sat talking about the issues. He had confidence that Freddy would not be violent, but figured that everyone involved was in for a big surprise.

Mary brought up the fact that the nickname 'Mutant' was disturbing to Freddy.

Dr. Elliot thought about that for a few moments and then shocked everyone with the statement, "Well Fredrick, you know they just may be right. You do have a very unusual mind. Maybe you have mutated into one of those very unusual people. However, remember one thing, along with a great mind, comes great responsibility. You are responsible not only for yourself, but also for those of lesser minds. Sometimes that is the larger of the problems you face."

Dr, Elliot was very bright himself and he surmised that the easiest way to negate the mutant slur was to turn it around to something positive. His ploy worked beautifully.

Mary sensed that she had accomplished by this visit what she had hoped to accomplish, so she said, "Dr. Elliot I believe you have given Freddy the tools he needs to handle his problem. I think we need to go and let you get on with your work. I know you still need to make your hospital rounds. Thank you so very much for your time."

"Well thank you for giving me this opportunity to visit with you. Freddy, my door is always open to you. If you need to talk to me any time day or night, here is my private number where I can be reached."

Dr. Elliot wrote his private telephone number on the back of a business card and gave it to Freddy, admonishing him not to share that with anyone.

Mary and Freddy left. Their ride home was much different from their trip in. Freddy was almost back to himself. About halfway home Freddy asked, "What are we having for supper?"

Mary gasped, "Oh, I told your daddy I would pick up fried chicken." She wheeled the car around and headed back into town. At home, Luther was pacing the floor when they arrived.

The first words out of his mouth were, "Where have you been?"

Mary answered, "Well, we had a little problem and I wanted Freddy to talk to Dr. Elliot.

"What about?"

Mary related the problem to Luther.

Luther, being Luther, looked at Freddy and responded. "Son, you are going to have to stay away from that little girl."

Mary could have easily shot her husband at that moment. She feared that all the progress that she and Freddy had made that afternoon was just been blown away by Luther's stupidity. Glancing at Freddy, she saw him cut his eyes ever so slightly at his daddy and stand looking at him for a moment. He then looked at Mary and stated rather emphatically, "I'm glad I mutated."

With that, he turned and went to his room to change into his 'comfortable clothes'.

Luther looked at Mary and asked, "What was that all about?"

Very sarcastically, Mary replied, "You wouldn't understand."

*　　*　　*

It did not take Freddy very long to put his plan into action. The next afternoon Freddy delayed getting on the bus until everyone else had gotten on. He climbed on and promptly went to Eva's seat, bent down and planted a kiss squarely on her lips. The bus driver was watching in the rearview mirror. He 'came unglued'. He jumped up and told Freddy and Eva to get off the bus. He went to a teacher on bus duty and asked her, "Will you watch my bus while I take these two to the principal's office?"

"Well yes, but what on earth happened, Mr. Simms?"

"This boy kissed this little 'nigger'."

The teacher gasped.

Mr. Simms went to the office and told the principal, "This kid got on my bus and kissed this Gal."

The principal glanced at Fredrick and he did not like what he saw. He had seen the look before and knew immediately, *"He is just letting this guy hang himself."*

Mr. Simms continued, "I ain't having white boys kissing 'niggers' on my bus."

The poor principal wanted to crawl under his desk. He could see it coming. Fredrick had a hold on him and had no intention turning loose for a better grip.

"Mr. Simms, you need to calm down and let me straighten this out. You go ahead and drive your bus. I will take care of these two. The old fellow looked somewhat stunned, but sensed a bite in the principal's voice."

Mr. Adams told Freddy and Eva to take a seat. He went to his secretary, asked her if she would call the primary school to see if she could reach Freddy's mother, and ask if she could come over. He also told her to try to reach Luther as well.

Mr. Adams went back into his office. Turning to Freddy he asked, "Fredrick, do you want to tell me about this?"

Fredrick asked, "Did you call my parents?"

"Yes I did."

Fredrick just sat back in his chair crossed his arms across his chest and said, "Then we will just wait for them."

Mr. Adams cringed. He thought to himself, "*This is not good. Something is going on that I don't know about and probably should. Lord, help me!*"

The High school was next door to the Middle School, so Luther arrived first. He came in excited wanting to know what was going on. Mr. Adams briefly told him what he knew.

Luther turned to Fredrick and asked, "Why, Son! Why did you do that?"

"We will wait for Mom. I don't want to have to repeat myself." That said, Freddy simply folded his arms across his chest again and sat back, as though, '*Case closed as far as I am concerned.*'

In just a few minutes, Mary arrived. She was shocked to see that Eva present.

Mr. Adams invited her to take a seat, and then he began, "I really don't know very much about what is going on except that Mr. Simms brought Fredrick and this little girl to my office and said that Fredrick kissed her on his bus. He was very upset and said some things that I am sure he will regret. I suspect there is more going on than we know about. I have observed that Fredrick does not do anything without a reason. Perhaps we should let him tell us what happened.

"Fredrick what can you tell us about this incident?

Freddy flippantly replied, "Oh, I was just overcome with love, so I kissed her."

Everyone was stunned but Mary recovered first. She was a bit miffed at her son at this point and he could tell that by the tone of her voice. "Freddy, you have placed Eva in a very embarrassing position. Aren't you at least sorry for that?"

Fredrick was sitting with his arms folded across his chest in a slouched position, looking more or less disinterested. He straightened up, dropped his arms to his side, and took on an icy look that stunned everyone in the room. He paused before he spoke but, when he did speak, everyone listened.

"Yes, mother. I do care about that. I am sorry that she was called a 'nigger' by someone who is in authority over us. I am sorry that for months she has been subjected to taunts, jeers, 'catcalls' and all manner of ridicule while those in authority simply sat by and let it happen without raising a hand to stop it. I thought it time that I drew attention to this fact and figured this was the way to do it. Was I right?"

With that, he simply sat back refolded his arms across his chest as if to say, *"Now the ball is in your court. What are you going to do with it?"*

Mr. Adams removed his glasses, rubbed his eyes and put his glasses back on. Mary and Luther looked at one another. About this time Mr. Adam's secretary came in and quietly said, Mr. Adams, Mrs. Burks is on the phone. She is trying to find her daughter since she was not on the bus. What should I tell her?"

Mary arose, "Let me talk to her. I will take Eva home."

While Mary was out of the room, Mr. Adams looked at Luther and asked, "What do we do?"

Under his breath Luther responded, "Hell, I don't know."

Mary came back in the room and Mr. Adams posed the same question to her.

Mary was not at a loss of words. "For one thing you are going to stop the abuse on the bus. That has gone much too far. Freddy, you need to apologize to Eva. You have placed her in a very bad position, and I think you need to apologize to Mr. Adams as well."

Freddy turned to Eva and said, 'Eva, I am truly sorry. I guess I didn't think this through. I sure didn't intend for you to get mixed up in this mess. I thought I would take all the heat."

He then turned to Mr. Adams, "Sir, it is going to be harder to apologize to you. I am sorry that I have made your job difficult, but something has to change. Eva and I have been abused enough."

Mr. Adams sat looking at Fredrick for an extended moment. He really saw him for the first time for who he was. Up until now, he had simply been a thorn in his side, not knowing how to handle a kid too young to be in the grade where he was, but too bright not to be. Now he saw a young man—mature well beyond his years and one who would take on a 'buzz saw' for those he cared about. He sat thinking, *"This kid would have sat there and taken all the abuse if this little girl had not been involved. He did this for her benefit and it backfired on him."*

"Son, you don't owe me an apology. I am the one who should apologize to you. You are unique and we just don't know how to cope with that. Please forgive us and help us.

"Eva, I apologize to you also. You are very fortunate. You have a true friend. That is a rich blessing."

"Thank you, Mr. Adams."

Mary spoke up. "Why don't we all go home and think about this. And work it out later."

"Good idea, Mrs. Overall. I'm sure that Mr. Overall needs to get back to practice, and I need to start some damage control."

Luther commented, "I think I need a shot of whiskey."

*   *   *

Mary took Freddy and Eva Mae home. She stopped at the Burks and tried to explain what had happened as tactfully as possible. She was very much aware of what Mr. Adams had meant by 'damage control' and that what had transpired constituted liable by a representative of the school system. The bus driver calling their daughter a 'nigger' was outside the bounds of decency and she very well knew this could cause ripples all the way to the top if the Burks decided to pursue it.

Freddy and Mr. Burk were very close. Freddy spent hours on end following him around over the farm. He was most embarrassed that the incident had gotten out of hand. He had simply intended to taunt his distracters. He suspected that the driver would be offended, but he had not expected him to react in the manner that he had.

His first words after Mary explained to Duke and Rosalie what had happened were, "I am sorry for what happened. It got out of hand and went further than I intended it to."

Duke thought the situation over, smiled at Freddy and commented. "Lawd have mercy Mr. Freddy. You don't know much about white folks do you. They all think that black is 'catching'. If I was you, I wouldn't worry too much about all of this. I imagine that what you did is going to put a stop to the pestering. I ought to spank you for kissin' my dauter though."

Duke and Freddy smiled at one another. Duke understood how Freddy's mind worked better than most.

Although the town's most unscrupulous lawyer approached and badgered the Burks to file a civil suit, they just laughed it off and went on about their business. Rosalie was tremendously angry with the bus driver and she was ready to 'nail his hide to the wall'. However, Duke simply responded, "Baby, if we sued the school, the lawyer would wind up getting most of the money—our reputation would be hurt, the school would be out a lot of money and the lawyer would be the only one that really benefited out of this. I don't think it is worth it."

Rosalie could see the wisdom in Duke's reasoning and she backed off.

Mr. Adams called the School Superintendent and the Superintendent called the Director of Transportation who in turn called Mr. Simms and instructed him to come to the Transportation office the next morning after he finished his route.

Mr. Rogers' secretary invited Mr. Simms into, the Transportation Director's office and Mr. Rogers opened the meeting with, "Mr. Simms, I have a report that you called a little black girl a 'nigger' in her presence. Is that correct?"

"Well I might have. I was so upset with that idiot kid kissing her and all."

"Mr. Simms, this is unacceptable. You will have to go to this family's home and apologize to her and her parents."

"I ain't gonna do it."

"Mr. Simms this is a requirement for you keeping this job."

"Well, I ain't gonna do it. I'll quit first."

"Mr. Simms, you have been a good, loyal and faithful employee. I hate to see you give up your job as bus driver like this. I am going to ask you one more time to reconsider and go to this family and apologize."

"No! Hell will freeze over before I will go apologize to them 'niggers'."

"Well then, I will have to ask you for the keys. You can pick up your pay later today. I will have your check cut."

Ed Simms gave Mr. Rogers a look that could kill, reached in his pocket, pulled out the bus keys and slammed them down on his desk. He turned and walked out.

Word on the street was that Freddy Overall single handedly brought Mr. Simms down. Mr. Simms was a crusty, mean spirited old man most of the kids disliked and were afraid of. Freddy's reasoning for kissing Eva Mae became a debated issue throughout the school and town. Most felt that he was setting a trap for Mr. Simms and that became the prevailing and accepted fact. Freddy Overall became someone 'not to be trifled with'. The taunting on the bus stopped. Pressleyites simply could not come to grips that a white boy could care this deeply for one they considered black.

*　　*　　*

Luther suddenly realized that he had been working on his Master's degree for five years, and lacked six hour to finish. He was running out of time. Normally a six-year window for completing the work is assumed. He decided to sign up for a Saturday class at Texas A&M during the spring semester and then take his final class during the first summer semester which would leave him the second summer semester to take his Comprehensive exam. One of his big assignments was a research paper for the class. It could be anything the student chose about school administration, with the professor's approval of course. One evening at dinner, Luther was fretting about what he should choose for his topic.

He commented to Mary, "I just wish he had assigned a topic and then let me work on it. I don't have a clue what to write about."

Mary was sympathetic but she did not know what to suggest. As a lark, she looked at Fredrick and simply asked, "If you were your dad, what would you choose as a topic?"

Fredrick sat back crossed his arms across his chest and got that look on his face that was so unsettling to his father. He looked intently at him as though he were studying every feature.

After about a minute he thoughtfully commented, "Well, I guess if I were you, I would probably choose something I was interested in. Now let's see—what are you interested in? Sports—sports and more sports. I guess I would write something about the importance of the athletic program to the educational process."

Luther did not know whether to be angry, to feel put down, or if Freddy was really being serious. He never knew with Freddy, but as he thought about Freddy's suggestion, it became readily apparent to him that his idea was a good fit. He turned to Mary and commented, "You know I could do that. I have harped on that for years. Why didn't I think of that?"

He turned to Freddy, "Thanks, Son."

It was a rare occasion that Luther referred to Freddy as Son—a mild breakthrough.

*   *   *

Luther never did figure out if Freddy was simply being sarcastic or if he was really offering him a good suggestion. Over the next couple of weeks, he struggled to find time to work on his research paper, finish the basketball season, and prepare to start baseball.

One evening during dinner, Luther was complaining that he just couldn't find time to work on his paper. Mary spoke up and offered, "Luther, if you will give me a brief idea of where you want to go with this, I will try to help you make an outline. Perhaps Freddy could do some research for you at the Library."

Freddy's eyelids went up ever so slightly as he cast his eyes toward his mother, giving her his look that said, *"Now do I really want to get involved in this?"*

Mary continued on, "He knows how to do research in the library and I am sure he would be a big help."

Luther responded, "Well, now I don't want someone else to do my work for me."

"Oh, we won't be doing your work, you will write the paper. We will just be helping gather information."

Luther gave Mary a general idea of where he wanted to head with the paper. One overwhelming thought that he had was to look at the growing obesity problem among teenagers. Freddy took that and ran with it.

At the end of the month, The Overalls received a long distance phone bill for $217.18. Luther hit the ceiling, ranting, "What are all of these long distance calls for?"

Mary replied, "You had better ask Freddy."

Luther went to Freddy's room and asked, "Son, what are all of these long distance telephone calls for?"

Freddy took the bill, studied it and then began, "Well, I called Mayo Clinic to see what information they had on Teenage Obesity. I got hung up there with a lady who was passionate about the subject, and then I called the American Medical Association. They wanted to tell me a lot about it also, and then I called the University of Texas Library, A&M library, Harvard Medical School Library, Rice Library, Johns Hopkins Medical School Library, and a few others requesting information. Information should be rolling in shortly. I don't think you will have any problem writing your paper, Dad. It is just the cost of education."

Luther went away feeling strangely as though he was chastened. For some strange reason, every time he engaged in a confrontation with Freddy, he had this feeling and Freddy never raised his voice.

*   *   *

Freddy had just about explored all of the possibilities with his Commodore 64 computer. It had a word processor, "Quick Brown Fox" that was in a module that plugged into a slot on the back of the computer. It was a good word processor, except text was broken into two lines, each with forty characters rather than the normal eighty character lines. This was somewhat disconcerting when typing documents. Freddy decided that while his daddy was working on his paper, this was a good time to push for an upgrade. IBM released their first personal Computer August 12, 1981. They called it a Personal Computer. That name stuck and became shortened to PC. The first IBM PC ran on a 4.77 MHz Intel 8088 microprocessor. The PC came equipped with 16 kilobytes of memory, expandable to 256k. The PC was available with one or two 160k floppy disk drives and an optional color monitor. The price tag started at $1,565.

Luther almost herniated himself when Freddy asked for the $700 for the Commodore 64, so he was a little hesitant to approach his dad about upgrading to the IBM PC, but clones were hitting the market by 1986 and Freddy saw his daddy's research paper as a corridor to obtaining a new PC. He began researching Personal Computers in earnest and became acquainted with Lotus 1 2 3 and the power of spread sheets. He saw this as an opportunity to align his mom as an ally in his push for a new computer since she was the family bookkeeper.

Freddy learned that Dr. Elliot had bought an IBM PC early on for use in his office and that he had Lotus 1 2 3 installed on his machine; He cornered him at church one morning and began quizzing him about the program. The depth of Freddy's questions intrigued Dr. Elliot. Finally, he suggested, "Freddy, why don't you and your folks join Mrs. Elliot and I for lunch and then you and I will go to the office and play with the computer?"

Freddy turned to his mom and dad and asked if they could do that, and received a reluctant approval. Both Luther and Mary could already see a new Computer on the horizon.

Freddy generally sat rather stoically through the sermon and read. On this day however, he was extremely antsy. He fidgeted throughout the pastor's homily. Mary was amused because Freddy was a master at covering his feelings, but this particular day they stood out like a sore thumb.

All during lunch, Freddy quizzed Dr. Elliot. Dr. Elliot had also researched computers and he fielded all of Freddy's questions. Fredrick wanted to know about serial ports, open architecture, software compatibility, printing options, graphics, and what BIOS Dr. Elliot would recommend.

After lunch, Dr, Elliot asked, may I borrow Freddy for a little while? We are going to my office to play computers.

Luther responded, "If you can stand him. He makes me tired just listening when he gets started on computers. He is pretty hyper today."

Dr. Elliot laughed, "Oh, I hadn't noticed."

At the office, Freddy learned that Dr. Elliot had bought the computer and taught himself how to program the Lotus Software to do his bookkeeping for him. He wrote his own program to keep all of his office billing and financial records.

He told Freddy, "At income tax time it is all there. If you can get your folks to buy you a computer, I will give you a copy of my program and your Mom can keep your farm records. Freddy and Dr. Elliot played computers from two until six when Dr. Elliot had to go to the hospital to make his rounds. Freddy called his mother and asked her to pick him up at the hospital, which she did.

When Mary came to pick him up, Freddy had a floppy disk in hand. That was the key to his new computer. His first words were, "Mom, I have you a new tax deduction for the farm. Dr Elliot gave me a copy of his Lotus program that you can keep all of our financial records on. You can add the computer to your tax deductions."

"What on earth are you talking about Freddy?"

Waving the disk, he excitedly told her all about the program, how easy it was to input data and how it made all of the calculations automatically. Before they arrived back at the farm, he sold Mary on the idea that the computer really was a good idea. He did not even need to ask Luther. Mary simply told him to find what they needed and she would purchase it.

Freddy poured over computer specifications for days and finally decided on an IBM Clone assembled by a small computer house in Dallas. One of the stipulations was that he must be assured that the Lotus program worked on the computer. The company agreed that if he brought his disk, they would load it and he could see the program work before he accepted delivery. The computer was purchased with two floppy disk drives, Microsoft Basic, Word Perfect word processor and Lotus 123 spreadsheet loaded. The cost was $2,280.00. The machine had a hefty power supply and five expansion slots. It came with a two year, un-limited warranty. This impressed Mary because she was very well aware that Freddy would have his hands deep into the guts of the machine. She was not wrong.

Mary drove to Dallas for Freddy to load Dr. Elliot's Lotus program and bring the computer home. The Financial software was loaded and worked correctly. Freddy was on cloud nine. On the way home, he decided to give his commodore 64 to Eva. Freddy had enjoyed the Commodore 64, but the Clone was the beginning of his love affair with computers and his salvation for the many dark days ahead of him.

*   *   *

As Freddy had predicted, information regarding youth obesity coupled with sedentary lifestyles and lack of proper exercise came rolling in. In two short weeks, Luther had enough information to write six research papers. Mary began to sort the information for him and put together an outline. Mary was struggling with Word Perfect, but Freddy read the manual and knew all of the macros and commands, so, in short order he had her trained to a high degree of proficiency. Mary discussed the paper with Luther over dinner a couple of evenings and then she simply started typing. Freddy had great fun learning how to input data into Lotus and make charts and graphs. It took Mary and Fredrick three evenings to teach Luther all he needed to know to present and defend his paper, but Luther was a good visual and verbal learner, so when time came he was ready.

Since Freddy had talked Dr. Elliot out of a financial program, he and Mary began inputting all of the farm and personal finances into the spreadsheet. They had all of their records up to date. Freddy found a check-writing program that was coupled directly to the spreadsheet, which would deduct checks from the bank balance, and he soon had that running ~ *after several calls to the software developer.*

The computer was a big mystery to Luther. He would not go in the office with it if he could keep away. He looked at it as some monster that was going to gobble up their entire family. Mary had coaxed him into using only credit cards or cash and not checks, so all of their checks were generated from the computer program. This did not set well, but he reluctantly agreed to hand over his checkbook.

*　　*　　*

Freddy was finishing eighth grade and he would be starting high school the next year. Velma graduated from college and she had taught for a year at a small school in East Texas when a job opened up for a girl's basketball Coach in Pressley. She applied for the job and got it almost immediately. The name Overall and sports were spoken in the same breath in Pressley. Freddy was not enamored that his sister was moving back to Pressley. They were not on the same page; in fact they were not even in the same tablet. Mary and Luther invited Velma to live with them, but she informed them, "No, I am going to get an apartment in town. I am not going to live in the same house with that little 'twerp'."

Of course, she made this statement in Freddy's presence. He put his hands together as if in prayer and mouthed "Oh thank you, Lord."

This action simply added fuel to the fire.

*　　*　　*

Freddy had let his hair grow out and it was almost long enough for a ponytail. This angered Velma and her brothers and certainly fed Freddy's desire to leave it long. He kept it clean and neat and actually, it improved his looks and distracted from the thick glasses. It also made him look more mature. Unfortunately, some of the kids in his class started to copy his hairstyle. They were beginning to push the envelope as far as it would go. At the last school board meeting of the year, a dress code was adopted. With the superintendent's recommendation, it included the length of students' hair. Dr. Elliot opposed the measure because of his friendship with Freddy, but was out voted.

The school board meeting was on Tuesday night, so Wednesday morning the principal called all of the students, that had long hair, to his office and told them that their hair must be cut by the next morning or they would be sent home. He was looking directly at Freddy when he made the statement. Freddy's looks did not change. He just sat stoically as if waiting for further instruction.

After a long moment, looking directly at Freddy, Mr. Adams asked, "Do you have any questions?"

One student asked, "How short does it have to be cut?"

"The dress code says it cannot hang down in the back, ponytails are not allowed, and it has to be trimmed above the ears."

Freddy's expression still did not change. Mr. Adams shuddered inside.

The next morning Mr. Adams was 'parked' at the front door observing all the students when they arrived. He saw Mary's car drive up as she came to drop Freddy off. When he exited the car, Mr. Adams could not believe his eyes. Freddy had obviously taken a bowl, placed it over his head, and then cut or shaved off everything beneath it. He looked like he came straight out of MAD Magazine as he slowly made his way up the walk. As he entered the door, he smiled at Mr. Adams and said in his usual manner, "Good morning, Mr. Adams."

"Good morning, Fredrick. I like your haircut. I believe you are a trend setter."

"Thank you, sir."

Freddy walked on down the hall just as though nothing had transpired.

Mr. Adams went to his office, closed the door and burst into laughter. His secretary came in and brought him a cup of coffee. He was still laughing uncontrollably. When he finally got control of his emotions he asked, "Mrs. Jones, how can anyone not like that kid? He is smart, poised, self confident and has a grand sense of humor."

Mrs. Jones stood reflectively for a moment and then answered, "Well, Mr. Adams, people don't like Fredrick because he is different. He is so much smarter than the rest of us that we feel inferior. No one likes to feel inferior."

"I believe you are right, Mrs. Jones. A person can be too smart. But you know what I have observed? If they are just a little bit too smart then people just get in their way, but if they are far out, then they are smart enough to overcome. Fredrick fits into that latter category. Just like this haircut. He followed the rules we gave him and turned the tables right back in our face. His long hair looked so much better than what he has now. Now we have to look at this for the rest of the school term. I love that kid and I hope he goes far."

"Well, Mr. Adams, I don't think you have to worry too much about Fredrick. He has skills far beyond his years. It is the poor teachers and staff you had better worry about. We are all afraid of him."

Mr. Adams laughed again and replied, "So am I, Mrs. Jones. So am I."

Dr. Elliot walked into church on Sunday, took one look at Fredrick and burst into laughter. He walked to his pew and sat down beside him and whispered in his ear. "Way to go Fred."

Fredrick just smiled; He continued to keep his head shaved below the bowl for the rest of the school term. Just as soon as school was out, he went to the barbershop and got a burr.

Freddy's haircut was already a burr under Luther's saddle and he demanded that he have it trimmed. Mary on the other hand admonished Luther that Fredrick obeyed the rules.

Luther exploded, "Rules, hell. He looks like a damn freak."

"Maybe so, but they made the rules—he didn't. Now he has obeyed them, so you need to back off . . ."

Luther was not happy but since he did not understand his son and figured that Mary did, he backed off. Still, Luther was not happy with Fredrick and he was embarrassed to be seen with him.

Mark and James came home from school for the weekend and they threatened to shave Freddy's head. They would have if Mary had not stopped them. They were both livid and told their mother they would not come home again as long as his hair was like that. They got in their car and went back to school. Luther was angered because he had looked forward to a weekend with the boys and this caused a serious rift between him and Fredrick.

*   *   *

Luther presented his research paper and received an A. He could not stay mad at Fredrick very long, because he needed him. He still had one course before he was to take his comps and that meant another research paper. This time he chose, on a recommendation from Freddy, Implementing Dress Codes in the Schools, Using before and after pictures of Freddy in his presentation, how could he not make an A on that paper?

All week before he took the Comprehensive Examination, Luther was 'a bowl of jello'. He fretted each night at dinner. Finally one night just before he was going to take the exam, Freddy looked at him through his thick glasses and remarked, "Dad, you have been a coach for over 20 years. You have administered the athletic program for a reasonably large school all that time. If you can't pass this little old exam, shame on you!"

Luther looked at Fredrick for a pregnant moment and saw him with new eyes. It was the first time that he ever felt that his son showed him any manner of respect. He always felt that Fredrick really looked at him as being inferior. The fact that he now understood that his son recognized the job he was doing was a tremendous boost to his self-esteem. His eyes misted. He said in a choked voice, "Thanks, Son. I needed that shot of confidence. I'll just go do it."

Fredrick gave him a thumbs up sign, got up and walked out of the room.

Luther turned to Mary with tears in his eyes and commented. "I didn't even know that he recognized the job I did."

Mary reached over and placing a hand on his arm and replied, "Oh Luther. I wish you knew Fredrick. I think you would like him."

This pushed Luther over the edge. He wept as though his heart was breaking. When he finally got control of his emotions he asked, "Mary, do you think I will ever know my son?"

"I hope so, Luther. I truly hope so."

Little did they know that tragedy was going to push Fredrick and Luther together.

Luther took his comps and passed with flying colors. Life was good at the Overall farm. Luther seemed to be making progress in learning to accept his unusual son. Fredrick was starting high school. Since he had started school in the third grade, he was eleven years old when he began the ninth grade. His birthday was in September, and he would be twelve soon. Mary had outfitted him with contact lenses over the summer, but he seldom wore them because they were simply too much trouble.

It was the end of the first day of school in 1986. Almost everyone had already left school and Mary was preparing to leave when a custodian came into her room with a small shy first grader. She said, "Miss Mary, I found this child hiding in the restroom."

*   *   *

Mary placed her arm around the child's shoulder, and asked him his name. She discovered that he was Timmy Watson. She knew his parents and where they lived. Upon quizzing the child, she learned that he had been traumatized by the fact that he did not know which bus to get on. Not knowing what to do, and too shy to ask a teacher, he slipped out of line and hid in the restroom. Since Mary had already signed out for the day and was preparing to leave by a side door, she asked the custodian to go report the incident to the principal and tell him that she was taking the child home.

Mary and Timmy got in her car and she took him home. Mrs. Watson was most grateful and graciously thanked Mary for her kindness. When Mary left the Watson's home, she took a shortcut on a Farm to Market road that intersected with the county road, which went past the Overall farm.

After losing his bus-driving job, Ed Simms had gone to work as a truck driver for the county driving a dump truck. He was hauling a load of crushed rock to a work location on a county road, which crossed the Farm to Market Road. He came to the intersection of the two roads at the same instant that Mary Overall's car arrived. Not seeing a stop sign at this blind intersection, Ed went barreling through at about 45 miles per hour, striking Mary broadside. Mary's Chevy Impala was no match for Ed's Mack R686RST Dump truck loaded with twelve yards of crushed limestone. She never had a chance, and died immediately on impact.

Fortunately, the battery was still working in the truck, so Ed was able to radio the office and ask for help. Within ten minutes the sheriff and two deputies were on the scene and an ambulance was on the way. The Sheriff immediately called for a "jaws of life team" to come to remove Mary from the car.

Ed knew that he had struck Mary Overall's car and he told the girl in the county office who was involved in the accident. She called the Overall home first and Fredrick answered. The young lady informed him that his mother had been in a wreck and asked how to reach his father. He told her to call the school. Fredrick had the presence of mind to find out where the accident occurred. The young lady could give him no other details other than to tell him that Mary had been struck by a county dump truck.

When Freddy got off the phone, he ran to find Duke to get him to take him to the sight of the accident. From Rosalie he learned that he was out in the middle of the field on the corn picker. After briefly explaining to Rosalie and Eva, Fredrick ran as fast as his legs could carry him, but it takes a while to get to the middle of a four hundred acre field. When Duke saw Fredrick running toward him, he immediately shut the corn picker down. He went running to meet him. Before Duke reached him, Freddy screamed, "Mr. Duke, Mama has been in a car wreck. Can you take me to see about her?"

"Oh, I sho' can son. Where did it happen?"

"Intersection of FM1680 and County Road 387."

"Duke and Freddy went running toward the Burks' house as Duke quizzed Freddy. "Do you know what happened, son?"

"Dump truck hit her car."

"Oh Lord Jesus, Please let Mis Mary be OK. Oh please!"

Duke's prayer was unsettling to Freddy. Rosalie and Eva Mae were waiting in the yard weeping when Duke and Freddy got to Duke's truck. Duke simply said, "We going."

They climbed into the truck and headed to the scene of the accident. The ambulance with Mary's body had just left when they arrived. Duke stopped the truck and went running to the scene. A deputy stepped in front of Duke and said, "You are not needed here. You need to move along."

Freddy got in his face. "My mother was in that car! How badly was she hurt?"

"Well, son, I don't know. You will have to talk to the Dr."

From the look on the deputy's face and observing the car, and Duke weeping uncontrollably, Fredrick knew immediately. Luther arrived at this moment and went running to the deputy. The deputy pulled him aside and from the anguished, "Oh no!", and his father breaking down, No one had to tell Freddy.

But, Fredrick Overall's mind did not work like most. His grief would come later when he was alone and no one could see. Right now, he was studying the scene and processing the information he was taking in.

Luther and Fredrick went to the hospital. Dr. Elliot was there. Fredrick's first question to him startled him. "Dr. Elliot, did she know?"

Dr. Elliot was slow in processing the question and answering. "Only for a split second son. She did not suffer."

Fredrick thoughtfully replied, "Well, at least that is something."

He looked at Dr. Elliot. "You better give Dad something. He is falling apart."

"What about you, Fredrick?"

"I'll be okay. Dr. Elliot, I loved my mother more than life itself. I wish this had been me rather than her. At least she is not suffering. We have to live with the hurt."

Dr. Elliot knew this was the response of an adult mind. "Son, I wish I had some words to comfort, but I simply do not. It is a hard thing to have to live with."

Fredrick looked at Dr. Elliot. He very much appreciated that he did not utter pious platitudes, and respected him for that. "Dr. Elliot, I have thought on this some. I don't know why Mama was on that road. It was not her normal route. Mr. Simms was driving the truck. I was responsible for him being fired as a bus driver; otherwise, he wouldn't have been there. It looks to me like God placed them at that intersection for this purpose. I am not very happy with God right now."

"That is a reasonable response, Fredrick. God is big enough that he can take your anger."

Dr. Elliot was not a tremendously religious man, but he did have an active faith and he knew the Bible. He continued, "Fredrick, God's ways are not man's ways, but I believe that God is heartbroken for you right now. You tell him how angry you are at him and ask him to comfort your heart, help you bear this and help you move on to become all that your mother wanted you to be. You owe her that, Fredrick."

"She was my best friend—the only person in this world who understood who I am. I feel terribly lost and alone right now. I do not know how I will handle this just yet, but I do know one thing, I will not let my mother down. Thanks, Doc."

With that, Fredrick turned and walked away. Luther had been listening to the conversation. He looked at Dr. Elliot with eyes full of tears and asked, "Lord, what in the world am I gonna do. Mary was my strength. I don't have a clue how to get along with Fredrick."

"He will teach you, Luther. Just let him teach you."

Dr. Elliot had been writing a prescription during the conversation; He handed it to Luther and instructed, "Get this filled and take it as prescribed. Try to get Fredrick to take it also, but don't attempt to force him."

Luther smiled faintly, turned, and went to catch up with Freddy who was plodding toward the car.

Once in the car, Fredrick looked at his dad, "Daddy, it is going to be hell . . . Pure living hell, without Mama! You are going to have to learn that I am not Mark and I am not James. *I am Fredrick.* You must somehow learn to live with that."

"Oh. Son, I know that you are different. I accept that."

"No, Dad, you don't. You want to, but you *don't.* You did not want me when I was born. Bottom line, you still *don't,* but you have me anyhow and you are going to need me. You do not have a clue about how to run the farm or anything at all about the family business. I am going to have to take that over. You do your coaching; I will run the business. Mama taught me well. Somehow, some way, somewhere along the line, perhaps we will learn to understand one another."

With that salvo, Fredrick sat back in his seat and buckled his seat belt. Luther wanted to respond, but simply had no response for his son. Fredrick pretty well summed things up, and Luther knew it. He started the car and drove to the pharmacy, picked up the prescription and headed to the farm and the arduous task of letting Velma, James and Mark know about their mother.

Once at home, Luther totally fell apart. Fredrick called James and told him what happened and asked him to tell Mark. Then he called Velma at her apartment in town. James told him they would be home late in the evening. Velma said she would be out immediately. Fredrick then went to his favorite crying spot down by the creek and wept his heart out. Strangely, Fredrick still felt that his mother was near and comforting him. He accepted that as God's grace to him and the comfort that Dr. Elliot had mentioned. Although he still had not been able to pray, his anger toward God was lessening somewhat. He had been on the creek bank for about an hour when Eva Mae slipped in beside him. They embraced and wept together for a few moments.

Eva was finally able to remember her mission, "Mama is worried about you and sent me to find you"

Fredrick was all cried out at this point, so he got up, took Eva's hand and they walked hand in hand back to the house. Luther had taken the prescription, sat down in his recliner to weep and fallen asleep. Velma had arrived and she lit into Fredrick for running off like a fool. He did not even respond, but simply ignored her, which just elevated her anger level.

Bill Hinds, Luther's assistant coach, heard about the accident and he and his wife came bringing a tray of sandwich meat and buns. Mary's principal,

Mr. Griffin also came, but he was a basket case. Their pastor came in just as soon as he received word. He was a good pastor. He simply gathered the family together in a room and had prayer for their comfort and strength. He then offered his services in any way that he could help. Luther asked him to handle Mary's funeral, which he readily agreed to do, and then he left.

The entire town of Pressley was shaken by Mary's death. Although not well liked by many people, she won the respect of all. Fredrick was a growing phenomenon in the town and many of his successes were attributed to Mary. Through Freddy, Mary's intellect became recognized.

Mary's funeral was one of the largest ever held in the town and the flowers were prolific. Fredrick never shed a tear during the entire service. Velma, Mark, James and Luther wept uncontrollably. As is so often the case, they suddenly recognized the impact this mother and wife exerted in their lives and this loss was crushing. Freddy was very gracious before and after the service to all well wishers—more so than the rest of the family. They were simply overcome with grief.

Back at the house after the funeral there was an attempt at a family meeting before Mark and James went back to school. Velma had planned to be in charge. Her opening remarks were, "I guess I will have to give up my apartment and move in here."

Fredrick asked. "Why?"

"Well, someone will have to look out after things and take care of you and dad."

"Velma, you don't know how to do anything but cuss and play basketball. We don't need you here. Rosalie will continue to cook and keep house for us. You just stay in town where you belong. Dad and I will learn to live together without killing one another."

With that, he got up and left before Velma could recover from shock and respond. Velma was livid, but Luther backed Fredrick. "Velma, you are just starting a new job here in Pressley. You just go on with your life. We will all learn how to cope."

*   *   *

Luther and Fredrick began their adjustment and things went pretty well. About two weeks after the accident, the county attorney came to Luther's office and began, "Luther, the county realizes there is a liability on our part for Mary's death. We are so very sorry that this happened. I have recommended a settlement offer to the county commissioners and they have agreed to the amount thus relieving you of the trouble of having to go through an attorney and the long drawn out process of litigation. We are prepared to offer you one million dollars."

Luther was stunned. He felt it was a reasonable offer, but he responded, "That sounds reasonable to me, but I need to discuss this with the rest of the family before we make a decision. I will try to get back with you next Monday. I will talk to the boys and Velma this weekend."

A local attorney had already approached Luther, but he told him that he was not ready to deal with that just yet. He called the attorney and informed him about the offer. The attorney responded, "Luther you would be crazy to take that. I can get you ten times that amount."

Luther called the boys and asked them to come home Sunday for a family meeting. All of the family met together on Sunday afternoon. Luther outlined the county's offer and then told them what the attorney had said. He then asked, "What do you guys say?"

Velma, never at a loss for an opinion stated flatly, "I say we go with the attorney."

James and Mark were waffling and discussing the offer among themselves. Fredrick remained quiet. After discussing the matter Mark and James spoke up and said, "We vote to go with the attorney."

Fredrick, who was sitting stoically, slouched in a platform rocker raised up, "No!!!"

Velma screamed, "Shut up you little twerp. You don't know anything about this."

Fredrick turned a cold hard stare at Velma and did not speak for an extended moment. He then began, "Has anyone considered why the county is so anxious to settle right away?"

Velma, in a very angry voice, answered, "Well yes, they don't want us to get an attorney."

Fredrick smiled. "No! Someone does not want this looked at too closely. They want it settled and behind them. You see, Mr. Simms was not at fault. There was no stop sign. There was a post, but no sign. Someone had stolen the sign. Mr. Simms was not familiar with the road since it was not on his bus route. Don't you see, if we sue, the county will not be totally at fault? The person who took the sign will bear most of the responsibility, and they don't have any money. Someone in a position of authority wants this over and done before too many questions are asked. They know who took the sign."

Luther, Mark and James were all on the edge of their seats. Luther gushed, "Well, who do you think took the sign, Freddy?"

"Think, Dad. Who has two teenage sons who are always into mischief?"

"Just tell us, Freddy."

"Lawrence Spears, the county attorney and Joe Smith, the sheriff. I think Larry and Jody took the sign ~ they are always together. I also think their parents know and were intending to make them put the sign back up, but this happened before they got the chance. I say we take the one million dollars because the county has two unscrupulous employees who are letting someone else take the blame for what their kids did. I hate the fact that Mr. Simms has to go through life thinking he ran a stop sign that took my mother's life, but in time I think all of this will come out."

Velma asked, "How do you know there was no stop sign there? There is because I looked."

"I studied the scene the day of the accident. The nuts used for bolting the sign to the post were lying on the ground."

"Well, why didn't Mr. Simms realize there was no stop sign?" Mark spurted out.

"Too rattled. "The Sheriff shuffled him off to the hospital for observation before he discovered it. They got the sign back up before he realized it was missing."

Velma exploded at Fredrick, "Then why in the hell didn't you say something before now?"

Fredrick leaned back in his chair and executed a maneuver that always irritated Velma. He took his left index finger, placed it on the nose bridge of his glasses and pushed his glasses back to their proper position and sat looking at Velma for a long and extended moment, and then asked, "About what?"

That look infuriated Velma. It made his eyes look huge, and gave the impression that he was looking through you. His answer pushed her over the edge. She jumped up, stomped her foot and screamed at him, "About the damn sign, you idiot!"

Freddy simply shrugged his shoulders and replied, "No one asked me."

As an afterthought he added, "Velma, you need to watch your language. There is a child present."

Velma was totally outraged and stood up to strike Fredrick, but Luther got between them and told her rather curtly, "Sit down!"

Velma sat down, but she exploded again, "Well, those kids will have to pay for what they did! They are not going to get off 'Scott free'!"

In his quiet manner Fredrick continued, "Oh they will pay alright. Larry dates Janette Nelson, and Jodie dates Rita Lloyd. They were probably with them. They can't keep that bottled up. Besides that Velma, just like you, they have to look in the mirror every morning."

Velma bristled, but kept her seat.

James looked at Fredrick. He was awestricken that his little brother had reasoned this entire scenario out at a time when he must have been experiencing tremendous grief, and then, his handling of Velma and manipulating her causing her to make a fool of herself was entertaining. He got up from his chair, walked over to Freddy and hugged him. That was a first . . .

Fredrick then continued, "I didn't say anything because I wanted to wait and see what happened. We had better move fast though before all of this gets out or the offer may be withdrawn. I called the State Insurance Board and asked them if the amount was reasonable. The person I discussed the issue with thought it was a reasonable offer."

Luther just wanted to get this behind him. He was tremendously grieved by Mary's death and the money was not an issue with him. He looked at each of the kids and they appeared numb, except for Fredrick. "Then are we all in agreement that we go with the county's offer?" he asked.

Everyone nodded in agreement. Luther then stated, "I am going to split the money four ways. That should give each of you a boost toward success. Velma, I suggest you use part to purchase a home. James and Mark, you should have plenty to go as far as you wish in school and still have some left for a home. Freddy, that should allow you to pursue any type of education you choose."

Freddy spoke up, "Dad that is your choice. You don't have to do that, but if you do, have the money divided before they issue it, otherwise we will have to pay taxes when you give each one our part."

Luther shook his head, "I never thought of that."

After the meeting, Luther went to the phone and called Lawrence Spears. He informed that the family had decided to take the county's offer. He stated that the funds were to be divided four ways. Lawrence told him the county would issue one check made out to all four parties and that all four would have to endorse the check. They could then divide the funds and avoid taxes.

Lawrence instructed, "Luther since the kids will be involved in the settlement, I will also need their signatures. Can they be in my office Monday morning? Luther went back to the family room and asked the boys if they could stay over. They both needed to get back for football practice at 10 am the next morn. He came back and relayed that word to Lawrence.

Lawrence asked, "Luther, will the boys sign a blank document and you can look it over after it is typed up before you sign?"

"Yes, I think they will do that."

"Then meet me in my office in one hour and I will have it ready for them to sign."

Luther went back and told the boys what had transpired and they both agreed.

Velma spoke up and said, "I may as well go with you and sign the blank document and get that over with. The Twerp can read it before he signs."

Fredrick did not need the dictionary since he had looked the word up before, but he reached for his dictionary and read, "Twerp—a silly, insignificant, or contemptible person."

Fredrick just shrugged his shoulders.

Velma gave him a hard disgusted look and replied, "You got it buddy."

Fredrick pushed his glasses back in place, crossed his arms across his chest and just stood staring at her."

Luther admonished, "We need to keep all of this in our family. You are not to discuss this with anyone. I have some concern about the moral issues here, but the county is responsible for their employees and that includes the sheriff and the county attorney. They made the offer, we did not ask for it, so I guess it is okay to accept.

"At some point, if word does not leak out, Fredrick you must tell what you know. We are not going to be popular at that time."

Freddy smiled and replied, "It is already out Dad. I have been staring at Larry and Jodie and telling them by telepathy that I know. I have seen them whispering to each other and I see the same thing with Janette and Rita. Guilt simply stands out all over them. They are tremendously uncomfortable around me. It is just about to break all over the place."

Luther looked at his son. In many ways, Fredrick scared him. He was quietly thinking, "That kid has a way of getting in your mind."

Luther, James, Mark and Velma went to Lawrence Spears office, and Freddy went to his crying spot. The fact that he would be receiving money and profiting from his mother's death pushed him to his limit. He broke down and wept his heart out. When he finished his cry, he made a vow to his mother that he would use the money wisely. First, he would educate himself as she would have wished and second he would make the world a better place. When he got up and turned to leave, he discovered that Eva Mae was sitting behind him. He could tell that she had also been crying; she rushed to him and hugged him. He kissed her and then they walked hand in hand back to her house.

*   *   *

A charge of involuntary Manslaughter was pending against Ed Simms; He was suspended from his job as truck driver for the county after the accident and awaiting the grand jury decision to indict. The grand jury hearing was still almost a month away.

On Wednesday after the Sunday meeting, Lawrence Spears called Luther and told him the check was ready. He asked, "Can you and the kids come in to sign for the check."

Luther asked, "Can I come in, sign and pick up the check? Don't you just need a legal document that one of us has received the check?

"Yes, I think that will be okay."

Luther went to pick up the check, and the District Attorney was in Lawrence Spears office. When Luther went in, Lawrence and the district attorney were standing in the door to the office. After Luther picked up the check, The DA stopped him and asked, "Mr. Overall, do you plan to file charges against Mr. Simms? I think we would need you to do that in order to convict him of involuntary manslaughter."

Thinking before he answered, *an unusual feat for Luther*, he commented, almost under his breath, "It is a blind intersection with brush grown up in each and every corner—I know that he punishes himself every day for what happened—I will have to talk to the kids about this."

"Well, think about this. You will have to decide before the grand jury meets.

Luther observed that Lawrence listened intently to what he said, and he observed that the two men went back in Lawrence's office as he was leaving. He thought, *"I wonder just how far reaching this cover up goes? I wonder what they would think if they knew that Freddy already had it all figured out?"* He broke out in a huge smile.

Luther carried the check and placed it in his safety deposit box to hold until the boys came and cosigned. After everyone had signed the check, it was deposited in each of their respective checking accounts to disperse into saving accounts.

Everyone in Pressley knew of the settlement and Velma fueled the gossip by immediately going out and purchasing a new Red Mustang Convertible. This made Fredrick livid and it would remain a burr under his saddle for years to come.

*   *   *

Just as Fredrick predicted, Janette told one of her friends about the boys removing the stop sign, they told another, and things began to snowball from there. Soon there were whispers all over the campus at school and then it spilled over to the homes. Word finally got back to Mr. Simms who then demanded an explanation. He was immediately reinstated to his job driving a truck for the county. It took lots of shuffling among the sheriff, district attorney and county attorney to keep the boys from being indicted for involuntary manslaughter, but with enough money under the table and enough political finagling, they pulled it off. Since Luther did not file criminal charges against the boys, the issue soon died down.

As the real story unfolded, Jody, Larry and the girls had been out joy riding Sunday night after church. They had parked to smooch on the old county road near the intersection and sign where the accident occurred. Larry got the wild idea to steal the sign for his room. He and Jody found a pair of pliers in the trunk of his dad's car and they took the sign down. Larry forgot to take the sign with him when he got out of the car that night and the next morning when Larry's mother took him to school, she noticed the sign. She quizzed him about it and learned the whole story. She called his dad and told him. Sheriff Smyth ran into Lawrence Spears in the courthouse and told him what the boys had done. Lawrence told the Sheriff, "I will come by tonight after I get off work and pick up the sign and Jody and those two young men can go put it back up."

Both men thought that would be the end of the incident, but later that day the accident occurred. The Sheriff and the county Attorney put their heads together and came up with the plan to offer the settlement before the Overalls discovered what had happened.

Fredrick watched all of this with interest, thinking, *"You know, folks can outsmart themselves sometime."* He then quoted scripture to himself, *"Be sure, your sins will find you out."*

There was lots of speculation about whether the Overalls knew about the missing sign, but no one outside their family ever knew the truth.

*   *   *

Fredrick's life at school moderated somewhat after the incident. All of the kids knew that he and his mom had been very close and that she was one of the few people who understood, *what they thought of as his quirky mind*, so most showed some compassion. Somewhat ironically, Larry Spears and Jody Smyth, before the incident, were his greatest persecutors and after this incident, they simply went away and left him alone. Both boys were on Luther's football team.

Jody was the second string quarterback behind Ben Burks. Ben had a slight ankle injury in one game and Luther sent Jody in the game replacing Ben as quarterback. Jody went running in, in a rather cocky manner as if to say, "And now we are going to play football." The first play he called was a long pass play. He threw a long wobbly pass, which was easily picked off near the right sideline. A defensive linebacker intercepted the ball and ran 50 yards before a fullback pushed him out of bounds on the ten yard line. Fortunately, the Offensive team received a ten yard penalty for unsportsmanlike conduct on the first play which pushed them back to the 25-yard line. Pressley held at the 20-yard line and the opposing team missed a field goal by inches.

Pressley took over on the 20-yard line and Jody attempted two running plays, which went a total of two yards. Wanting to redeem himself, he called another pass play. It too was intercepted and he was not so lucky this time. The defensive end ran 30 yards for a touchdown. The score placed the opposing team six points ahead with three minutes to go in the game.

Ben came running to Luther, "Coach, I can handle it."

Luther looked at Ben's ankle, which had been taped. "Are you sure, Ben."

"Yes Sir, I am sure."

"Well, go get'em!"

Ben went hobbling off to the huddle. The kickoff after the score had not gone well for Pressley and they had the ball on the nine-yard line. Ben hobbled into the huddle and a very dejected Jody came off the field.

Not expecting an injured quarterback to attempt a pass deep in his own territory, Ben completed a 25-yard pass, giving Pressley a little breathing room. He tried two running plays, giving Pressley another 22 yards, since the opposing team was willing to give up short yardage rather than allow a long pass play. Earlier in the game, Ben had run a play where he faked a quarterback sneak, but instead of running with the ball, tossed it back to a fullback who had thrown a pass for a touchdown. The opponents were fooled by that play and their coach warned them to watch for it again.

In the huddle, Ben told the team, "We gonna run that surprise play again, but this time I am gonna keep the ball and run with it."

His fullback asked, "Can you run?"

"Watch me."

With one minute and forty-four seconds left in the game, Ben faked the pass play: the fullback did an excellent job of faking that he had the ball. Ben with the ball tucked behind him, slipped through the line like he was going out to block for the pass play, slipped by the first two defensive backs, and headed down field. There was only one man left between him and the goal line. The crowd went wild. As the defensive player moved in to make his tackle, Ben did a quick spin, which was his trademark, and with a stiff arm, the tackler went face down on the field and Ben went to the goal line. The crowd went wild cheering Ben as he hobbled off the field, *all except Jody Smyth.* Pressley was again on its way to another district championship.

The consensus in Pressley was that Ben Burks was starting quarterback, chosen over Jody, because of Jody's involvement in the accident that caused Mary's death—that Luther held a grudge and would not let Jody take his rightful place as starting quarterback. These rumors were mainly fueled by Jody's mother. After this game, they simply 'fell on deaf ears'. Ben Burks had earned his wings. Playing while hurt and still eluding a quiet confidence, he not only earned Luther's respect, but that of the whole town.

*   *   *

Since Mary's death, Fredrick attended football games with Luther in order to support his father. He sat with Eva Mae at the games. This caused a lot of heartburn in Pressley, and several of Luther's friends chastened him for this. His principal called Luther in one day and admonished, "Luther, you are going to have to stop Fredrick from sitting with that little black gal. It is going to ruin your reputation. If you want that superintendent's job, you better put an end to that. Now I am telling you this as a friend, and I know what I am talking about."

Luther knew that Ben Green had heard talk and at that point, he essentially gave up on obtaining the job as superintendent. When it came open at the end of the year, he applied for the job, but there was lots of animosity and jealously toward the Overalls over the settlement for Mary's death. After the settlement, they were clearly the richest people in town, unseating a couple of other "old" families for that position, and these families were powerful and vicious. There had already been talk of firing Luther as head football coach, but it is hard to fire one who has just won another district championship, so Luther was set for at least one more year, and Velma also had a successful year.

Velma heard the talk about Fredrick and Eva Mae and she was very angry with Fredrick. After the announcement of who the new superintendent would be, Luther, Velma and Fredrick were eating lunch in town after church and Velma looked at her dad and said, "Daddy, that little ignoramus caused you not to get that superintendent's job," with an exaggerated gesture of pointing at Fredrick.

Luther was startled. "Oh, I don't think so. I think it is because of the Gibsons and the Turners. Word has it that they didn't like the idea of our settlement."

Velma was adamant, as she normally was, "No! It is because of that little 'nigger gal'. He is with her all the time."

Luther was horrified. He knew very well how much Eva Mae's friendship meant to Fredrick and how much she had helped him cope with his mother's death.

Luther glanced at Fredrick. He had not changed expressions except to push his glasses in place so he could stare at Velma. If Fredrick was angry, which he was, it did not show, but Luther was a different story. His face flamed and he almost screamed at Velma, "Well let me tell you something Velma, If this damn town is so narrow minded that they cannot accept Eva's friendship for my grieving son, I don't want the job as superintendent or any other job in this town."

With that salvo, Luther got up, went to the cash register, threw $30 on the counter and walked out. Fredrick got up, looked at Velma and remarked, "You know Velma, I am beginning to think you are only my half sister. You are living proof that my daddy had sex with a coon dog."

Fredrick went to the car, got in with his dad and they drove home, neither speaking until they got in the garage. Fredrick turned to Luther, "Dad. If what Velma said is true, I am truly sorry, but what you said meant more to me than you will ever know."

Luther sat with both hands white knuckled on the steering wheel. Luther was going to lose it and he knew it. Finally he could hold it in no longer. He wept as though his heart was breaking. Luther was a man's man and he was tremendously embarrassed for his son to see him cry, but what he could not know was the effect this was having on Fredrick. It was closing a gap between him and his father.

When Luther could speak, he gushed, "Son, I have seen Eva's kindness to you, and Duke and Rosalie have made life bearable for us here at the farm. Ben has quietly taken abuse for being starting quarterback, which was undeserved.

If this town cannot accept that, then they can go politely to hell. Sometimes, I think I hate this town, but I don't. We have roots here and this is where we belong."

"Dad, there may be some element of truth in what Velma said, but I really doubt that. The day Mom was killed, your chance of becoming superintendent ended. The dynamics of human nature is such that the town feels certain guilt over this that they somehow need to assuage. Now I cannot explain exactly what I mean, but it is similar to a bunch of chickens. You have seen how chickens act toward one that is hurt or different. Do you remember when we had the two old hens that grew spurs? The other hens pecked at them un-mercifully. Mom finally took the two old hens out of the pen and put them in a pen by themselves. They got along fine together. People can act like chickens, when one is hurting; they seem to want to add to the hurt. I don't understand the dynamics of that other than to believe it is somehow a mechanism of overcoming a fear of, 'What if that were me?' The feeling that if I can inflict pain, it will help me overcome my fear.

"I have read a lot about the holocaust lately and I find it interesting that the Germans had to dehumanize the Jews before they could treat them the way they did. I find it frightening that I see this everywhere in human nature. We think that could not happen here, but I fear that it could. I do not know if it is the presence of evil in human nature or simply the absence of good. I really believe it has to do with the place in our lives—that empty space left when we push God out. We are hurting and I think the town could not give that job to you because of the dynamics of what I have just described. You have had a successful year in football. Denying you the job made individuals feel somehow superior to you.

"Poor Velma is so simplistic. There is seldom just one element involved in this sort of thing. I am somewhat different, you know, my eyes, my looks, everything about me is different. I feel the brunt of being the pecked chicken, but Mom taught me how to cope. She taught me to learn as much as I could about everything and she taught me how to study human nature. I find that is an invaluable tool. Humans are one of the most interesting critters on earth. There is never a dull moment when you are studying humans.

"Don't be too disappointed about not getting the superintendent's job. I have looked at the new guy's credentials. He has a mail order Masters and Doctorate from one of those, 'you pay your money and you receive your degree'. Just bide your time. He won't last long."

"How do you know that, Fredrick?"

"Well, he spoke at an assembly we had at school. He doesn't use correct English, so I decided I would see where he went to school and got all of those degrees that everyone keeps touting. I went to the administration office and asked to see his credentials. They told me it was confidential. I told them it was public record. They told me I couldn't see them. I told them I would get a court order and they relented. Then I went to the library and told Mrs. Cranford, the head Librarian, that I was researching a school I was thinking about attending when I graduate from High School. I asked her if she could help me gather some information. She went to a directory, and came back just livid and blurted out, "Fredrick Overall, why in the world would you even consider that school! They give *Mail Order Degrees*! Shame on you!!! Shame, shame shame!!!'"

I simply smiled and replied, "Well, I thought that since that is where our new superintendent received his touted PhD, I would consider going there. Her jaw dropped a foot."

Luther was still holding on to the steering wheel listening to Fredrick. He never ceased to be amazed at his son.

He was having trouble processing all he heard. It was apparent that Freddy had not expected him to get the superintendent's job, although it had essentially been promised if he would get his Masters in Administrative Education, which he had done.

He had to smile as he thought of Fredrick's subtle revelation of the new superintendent's shabby credentials to the town. If Mrs. Cranford knew, then the whole town was going to hear and they were going to hear loudly. Until learning this information, he had felt no animosity toward the man for getting the job because he had a PhD and was well qualified. Now that he had learned the truth, he was livid.

He finally released his hold on the steering wheel, opened the door and exited the car. He had lots to think about. One thing he was certain of though, was, he did not ever want to get on that kid's bad side.

Chapter 3

The new superintendent came in and immediately began to try to change every aspect of the Pressley educational system. He quickly learned that Luther had been slated for the job and immediately set his sights at running him off. He felt threatened by Luther. The only problem was that he was not very smart and did not realize that Luther was a very popular winning coach. In a football crazed town, to try to fire a winning coach is not a good political move. He also did not realize that Fredrick had cut his legs out from under him in the academic community. Luther did at least have a legitimate degree from a prestigious University. One other problem that he was unaware of was that the school board had hired him over the objections of the president, Dr. Elliot. Dr. Elliot had gone on record objecting to his credentials before the rest of the board voted him into the position. Now he was not going to let them forget that he had objected. By raw grapevine, superintendent Weems learned that the school system had a twelve year old high school junior. When he learned that this was Luther Overall's son, he set his sights on correcting the obvious blunder.

He immediately ordered that child placed back in seventh grade where he belonged. Luther went straight to Dr. Elliot when he learned this. Dr. Elliot, after being badgered by Superintendent Weems, called a special board meeting to discuss the issue. Dr. Elliot asked both Luther and Fredrick to be present at the meeting. On the drive into town, Fredrick was quiet most of the way.

Just before they arrived at the administration building Fredrick cautioned, "Dad, this guy is not very smart. I suspect we had best simply sit back and let him hang himself."

Luther sat thoughtfully for a moment and then asked, "You want me to keep my mouth shut; is this correct?"

Fredrick did not respond immediately. "Sometimes, it is just better to let the other person stew in their own juices, especially when they are in a weak position. I believe we can handle him with a derringer. I don't think we will need a howitzer."

Luther smiled. He was thinking, "I *sure would hate to be in this guy's position between Freddy and Dr. Elliot. This is going to be interesting.*"

Freddy and Luther were early. They went in and immediately Dr. Elliot and Fredrick struck up a conversation about the latest computer software. Fredrick asked Dr. Elliot if he was familiar with Harvard Graphics. Dr. Elliot had read about it, and they discussed which BIOS might be best for graphics software. They then switched to a discussion of whether Pascal was going to replace Fortran as the programming language of choice. Their discussion became more animated by the moment.

Dr. Weems was late. This had become his trademark and it was a very sore point with Dr. Elliot who often had to rush his hospital visits and skip dinner in order to chair the meetings. Just as soon as Dr. Weems came in the room, Dr. Elliot rapped his gavel and said rather curtly, "We need to start the meeting since we are already ten minutes late, so I call the meeting to order.

"*Doctor*, and he strung out the *Doctor*. I believe this meeting was requested because you made the administrative decision to place Fredrick Overall back to seventh grade. I turn the floor over to you."

"Yes, thank you, Dr. Elliot. It has come to my attention that we have a student in our system who has been promoted to a level far above his age group and I personally feel that this is not in the best interest of that student. Over the years, I have learned that students undergo and learn certain developmental skills other than simply their academics. Personally, I believe these skills are crucial to their development into responsible adults. I am recommending to the school board that we require this student to be returned to his own grade level."

Dr. Elliot looked at Fredrick and knowing this young man he decided to take a gamble, "Fredrick, you are the person most involved, do you have any questions for Dr. Weems."

Dr. Elliot had been watching Fredrick out of the corner of his eye and he was sitting in a rather slouched position in his chair and would have given the impression to the unknowing eye that he was totally disinterested. He slowly sat up and with a deliberate and intense gesture with his middle finger on the bridge of his glasses pushed his glasses firmly back against his face and into position. He then just sat staring at Dr. Weems for an uncomfortable moment and then asked, "What kind of personal developmental skills? Do you mean like sex education?"

Dr. Weems blushed slightly and stammered, "Well, that, that is certainly one of the things that students learn all through their academic endeavors. It is simply a part of going to school and interacting with other students."

"Well, I already know all that. I watched my Dad teach my brothers. He just threw them the car key and said, 'Boys, the rest is up to you'."

With that, Fredrick sat back in his seat, stared at Dr. Weems and let his statement hang. It was not original, but it was well placed. Fredrick had heard that line by Charlie Weaver on Hollywood Squares as he walked through the den once when no one thought he was listening.

Dr. Elliot could not contain himself. He burst into laughter along with the rest of the school board. Luther put his face in his hands, but he just couldn't hold it in. He too burst into laughter. Fredrick never cracked a smile; he just sat staring at Dr. Weems.

Dr. Weems could not meet his stare and he turned five shades of red. He was totally livid. Marlan Burns, one of the school board members spoke up and said, "I move we deny that request. I believe this boy can handle himself."

Mack Turner seconded the motion. Jim Bailey called for the question. Dr. Elliot asked. "All in favor of denying the request to move Fredrick Overall back three grades signify by raising your right hand."

All hands went up except Dr Weems. Dr. Elliot stated emphatically. "Request denied, I would entertain a motion that we adjourn." He got a motion and second, and a vote of acclamation. The meeting was adjourned.

At the end of the meeting, Dr. Weems was livid. He attempted to corner a couple of board members and educate them regarding the big mistake they had just made, but his exposition 'fell on deaf ears.' Suddenly he found himself face to face with Luther Overall. Now, Jim Weems was a big man; fifty pounds overweight and about six feet tall, but Luther Overall was six feet three, trim, and fit; very athletic. He not so gently poked his finger in Dr. Weems chest and in his booming voice informed him, "You listen to me, Buster—If you ever pull a stunt like this again and try to get at me through my son, I will kick your butt up between your shoulders and then beat the hell out of you."

Dr Weems was terrified. He stepped back from Luther and two board members stepped up to try separating the two big men if necessary. Dr. Weems regained control of his voice; glaring at Luther almost screamed, "Overall, you are finished as coach here. I will fire you if it is the last thing I ever do."

Luther was calming down and bringing his anger in check. He just smiled and replied, "I really doubt that you are man enough to do that, but if you should be so lucky though, I would not consider that a big loss if this town is stupid enough to hire an idiot like you. Come Fredrick, I don't like the company here."

Luther and Fredrick walked out. Three board members followed, all three trying to apologize to Luther as he headed to his car. Dr. Weems found himself left alone with Dr. Elliot. Dr. Elliot looked at him and in a calm, cool voice began, "Dr. Weems, you have two years left on yorr contract which we will honor, but I suggest that it might be a good idea for you start looking for a new position. I doubt very seriously that we will need your services here in Pressley. When you took on Fredrick Overall, you took on a tiger. That frail look and mild manner are a cover up for an atom bomb."

By the time Dr. Weems left the administration building, he truly felt that he had been at 'Ground Zero'. He had come into the meeting like a proud peacock. He left a plucked chicken.

In the car and headed for the Dairy Queen, Luther looked at his son and remarked, "You did yourself proud, Son. You cut his legs out from under him and he never knew what hit him."

Fredrick pushed his glasses back against his face and after a thoughtful moment replied, "Well Dad, you didn't do too badly yourself, and I think he did know what hit him."

They both laughed. Fredrick then asked, "Dad, are you thinking about giving up your job here in Pressley?"

Luther didn't answer for a moment but then replied, "Son, I have been offered a job at Markel. I'm not sure I want to stay in Pressley. Markel is only twenty-five miles away. We wouldn't have to move."

Fredrick was quiet for a few moments and then replied, "You would have to drive an extra fifty miles per day. I am always uneasy when you are not at home."

This statement pricked Luther's heart ~ It spoke volumes. It reflected the pain that his son was still feeling over his mother's death, but most of all it communicated to Luther that he was important to his son. Luther broke down and started crying. He had to pull off the road and get control of his emotions. When he regained control he looked at Fredrick and said, "I still miss her too, Son."

Luther reached over and placed his arm around Fredrick's shoulders and for the first time ever finally said, "I love you, Son."

Fredrick reciprocated, "I love you too, Dad."

*   *   *

This night was a breakthrough of gargantuan proportion. Luther began to discuss game strategy with Fredrick and Fredrick began to study football, basketball and baseball in depth. Fredrick didn't just scratch the surface of any subject. If he decided to research something, he did a thorough job. Luther became amazed at the depth of understanding of all aspects of the sports that Fredrick exhibited. He studied the physics, the psychology, and the political aspects of the sport. Luther began to depend on him for insight into different aspects of the game. Although Fredrick did not really care for sports, he wanted to be a part of his father's life to help him cope with the loss of Mary, and he succeeded in doing that. Luther responded in kind, and listened to Fredrick's views on the farm operation. Luther simply turned the farm over to Fredrick and Duke. Together they made all of the decisions; Fredrick paid all the bills and kept all the records. Duke was a good farmer and Fredrick was like a sponge, learning from him. However, Fredrick never took anything at face value, so when

Duke's empirical knowledge did not align itself with Fredrick's gut feelings, he went to the library and researched the problem. Many, many times he came away with a scientific basis for what Duke had learned from trial and error.

*   *   *

Mary Overall was a Lane before she married Luther. Her family consisted of her mom and dad, Mr. and Mrs. Lane, Mary, the oldest and Evelyn. Evelyn and her father were constantly at odds. Mr. Lane was a very harsh disciplinarian. He whipped Evelyn with his belt when she was a sophomore in High School. She had on a full skirt at the time of the whipping and her daddy had pulled her dress up and whipped her on her bare legs and panties. She never forgave him for this. She felt it terribly degrading. Just as soon as she was old enough to leave home, she left and went to Houston and got a job with an oil company. She would not come home and the only time she saw her mother was when her mother went to visit her. She had no interest at all in the farm and let it be clearly known that as soon as her daddy died they could sell it.

Mr. Lane had a serious stroke after Mary's death. Luther called Evelyn, but she did not come home. The burden of caring for the old fellow fell on Luther and Fredrick's shoulders. Mr. Lane thought Luther 'hung the moon', but he could not stand the sight of Fredrick. Mr. Lane went into rehabilitation after his stroke. When he came out, Luther and Fredrick tried to get him to come live with them for a while, but he flatly refused. He was a cantankerous old man before his stroke and now he was even worse.

Mr. Lane operated a 700-acre farm of his own plus a section of leased land, one mile from the Overall farm. Fredrick's grandmother died before Fredrick was born. He never had a real relationship with his grandfather. After Mr. Lane's stroke, management of his farm fell on Luther's shoulders. The Clooney family lived on the farm and worked for Mr. Lane. Mr. Clooney and Duke were good friends, and Mr. Clooney was a reasonably good farmer. Luther delegated record keeping and financial oversight to Fredrick. This did not set well with Mr. Clooney, and there were a few rough edges to this arrangement at first. Fredrick set up a computer program to keep all of the farm records.

When Fredrick took over the record keeping task, he discovered that his grandfather's records were sparse and incomplete. He and Mr. Clooney had a serious confrontation because Mr. Clooney would not give Fredrick all receipts for purchases. Resolving this problem required Luther's involvement. Luther finally told Mr. Clooney that Fredrick was representing him and unless he had serious questions he was to do as Fredrick instructed. This almost caused the Clooneys to leave, but jobs were scarce and the Lanes had a good tenant house. The best home they had ever lived in. After a little while, Mr. Clooney's respect for Freddy's knowledge slowly began to grow. It took a huge leap when

Fredrick convinced Luther that the Clooney family was underpaid for the job they did. Grandfather Lane was very tight fisted and paid the Clooneys just enough to keep them on his farm. Fredrick suggested that they instate a profit sharing plan to stimulate job ownership. Being a coach, Luther saw the merits of this plan easily and bought in.

Mr. Lane, although he was not mentally competent to run the farm, somehow found out about the profit sharing plan. He threw a fit, and threatened to beat Fredrick. Fredrick in characteristic manner, simply stood toe to toe with him, and with his index finger pushed his glasses firmly back against his face and looked the old fellow in the eye. The old man could not stand to look at Freddy's eyes through his thick glasses—even before the stroke, this drove him up the wall, and now it pushed him over the edge. He turned and went screaming into the house and started pounding on the table and screaming at Mrs. Clooney who was there cleaning and cooking for him. She came running outside terrified. Mr. Clooney went to her to try to calm her down and he told Fredrick to go get his daddy.

Fredrick calmly replied, "I'll handle it."

He went inside, poured his grandfather a cup of coffee and handed it to him. In a calm voice he said, "Granddad, you are getting a little worked up and scaring folks. You need to calm down."

The old man looked at his grandson, sat down at the table and started adding sugar to his coffee. He liked his coffee strong and sweet. Fredrick sat watching him add three teaspoons of sugar. When he finished adding the sugar, he stirred it and took a sip.

"Fredrick asked, "How's your syrup Granddad?"

"Hush yo mouth boy. You know I like my coffee sweet."

"Well, maybe it will sweeten your disposition. You are a mean old cuss—you know that?"

"I don't like folks meddling in my business."

Fredrick sat staring at the old fellow for a very long and extended moment and then stated as gently as possible, "Granddad, I hate to tell you this, but your days of managing this farm are over. It is a hard thing. You have put your life into your farm. I give you my promise that I will keep it in the family and cherish it after you are gone. I won't promise that I will not make changes, but I promise to love the place as you have always loved it. I don't think that is a bad legacy to leave behind, do you? Why don't you just sit back and enjoy what you have built here for the rest of your life?"

The old man was having one of his more lucid moments. He sat staring at Fredrick for a few moments before answering. "I dun worked hard here, I raised yore Maw here and Evelyn. I made a bad mistake with Evelyn and she ain't never forgiven me. Your Maw was all I had after Mattie died. Now she is gone and I ain't got nobody."

Freddy did not cut him any slack. There were many issues that needed to be addressed, and the time had come for addressing them. "Well, granddad, it is your own fault. You won't let anyone else in. Your hurt has been great and we understand that. All of us are hurting over Mom's death, but we don't shut everyone else out."

This angered Mr. Lane, "Just shut up. You don't know nuthin about it."

Fredrick still did not back off. "Don't I? Look at me, Granddad." The old man cut his eyes up at Fredrick and then back at his feet."

Freddy very firmly repeated. "Look at me!"

The old man looked back up and looked directly into Fredrick's eyes.

"You can't stand to look at me can you? You sit there and tell me that I don't know anything about it when my own grandfather can't even stand to look at me! Who do you think my only friend in this world was? You have the audacity to tell me that I don't know anything about it?"

The old man saw his grandson for the first time. He broke into uncontrollable sobs. "I'm sorry, son. I am so sorry."

"Granddad, maybe you should tell Evelyn that also before it is too late. You must have hurt her deeply to cause her to feel the way she does."

"Well, I don't know what to say to her."

"You could start with 'I'm sorry.' If you truly are, then that is the place to start."

"Will you write her for me son? You know I can't write no more."

"What do you want me to say?"

"Just tell her, 'I know I was wrong and that I am real sorry'.

"I'll type a letter tonight and bring it over tomorrow and read it to you. If you can't write, at least you can make a mark on the paper to let her know it is from you.

"Granddad, you need to finish your coffee and go lie down. You look tired and you need to rest."

The old man turned his cup up and drained it. Fredrick came around the table, helped him up and led him over to his recliner. He sat down, leaned back, and almost before he was stretched out, he was asleep. The Clooneys had come inside and heard the whole exchange. They had just gotten their first glimpse of the real Fredrick Overall.

From that day forward, Fredrick was in charge of the Lane farm. His grandfather never questioned.

*   *   *

Fredrick typed the letter on his word processor and carried it to Mr. Lane to look at. He couldn't read it, but Fredrick read it to him. It said,

Dear Evelyn,

I know that I did wrong by whipping you in the manner that
I did, I was just an old fool and I am so very sorry for what I did.
I have laid awake many, many nights and cried over my mistake. I
hope that somehow you can find it in your heart to forgive me.

Your Daddy,
Isaac

Fredrick read the letter to Mr. Lane and the old man struggled to try to sign
his name. He made a few marks that somewhat resembled Isaac.

Freddy addressed it and mailed it. The old man did not receive a response.

*   *   *

During the summer after Fredrick's second year of high school, Bud Clooney,
Mr. Lanes farm manager, was struggling with a big John Deere Tractor. It was
missing terribly. The tractor had ten thousand hours on it. In reality, it was just
about worn out. Fredrick remarked to Bud, "We need to overhaul that tractor."

"Fredrick, it would cost more to have that tractor overhauled than it is worth."

Fredrick pushed his glasses back against his face and replied, "I did not
say, have that tractor overhauled', I said, overhaul that tractor."

"What are you talking about boy? We can't overhaul that tractor."

"Why not?"

"Well, we don't know how."

"Who says?"

Bud looked puzzled. "Well, we just don't. Do we?"

Fredrick shrugged his shoulders. "I don't know. We haven't tried yet."

Bud was amused, curious, and his adrenalin started pumping. He hated to
go into harvest with the tractor operating at only 50%.

He pushed his hat back on his head and looked at the tractor and then at
Fredrick. "How do we start?"

"We drive it in the shop."

Bud pulled his hat off and wiped his forehead with his handkerchief.

"What's your daddy gonna say?"

"Are you going to tell him?"

"I figured that was your responsibility."

"Well, if I happen to remember and get around to it."

Bud smiled at Fredrick. He did not have a clue how to start to overhaul a
big diesel tractor, but he had always wanted to try. He overhauled his old truck
engine and was able to get it running.

"What are your plans, Freddy?"

"Well I have studied some. We will pull the injector pump, send it out and have it refurbished. We will have to figure out a way to support the tractor when we pull the engine. I think it best that we carry it to our shop. We are better equipped than Granddad. While the machine shop has the engine, we can change the clutch and pressure plate, pack all the wheel bearings and replace all the seals. The machine shop will grind the valves and push in new sleeves. We may just get them to install the pistons and rings and reassemble the engine. If they do that, then they stand behind their work. They will do the reassembly for $250."

Bud was getting excited. Fredrick had obviously studied this project and had done his homework. He had just blown away Bud's greatest anxiety—fear of engine re-assembly ~ which might result in catastrophic failure.

"When do we start, Freddy?"

"I figure that by the time we get it down to the shop, it will be about lunch time. Dad is gone today and we can slip it in before he sees it."

That slowed Bud down only for a moment. Freddy climbed up on the tractor and started it. He took off down the road with the hazard light flashing. Bud followed in his truck. Duke heard them come in and went to the shop to see what was going on. Fredrick pulled the tractor into the shop and closed the door.

Duke heard the tractor running and knew immediately what Fredrick had in mind. He smiled and asked, "Guess you told Mr. Luther 'bout this?"

"He has lots on his mind. I don't think he will be too interested in this project." Showing his mischievous side, Freddy added—"Unless we really mess up."

Duke smiled and Bud frowned.

*   *   *

Poor Bud did not know where to start with supporting the tractor. Fredrick took a tape and measured from the bottom of the tractor bell housing to the floor and from the front engine support to the floor. He then picked up a chain saw and asked Duke and Bud if they would go down in the pasture with him on the tractor with the front-end loader. Duke climbed up on the tractor and Bud and Fredrick climbed in the bucket. Fredrick directed Duke to a fallen oak tree, which had blown over during a windstorm. Fredrick started the chainsaw and whacked off the tree just above the root base. The base with the root ball sprung back into the hole left when the tree blew over. He measured off two sections of trunk and cut them off the tree. He then asked Duke and Bud to help him load the chunks into the tractor bucket.

Back in the shop, they unloaded the sections of tree trunk and rolled them over to the tractor. They were slightly shorter than the distance under the tractor. He found some boards to make up the height. Fredrick got the floor jack, jacked up the front end of the tractor, slid a stump under, blocked up with the boards, and let down the jack.

He said, "All right we are ready. Let's get the sheet iron off so we can get to everything."

Bud looked at him and said, "You really are gonna try this aren't you?"

Fredrick, with finger, pressed his glasses back against his face and just stared at Bud for a long moment. "Of course I'm gonna try it. Did you think I was playing Lincoln Logs?"

Duke cracked up. He knew Bud's anxiety. He had worked for Old Man Lane way too long and had felt the heat of his anger on more than one occasion. Duke well understood why he was so uneasy about starting this project. He eased his mind somewhat. "Mr. Bud, Fredrick won't get you in a mess and leave you. He will stick it out and see this finished."

With that, Bud grabbed a hand full of tools and started taking things apart. Fredrick reached for his ITI Manual and began to read and explain. Once the hood was off, the radiator was drained, and the oil was removed from the oil sump, Fredrick then asked Duke to bolt a chain to the bucket on the front-end loader and raise it above the tractor engine. He instructed, "We will unbolt the engine from the bell housing, move the engine and front end away from the rear end with the tractor. Then we will let the front end down on the other stump and unbolt the engine from it."

Duke cautioned, "Mr. Fredrick, you sho' got to be careful that that front end don't roll and get away from you when you take that engine loose."

"You are right. We should block the front wheels, front and back."

Duke was still uneasy. "Son, I got to tell your daddy what you are doing. If something happened and you got hurt, he would skin me alive."

Fredrick appreciated Duke's position. "Don't worry, I'll tell him."

"You are sure now?"

"Just as soon as he gets home. Come on, we have to get this tractor apart before he gets home. If we get far enough along, then he won't try to stop us."

Bud was worried now. He had been frustrated all year trying to use this tractor. The thought of having a machine that performed properly was very appealing, but the thought of facing Luther put a real damper on his enthusiasm. "Freddy, you are going to get me run off. I got a family to think about."

"Don't worry, Mr. Clooney. I'll take the heat. It doesn't bother me."

Freddy grabbed up a pneumatic impact wrench and started loosening bolts. Bud decided that Fredrick was going to tear the tractor down whether he helped or not, so he tore in with a vengeance. Duke mostly watched, and this worried Bud. He knew that Duke knew Luther better than he did and wondered if he knew more what to expect. About five o'clock, Luther drove in.

Fredrick looked at Bud when he heard his Daddy's car. "Well, I guess I will call him and we will take our licks."

Bud screamed, "We! I thought you said you were going to take the heat."

Fredrick pushed his glasses back against his face and looked at Bud. "But Mr. Clooney, I'm just a little old kid!"

Freddy didn't crack a smile. Bud's knees almost buckled on him. Duke burst into laughter. "Mr. Bud, don't let him git to you. He is just full of himself sometimes. He plays his daddy like a fiddle. You not in trouble."

Freddy went to the house and met his dad coming into the kitchen. "Dad, come out to the shop and let me show you my project."

This was not the "welcome home" that Luther wanted to hear after spending all day in a NCAA "rules change" meeting, especially when he thought some of the new rules were ridiculous.

"What are you doing, Fredrick?"

"Working on a tractor."

"Let me get out of this tie and change clothes and I will be right out."

Fredrick walked back into the barn, and told Bud and Duke, "I don't think he is in a good mood. You two had better scat."

He did not have to tell Duke and Bud twice. They both headed out. Bud said over his shoulder, "I will be back after supper to load the engine in my truck." He then got in his pickup and left.

Duke, also over his shoulder said, "I got to go feed."

Fredrick began to clean up around the work area. He and Bud had separated bolts as they disassembled. Fredrick made tags from a slip of paper and dropped them in the cans to identify the various bolts. He was inspecting the clutch when Luther came in.

Luther almost fell out when he entered the shop. "What in the world are you doing, Freddy?"

"Overhauling Granddad's tractor. It was barely running. He hasn't taken very good care of it and it is just about worn out. I don't think he changed the oil until you had to chisel it out."

Luther was almost circling the ceiling. "Son, you don't know how to do this. How in the world do you think you can overhaul the big old tractor?"

Fredrick pushed his glasses back against his face and looked at his dad. "Well I was planning to do it one bolt at a time."

"But son, you don't know how to do this."

"Do you know how to coach, Dad?"

"Of course I know how to coach. I spent four years in college learning how to coach plus I have twenty years experience."

"But every game is different. Every play is different. How can you learn that? These tractors are all built the same."

"But son, you don't have any experience."

"I've got a book. I'm on page 17."

Luther stood looking at his son with a mixture of awe, admiration, frustration, irritation, and just a hint of envy."

Although he had coached for twenty years, he still felt a nagging feeling of inadequacy before each game. He was a winning coach with a very fine track record, but there was still a nagging lack of the type of confidence which he saw exhibited here in his thirteen year old son.

Fredrick grinned at his dad and admonished, "Lighten up, dad. It is just a machine."

Luther was whipped. "Is Bud helping you?"

"Yes Sir."

"Where is he?"

"He got scared and ran off when you came in."

"And Duke?"

"Same."

"I guess you told them you would take the heat."

"It was my idea."

Luther looked around the shop at all of the pieces. He walked over to the workbench and sure enough, Fredrick had his book open to Page 17. He looked at Fredrick and commented, "You had it all planned didn't you, down to the page 17 bit."

"Yes Sir."

Luther burst into laughter. He turned toward the door and started out. Over his shoulder he said, "Good luck, Son. If your grandpa has to buy a new tractor, he is not going to be happy. Can I watch when you tell him?"

"Oh don't worry Dad, we will get it."

After his daddy got outside the shop, he said under his breath, "Eventually!"

Velma knew that her dad was going to an NCAA meeting in Austin for the day so she came out to see what he had learned. She met her daddy coming back from the shop and asked, "What were you doing in the shop?"

"Looking at Freddy's project."

"What's the little Twerp doing now?"

"Go take a look."

Velma went to the shop and Freddy was still tidying up. "She asked, What in the world do you think you are doing?"

"I'm playing tractors."

"You are going to ruin this tractor, Idiot."

"It's already ruined Velma. It won't pull the hat off your head. Bud couldn't harvest with that tractor the way it was running. I can't hurt it."

Velma turned to her dad, "Why in the world did you let him tear up that tractor like that?"

"Why Velma, he has a book. He is on page 17."

With that he turned and went in the house. Fredrick, with a deliberate maneuver using his index finger, pushed his glasses back against his face and stood staring at Velma.

She just shuddered, stomped her foot and said, "Humf", then she turned and exited the shop as quickly as possible.

*   *   *

Freddy and Bud tore the engine down and carted it off to the Machine shop. The crank was badly worn and had to be turned to the maximum for available undersized bearings. New sleeves were installed and then the shop reassembled the engine. It looked brand new when they got it back. Fredrick and Bud installed a new clutch and pressure plate, and the reassembly began. The injector pump was refurbished and Fredrick and Bud went to the dealer's shop to talk to the shop foreman about timing the pump to the engine. Fredrick understood more than Bud that this was the critical process for them. He came away from the dealer with a good understanding of the procedure. All of the seals and worn bearings were replaced while they were waiting for the engine. Fredrick also had the hydraulic pump refurbished while they were in the process of overhaul.

The big day came for startup. Right off, the old battery would not turn the tight engine, so Fredrick and Bud got in Bud's truck and went to get a new battery. They wound up having to go to the John Deere dealer to get a battery large enough for the tractor. It was not cheap.

Back at the shop, with the new battery in place, the engine finally turned over. Priming the injectors turned out to be a major effort, but finally the engine began to fire on one cylinder. Soon all four cylinders were firing and the engine began to smooth out. It sounded brand new. Freddy beamed.

Luther was there for the big day. When the tractor sprung to life, he was all smiles. He hugged Fredrick and excitedly said, "Well, you guys did it."

Bud commented, "Well, Mr. Luther, it was mostly Freddy, He had it all planned out in his mind before we even started."

"Yeah! Right, Mr. Clooney. Just like when we came to the part in the manual and it said, 'disassembly is obvious at this point' and you looked at me and asked, 'To who?'."

Bud laughed. "Well there were a few anxious moments,"

Fredrick pushed his glasses back against his face and stared at Bud for a moment.

"A few?"

If Fredrick had experienced any anxiety over the project, it was never obvious to Luther, Bud or Duke.

Chapter 4

Bud used the refurbished tractor to pull the corn picker. Duke used the Overall's 90 horse to pull the trailer. Bud and Duke always worked together at harvest. They used the corn picker from the Lane farm and the combine from the Overalls farm. By sharing equipment, Luther and Mr. Lane were able to cut their equipment cost tremendously. Mr. Lane held a long term lease on an adjacent section of farm land which brought his total acreages up to 1350 acres. By using crop rotation, he had all of this under cultivation. Since Granddad Lane was not able to farm, Fredrick and Bud had to scramble to find help for harvest. Fortunately, they found a Latin American family to take up the slack left by Mr. Lane. Fredrick and Eva Mae both helped with the harvest by driving tractors as time permitted. With the "like new" tractor, Harvest went well and both farms showed a good profit.

*   *   *

At the end of the harvest season, a family dispute arose in the family who owned the leased section of land adjacent to the Lane property. The original owner died and the siblings were clamoring to sell. In his lease, Mr. Lane had stipulated that if the property was offered for sale, he was to have the first option to purchase. One evening, Jim Starnes, the delegated representative for the family, came to the Overall's and asked if they were interested, since Luther was representing Mr. Lane.

Luther stammered for a moment while thinking, but Fredrick spoke up and replied, "Yes! We are interested. Fredrick asked, "What price are you offering the farm for Mr. Starnes?"

"Well, we are asking $1500 per acre."

"That is $960,000. I don't believe it is worth that. Based on what we earned off it the past several years, it would take 52 years for payback. I think we can find something cheaper."

Jim was blown away by Fredrick computer like mental calculations but he became very defensive, "Well, we figure we can subdivide it and make a whole lot more than that."

Fredrick was ready for this approach. "Well, yes, sir. You are probably right. Real estate is down right now. Big time investors are still licking their wounds from the 84 turndown; I just read in a magazine that Dr. Denton Cooley from Houston went bankrupt listening to some fast-talking real estate brokers, but he is paying off all his creditors. I think that is commendable.

Fredrick went into his thinking mode with chin in hand and commented somewhat to himself like he was thinking through all the issues. "It's bottom land—an environmental impact statement will have to be filed before you can subdivide. That is going to take a study. I don't know just how much that costs. Surveying will be required to break it up. Roads will have to be built. That is going to require dozer work. Oh wee! That is expensive. You will lose your agricultural tax base and taxes will skyrocket, but if you can sell fairly soon that won't matter. However, on the other hand, if the property is slow to sell, that is going to eat away at your profit."

Fredrick suddenly looked at Jim Starnes and asked. "Have you talked to a real estate person about this and had it appraised?"

Jim Starnes answered, "Well, no we haven't had it appraised yet."

Fredrick replied, "Well, I would get someone out of the area to come in and look at it. All these local guys would see that as a gold mine if they can get you to sub divide. They would make a bundle off that. The place would probably support them for the next four or five years."

Luther was watching Fredrick and Jim. He could see Fredrick bursting every bubble in Jim's mind. He could envision the family sitting around discussing the farm and building pipe dreams. Just like the 'grim reaper', Fredrick had laid his sickle at the base of the stalk.

Jim asked, "Just how much would you be willing to pay?"

Luther looked at Fredrick. Fredrick commented, with chin in hand, "We might go $900 per acre simply because of the proximity to Granddad's place, but we are going to have to look at that. I need to do some more figuring to see just what the payback is. It is hard to make land pay for itself."

Jim left with *his tail between his legs*. Luther looked at Fredrick and commented, "Freddy, I believe you were ready for him. How did you know that was coming?"

"Dad, when you look like me, people don't notice you. You were talking to Bill in the post office and I was waiting in the car. Mr. Starnes was coming out of the Post Office when he ran into Mr. Banes, the realtor. They started talking about selling the Starnes place and I heard Granddad's name mentioned. I cracked the window and listened. I learned a lot and I began to study some on that."

"Well, son, just how much will we pay for the place?"

"I said, we might go $900. We will come up to that. Granddad didn't do a very good job with the place. He just guessed at fertilizer. I know it needs lime and we can probably come close to doubling the yield. That is where the profit is. It takes just about as much fuel and chemicals for a small yield as it does for a large and the labor is just about the same."

Luther shook his head and marveled at his son.

*　　*　　*

Jim Starnes went back to the family and related his discussion with Fredrick which scared all of the greedy heirs off the sub dividing idea. They came back with an offer of $1000, per acre, Fredrick countered with $750. Jim told the rest of the family that Fredrick had said that they might go $900 so they countered with $900. Fredrick appeared to be disinterested at this point, so the Starnes agreed to split the difference and the Overalls bought the place for $825 per acre.

Luther and Fredrick each invested $100,000 and got a six percent agricultural loan for the remainder. After Fredrick finished with it, the farm easily serviced the note each year.

*　　*　　*

Velma's basketball team was well on its way to winning a second district championship when she caught her star forward drunk on Saturday night after the next to last game. The last game would determine the championship. Velma was a tough coach. She was a tough disciplinarian just like her father. Because of this blatant disregard for training, Velma benched the young lady for the last game; which Pressley lost.

The benched player, Karen Boren, and the town were livid. Karen was the granddaughter of the bank president. He had a lot to say about the matter. Karen boasted all over town that she was going to get even with Velma Overall. One night, Fredrick had gone to a movie in town, alone of course, and after the movie he walked down to the Dairy Queen for a shake and to wait for his dad to come pick him up. Freddy could hear Karen and three other girls in a booth next to the one he occupied and Karen was bragging about how she would get even with Velma. Slashing her tires was discussed. Putting sugar in the gas tank of her new Mustang was mentioned, and finally when that ran down, the talk turned to boys. Fredrick heard Karen elucidating as to how she liked strong muscular men. Fredrick got an idea. It was a wonderful, terribly, 'Grinchey' idea.

That night, back in his room he sat down and wrote a letter to Karen claiming to be a left tackle on the Markel football team. He wrote that had seen her sitting on the bench at the last basketball game and that his heart broke for her. He wondered if she was hurt.

In his letter he bragged about how many pounds he could bench press, but he subtly wrote that he was very shy around girls and hoped that one day he would muster enough courage to ask her out for a date. He also asked if she would write to him and he gave a P.O. box in Markel. (he had to wait until he opened the P.O. box to fill in this information) He also mailed the letter in Markel. The next day, Fredrick enticed Rosalie and Eva Mae to take him to Markel to open a P.O. box. He signed his letter simply as Butch. He had to let Rosalie in on his ploy, which she thought was grand.

Karen answered immediately and doused her letter with a good liberal dose of perfume.

She wrote, "No, I was not hurt. That bitch we have for a coach caught me after I had a sip of beer and made me miss the game. It cost us the district championship. I know I could have won the championship. I am still trying to figure out a way to get even with that hussy."

She also wrote some steamy stuff that made Fredrick blush and indicated that she was ready and willing any time he worked up enough courage to take on a real woman. She included her telephone number at the end of her letter.

Fredrick wrote back very sympathetic. He also stated that he had an uncle in Houston who had just defended a teacher with a charge against her. Although his Uncle seldom lost a case, he couldn't win that one because folks believe almost anything against a teacher.

Karen wrote back immediately wanting to know more about his uncle's case.

Fredrick wrote, "Oh it was just too awful. The girl claimed that her teacher was a lesbian and tried to molest her, but surely you won't do anything like that because the teacher went to prison."

Karen was not very smart. She wrote back, "That is just what I will do. Everyone in Pressley thinks she is gay anyhow, and If I can put that bitch in prison, I will."

Fredrick had all he needed, but he continued to string Karen along. Within two days, Karen was in the principal's office bawling that she just couldn't keep it quiet any longer. She said she was forced out of the game because Miss Overall made sexual advances at her and became angry when she refused and she had made her sit out the game. She ended her little drama with, "I feel that I could have helped win the championship and I owe it to my teammates to make this known."

The principal called Velma in and immediately suspended her until the matter could come before the school board, informing her that criminal charges would most likely be filed. There was no investigation of the charges. Velma was simply summarily suspended.

Velma was devastated, the whole town turned nasty. Many folks were calling for Luther's resignation as well as Velma's.

Two days later a special school board meeting was called and the school board meeting room was packed. Fredrick had called Dr. Elliot and asked him to insist on an open hearing. Dr. Elliot sensed immediately that Fredrick had "something up his sleeve". His anticipation of an interesting meeting was peeked.

After Dr. Elliot called the meeting to order, Marlon Burns moved that the meeting enter into closed session to avoid embarrassment to persons present. Dr. Elliot raised his hand and suggested, "Mr. Burns, you have made a motion that I must honor, but I strongly suggest that this matter needs to be kept in open session since it seems such an important issue to the town. I believe it is in the best interest of everyone that all of the facts be heard and become known to all persons present here tonight. It is my hope that the motion will die due to lack of a second. Is there a second to this motion?"

Since almost everyone present wanted to watch Velma take her fall and see the Overalls publicly disgraced, no one spoke. The bank president and his wife, Karen's grandmother and grandfather had done an excellent job of inflaming the town.

Luther was livid with Dr. Elliot for blocking the closed session.

Dr. Elliot began, "We are here to discuss an impropriety by one of our teachers and to give her an opportunity to defend herself against the charges. First we will hear from the student making the charge.

"Miss Boren, will you come forward."

A tearful Karen Boren came forward supported by her mother on one side and her father on the other.

Dr. Elliot asked, "Would you like to take a seat, or would you prefer to stand, Miss Boren?".

"I would prefer to stand."

"Miss Boren, would you tell the schools board your view of the event that brought these charges against Miss Overall?"

Karen, with much drama began, "Well after practice one evening, Miss Overall offered to take me home. Instead of taking me home, we drove out into the country and she stopped the car and began to tell me how attracted she was to me. Before I knew what was happening, she started trying to kiss me and put her hand down the front of my dress. I fought her off and she took me home, but she told me I could not play in the last game. I didn't know what to do, I was just devastated."

Karen began to wail. "I'm sorry. I'm sorry. I know I could have helped win the Championship. I let my team down."

Her parents looked imploringly at Dr. Elliot as if to say, "Don't persecute our daughter."

Dr. Elliot sat thinking for a moment and admonished, "Miss Boren, those are very serious charges. If they are not true, you can be in lots of trouble" Bringing false charges against a person is a criminal offense." This brought Karen out of her remorse. She had not even considered that her story would be questioned. Dr. Elliot did not miss the startled look in her eyes.

Her father bucked up and almost screamed, "Of course they are true! Don't try to protect them Overalls!"

Dr. Elliot looked at Karen and said, "That is all for now."

"Miss Overall, Will you come forward?"

In reality, Velma was naïve. She had no idea that an angry student would blatantly lie about a teacher just to get the teacher in trouble.

Dr. Elliot asked, "Miss Overall, what is your response to these charges?"

"Dr. Elliot, they simply aren't true. I have never been in the car alone with that young lady. I categorically deny those charges. She was not allowed to play in the last game because she broke training. I caught her drinking."

"Miss Overall, these charges are very serious. It is beyond the authority of this board to deal with this issue. It is a matter for a criminal court to decide and then the board will act in accordance with their decision. Unless there is other information that can shed more light on this matter, I see no alternative other than for you to remain on suspension pending criminal charges.

"Is there other evidence which should come before this board before we accept a motion to that effect?"

Fredrick, who had been sitting as though disinterested, stood. In a long extended southern drawl, he started, "Dr. Elliot, I have a little information that you might be interested in."

Dr. Elliot smiled. He was thinking, "I wonder what in the world he is going to come out with now?"

Fredrick came forward. As he passed Velma who was still standing in front of the board, he, with index finger pushed his glasses back against his face and smiled at her. She looked terrified.

Dr, Elliot turned to Velma and said, "You may wish to be seated Miss Overall. Fredrick would you like to take a seat or do you wish to stand?"

"Maybe I ought to take a seat. This might take a few minutes."

"What can you tell this board, Fredrick?"

"Well, Dr. Elliot, when you look like me, folks don't notice you. My sister calls me a Twerp, meaning an insignificant or contemptible person. Well, being a Twerp can work to your advantage. People ignore you and you hear things that others do not hear. I just happened to be in the Dairy Queen one evening and I overheard a very interesting conversation. Miss Boren and three of her friends were in the booth next to mine. They didn't pay me any mind as they were talking. I heard Miss Boren remonstrating how she was going to get even with my sister for making her sit on the bench during the last game. They discussed slashing tires, putting sugar or sand in the gas tank of her car but I heard Miss Boren say, 'I want to do something so that she will know it was me'."

Fredrick paused at this point and Karen's dad stood and shook his fist at Dr. Elliot and asked, "Do we have to sit here and listen to this nut make up a story?"

Dr. Elliot raised his hand and replied, "We will hear the rest! Just be brief, Fredrick."

"Well, I thought to myself, 'They are going to hurt Velma. I can't sit idly by and let that happen.' I had also heard Karen talking about how much she liked strong muscular men, and that was when a plan hit me.

"I went to Markel got a P.O. Box and wrote to Karen pretending to be Butch. I told her how I had seen her sitting on the bench at the game in Markel, and asked if she was hurt, and if that was the reason she didn't play. I also told her I was a shy right Tackle on the Markel football team and could bench press 400 pounds, but I was too shy to talk to girls directly. She wrote back, calling my sister bad names and told me how she was trying to come up with a good way to get her. She added, 'All I had was one little sip of beer and she made me sit on the bench and we gave up the championship.'

"I wrote back and told her that I had an uncle in Houston who was an attorney and how he had just lost a case for a teacher who was accused of being gay and had tried to molest a student. I told her the teacher went to prison, although not guilty because people would believe anything against a teacher.

"Karen wrote me back and said. 'I am going to do it. I am going to send that'—well she used a word that you call a mama dog—'I am gonna send her to prison'."

Dr. Elliot looked at Fredrick and Fredrick pushed his glasses back against his face and looked straight back at him.

"I suppose you have the letters with you, Fredrick?"

Fredrick was slouched down in his chair as he related the story. He sat up, reached in his back pocket and pulled out all of Karen's letters along with a photocopy copy of his letters to her and the receipt for the P.O. Box.

He handed the letters to Dr. Elliot. All of the board members, plus the superintendent and principal crowded around Dr. Elliot to get a glimpse of the letters.

Dr. Elliot smiled at Fredrick and asked, "Freddy, have you been watching "Mission Impossible?"

Freddy added, "And The A Team."

Karen tried to get up and run out the room, but a deputy who had come to arrest Velma stepped in front of her.

Dr. Elliot had trouble bringing the meeting back to order with all of the buzzing going on between the crowd.

Dr. Elliot looked at Fredrick and commented, "Freddy, this is out of character for you. Can you tell me why you did this?"

Fredrick sat reflectively for a few moments and then answered, "Velma is not a bad person, in fact she is a good person and a good coach. She cares about the kids. She is naïve and vulnerable though. I couldn't sit idly by and let her be hurt while she was trying hard to do a good job. She very well may have given up the district championship by disciplining Karen for what she did. She thought she was doing it for Karen, not for herself. She really thought she could make a difference in Karens's life by this teaching experience. I guess she just doesn't understand the selfishness of some people. I thought hard to try to stem the inevitable. Karen seemed bound and determined to hurt Velma. I guess I just took the easy way out to keep that from happening. This was pretty easy to pull off you know."

Dr. Elliot had to use all of his will power to keep from laughing at Fredrick's last statement.

He then turned his attention back to the meeting. Are there any questions for Fredrick before he steps down.

Marlon Burns commented, *"Lord, son, you scare the hell out of me!"*

*   *   *

The deputy who was present to arrest Velma came up to Luther and Velma and asked, "Miss. Overall, do you want to press charges against this girl?"

Velma with a questioning look on her face turned to Luther and asked, "What do you think, Dad?"

Luther answered, "Tom, we are too stunned to make that decision right now. I'll have to talk to Velma and Fredrick."

Velma was visibly shaken. She was crying and having trouble controlling her emotions. Luther was trying to get her out of the room and to his car. On their way out, Bob Button stopped Velma and placed his hand on her arm and looked into her eyes. "Velma, I didn't believe the rumors. I thought the young lady's story was awfully weak. I'm glad your little brother took care of you."

Velma was able to get out a "Thank you", but there was something in his eyes that was unsettling to her; a kind of chemistry that passed between them. Naturally, Fredrick did not miss it.

Velma looked frail, and as Fredrick had stated, vulnerable as she and Luther made their way to the door. Up until now, she had always been Velma, the Amazon, tough, and hard as nails—the star basketball and volleyball player who almost single handedly carried Pressley to three district championships and then came back after college to coach them to two more. For the first time, people saw her as a real person. A quiet shame fell over the town of Pressley because of their eagerness to 'hang her and 'nail her hide to the wall'.

Karen's grandfather came to the car just as Luther and Velma got in. Luther rolled the window down and James Turner, Karen's maternal grandfather asked, "Luther, Y'all are not going to file charges on Karen are you? I know she is real sorry."

Luther looked at James and thought before he spoke, "James, your grandsons' action caused my wife's death. Now your granddaughter has tried to smear my daughter's name, and actually tried to get her sent to prison. I don't know how much more we can take off your family."

Luther rolled up the window; Fredrick had arrived at the car by this time and gotten in the back seat—Luther started the engine and the family headed out. Velma asked, "Dad, may I go home with you and Freddy. I don't think I could stand to be alone tonight".

"Of course you can go home with us. You can come home any time you wish. Velma looked at Fredrick in the back seat. "Thanks, Freddy. They would have hung me if it hadn't been for you. You caused me to spend a couple of rough days. Why did you have to tell her to say I was gay though?"

"Because it was believable. Velma, you need to get a boyfriend so people will quit talking."

"Maybe I don't want a boyfriend."

Fredrick did not back off. "And maybe you do! I saw that look that Mr. Button gave you. He is a very nice guy. He lost his wife to cancer three years ago. Do you want me to fix you up with him? He and I are friends."

Velma startled both Fredrick and his dad. "Yes!"

Fredrick grinned from ear to ear. Luther caught his face in a street light as they stopped at a red light. He also grinned. Velma finally smiled.

Luther, Velma and Fredrick talked well into the night. Velma felt abandoned by the town of Pressley and Luther and Fredrick struggled to point out that many were on her side. The power brokers in the town were on the other side backing Karen, but Fredrick had clearly cut the legs out from under them. They were somewhat disgraced by what had happened. This incident, coupled with the fact that their grandsons were partially responsible for the accident that took Mary's life, left them in a very precarious position.

At the end of the family discussion, Velma came to grips with what had transpired. She asked her dad, "Should I go back to school tomorrow?"

Luther thought for a moment and then answered, "I believe you were suspended until further notice. Have you received further notice?"

"Why no! I haven't heard anything!"

"Then by doggies, let them call you!"

Luther and Fredrick got up and went to school the next morning while Velma stayed home. Luther had been at school for about 30 minutes when Mr. Green came in. Rather sheepishly, he asked, "Luther, Velma hasn't come in. Do you know if she is planning to come in today?"

Luther turned and looked him in the eye. "Mr. Green, Velma was suspended until further notice. Have you given her further notice?"

Ben winced, "No I haven't, Luther. I just thought that after last night she would just come on in."

"Well, Ben, The Overalls play by the rules—even if other people don't."

Luther scored a direct hit. Ben Green felt guilty that he had not given Velma the benefit of the doubt. He knew that her suspension was the direct result of who Karen's grandparents were. He turned and went back to his office to lick his wounds.

*   *   *

Ben called Velma and suggested that she take the rest of the day off—with pay of course. The next morning bright and early, Velma was back on the job.

Mr. Green expelled Karen for one week and required that she apologize to Velma before she could go back to class. That was a bitter pill for Karen to swallow. The week she was expelled, her mother fretted that the Overalls were going to file charges. She had Karen convinced that she was going to reform school. Both mother and daughter were basket cases by the end of the week. When Karen came back to school and made her apology to Velma in front of Mr. Green, Velma graciously told her all was forgiven.

Mr. Green went with Karen to her first class and informed the teacher of reinstatement. He turned to Karen just before he left the room, "Miss Boren, you have seen what grace looks like. I hope you have learned something by what has transpired."

"I have, Mr. Green. I truly have." What she was really thinking was, "Don't mess with Fredrick Overall."

*   *   *

Fredrick followed up on his offer to Velma. He was in Mr. Button's Biology class. He worked out a deal with Mr. Button that he would write a research paper on any subject just as long as he didn't have to dissect a frog. He told Mr. Button, "I don't like blood and guts. I don't like cutting on stuff that has had a life. I even have trouble cutting up my steak when I eat it."

Mr. Button acquiesced and allowed Fredrick to watch a dissection and then write a research paper on the nervous system of the frog. Mr. Button learned more about a frog's nervous system than he really wanted to know before Fredrick was finished. Freddy wrote a fine paper. He had an appointment with Mr. Button after his last class on Thursday to discuss his paper. At the end of the discussion Fredrick weaseled in the question, "What do you think of my sister, Mr. Button?

Mr. Button was flabbergasted and he stammered, "Well, she is nice."

"Do you like her?"

"Well, well yes. I just told you she is a nice person."

Mr. Button was pale. Fredrick continued, "No, No! I mean do you like, as in L I K E—he spelled it out. Like oow, oow, like yeah man, as in yes, I am romantically attracted to her."

Mr. Button was amused and had this been anyone but Fredrick Overall he would have been affronted.

He smiled, let down his guard and admitted, "Yes Fredrick. I would very much like to ask your sister out but I don't know how to go about it. You see, I was married for eight years and I don't have a clue about how to start trying to court again."

"Well, that is what I figured, so I thought I would try to ooze you and Velma together slowly. She likes you also and she doesn't have a clue how to attract guys."

"Perhaps that is why she is so attractive to me."

"Makes sense to me. Can you come out to our place to dinner on Saturday evening? Say about six."

"Well I have a little girl. I will have to find a sitter."

"No! Just bring her with you. Eva Mae and I will babysit her. We like kids."

"Fredrick, I will just take you up on that offer."

"Good!"

"I'll let Velma know."

Fredrick went to the gym and found Velma. "Sis, you have a date Saturday evening. Mr. Button is coming for dinner."

"Fredrick, you didn't do something to embarrass me did you?"

Fredrick pushed his glasses back against his face and looking squarely at his sister he asked, "Velma, would I try to embarrass you?"

Velma was not comforted!

*   *   *

Karen had been waiting in Mr. Green's office Monday morning when he arrived. Her goal was to weave her web to entrap Velma. The school board meeting was held on Tuesday night. Velma missed school on Wednesday; Fredrick approached Mr. Button about Velma on Thursday, Friday was a miserable day for Velma and now it was the big day, Saturday. This was Velma's first real one on one date. It wasn't that she was not feminine and harbored deep emotional needs for a relationship. It was simply that she kept all of her own desires at bay and channeled all of her energies into sports and coaching.

The timing was not the best because of the events of the week, but in some ways this turned out to be a blessing in disguise.

Bob Button was a kind and compassionate man. He married his high school sweetheart and then became her primary caregiver as she fought and lost a battle with renal cancer. This was a devastating blow and left him with a three year old daughter to raise alone. He had done a fantastic job and she was now a dynamic, bright and precocious six year old. She had a million questions for Bob on their way to the Overall farm. Before they arrived, she had already figured out that her daddy had a date. She had never seen Velma, and Velma had never seen her, but she had extracted enough information from her daddy to know the reason for their trip to the farm. She was not real sure that she was interested in sharing her daddy with another woman. This fact did not go unnoticed by Bob and he was on 'pins and needles' by the time they arrived.

Bob was perceptive of human nature, he understood his emotions and knew what to expect of Velma. He would be in the presence of the commanding and dynamic Luther Overall—a prospective father in law who was bigger than life to him. The fact that Fredrick would also be present caused his knees to knock. His last thought as he exited the car was, *"Fredrick might just grab his Bible and try to marry us right on the spot."* Bob just wasn't quite that far along with his mental struggle of placing all the ducks in a row, even starting a relationship with Velma Overall. He was smart enough to know that Velma was undergoing similar struggles and he felt empathy for her.

What neither understood was that Fredrick Overall was a student of human nature and was three pages ahead of both of them making all kinds of mental notes of how to ease the tension. Bob arrived just a few minutes ahead of Velma. He was kicking himself for not having the presence of mind to offer to pick her up and bring her with him. Fredrick met Bob and Nelda at the car.

They exited the car and Bob introduced Nelda to Fredrick. Fredrick took Nelda's hand and immediately went into a long quotation of lines from Romeo and Juliet that ended with, Thy beauty is far beyond words to express." Then he bent down and kissed her hand. Nelda giggled. She liked Fredrick immediately.

Luther came around the corner of the house with an apron on and a fork in hand. Velma drove up about this time, and as she exited her car Fredrick exclaimed, "Hark! Who is that yon beauty I see exiting yon Mustang?"

Again Nelda giggled. "You talk funny."

As Velma approached the gathering in the yard, she looked grand. She was dressed in an immaculate gold pants suit, and her hair was pulled back in its standard pony tail, but it was exquisitely done and had a healthy look. Velma was six feet tall, but not an ounce of fat on her trim athletic body. She took Bob Button's breath away.

After greetings, Bob introduced Nelda to Velma. Nelda didn't bat an eye and the first words out of her mouth were, "Are you going to marry my daddy?"

Velma turned five shades of red. Bob wished for a well to jump in. Fredrick quickly stepped in and saved the day with an Indian routine. "Ug! Little beauty make heap big boo boo. Squaw turn red; brave become paleface."

Luther cracked up, Bob and Velma laughed. Fredrick never changed expression, but the mood became light and both Velma and Bob understood the anxiety of this little girl. Velma bent down and whispered, but loud enough for everyone to hear, "We hardly know one another. We don't even know if we like one another yet. Something like that would be a long way off."

She smiled at Nelda who smiled back as if to say, "Well maybe it will be okay."

Fredrick was thinking, "Maybe old Velma has a little more finesse than I imagined."

He pushed his glasses back against his face and stared at her briefly. She looked at him and he smiled. For the first time ever when Fredrick was giving her 'that look'. She smiled back.

Bob was not a handsome man, but he had a distinguished look about him and an air of self confidence that was appealing to Velma. He was seven years older, frugal and self sacrificing for his daughter and stories of his gentle care of his dying wife were well known throughout Pressley. Velma liked—L I K E D—Bob Button a lot.

Luther asked Bob how he preferred his steak cooked. Bob answered, "Well, I don't like it cremated, but I don't want it to jump up and run off either."

Luther understood. He commented, "That's the way Velma and I like ours, but Fredrick does not want to recognize his as something that has lived. He wants his black."

Remembering Freddy's exposition about dissecting frogs, Bob laughed. He was thinking, "Well, I guess medical school is out for Fredrick. I wonder just what he will do to challenge that mind."

Eva Mae simply appeared just like she had been a part of the gathering all along. Freddy had already introduced her to Nelda before Bob even realized she was there. He already knew her from school, and had heard the nasty comments about Fredrick Overall and that little "nigger" gal. He greeted her warmly. Eva and Velma weren't the best of friends, but that was slowly changing.

Eva essentially took over Nelda. There was a yard swing under an old oak tree in the back yard and Eva and Nelda wound up there talking like old friends.

Luther soon had the steaks ready. Fredrick had baked rolls and the house reeked with the smell of fresh baked bread. Potatoes were also baking in the oven. A fresh green salad had been tossed and new tomatoes were just beginning to arrive from Rosalie's garden. Rosalie had contributed a coconut pie and carrot cake for the occasion.

The meal went well with Fredrick carrying on a lively banter at the table. Eva was present for dinner and she and Fredrick shared a steak. Nelda and Eva bonded immediately. How Fredrick had suspected this would happen was a mystery to everyone since he had never met Nelda. What no one understood was that Fredrick understood the heart and compassion of Eva better than anyone. She knew Nelda's story and felt sympathy for the little girl.

After dinner, Fredrick suggested that he, Eva and Nelda would clean up the dishes and for Velma and Bob to take a drive through the farm and look at the crops. Corn was up about two feet and the soybeans were just beginning to pop through the ground. Fredrick suggested that Velma show Bob the bluff where they had all learned to swim, but cautioned them not to go 'skinny dippin'. This brought color to Velma's cheeks. Bob thought the color tremendously attractive. Bob and Velma climbed in the farm truck with Velma driving and they headed out. It was a welcomed respite from being on display in front of the family.

Bob and Velma began their conversation discussing and laughing about Fredrick's match making efforts. "Velma commented, "He likes you a lot and was dying to get us together."

Bob did not miss a grand opportunity and stated. "I am glad."

Velma glanced at him and could see nothing but adoration in his eyes.

Her eyes dilated and she smiled and countered, "Me too." Bob reached over and took her hand. She gave it freely.

Bob continued, "Velma, I didn't realize how beautiful you were until this evening."

Velma blushed, and responded, "Well, it's not true, but I sure do like to hear it."

"But it is."

Velma had stopped the truck at the bluff overlooking the creek."

Before they got out of the truck, she answered, "Thanks, Bob. I wish I had more social skills. I am scared to death to start a relationship with you, but at the same time I am so excited I'm about to pop a cork. Please help me; I am as dumb as a 'peach tree stump'."

Bob was amused at her honesty, but found it very appealing. Velma was a breath of fresh air when compared with all of the divorcees that had been after him ever since his wife's death. They got out of the truck, he placed his arm around her as they walked toward the bluff overlooking the creek.

Bob drew her close and whispered, "We will learn together." The sun was just dipping behind the trees. It was a romantic spot for this emotionally charged couple. Before either knew what was happening, they were in a passionate embrace that left each weak in the knees. Fredrick had planned well.

Thus began the courtship of Velma Overall. It blossomed, reached full bloom, and by mid December it was in full fruit. Just before Christmas of Fredrick's senior year of high school, Velma, Bob and Nelda stood up in the Overall living room in front of their pastor and became a family. Fredrick served as best man and Eva Mae was Velma's Bridesmaid.

Chapter 5

Time passed quickly and before anyone had time to grasp a slight hold on reality, Fredrick Lane Overall was standing at the podium giving the Valedictory address. The whole town of Pressley came to hear what he had to say. Fredrick looked rather stupid, sitting slouched down in his chair on the stage with his graduation cap slightly tilted to the side like it might fall off at any moment and the tassel slightly draped across his face giving the appearance that he was half asleep during the ceremony. His expression or posture did not change all during his introduction. When Mr. Green, the High School Principal, finished his introduction, he looked at Fredrick to see if he needed to wake him, but Fredrick was slowly moving into a position to rise from his seat.

Once standing, he ambled off to the podium, no notes in hand, and said, "Thank you, Mr. Green, but audience, don't believe a word of what he said. He is jumping with joy to be rid of me."

The audience burst into laughter. When the laughter finally died down, and Fredrick just stood waiting with no change of expression, he started over, "Seriously, Mr. Green, Thank you and thank you faculty and staff for four glorious years of high school. They have been grand years.

"As you recall, my mother was killed in a devastating accident my first day of high school and I thought at the time that my world had come crashing down. With the support of family and friends, and many of the staff here, I have learned that life is not always pleasant but it is always good. Life is always good in the fact that it is the hard knocks that teach the most important lessons.

"My dad, always the coach, likes to speak in clichés and little motivational phrases. One that I have heard many times and it has become part of my life is, 'It is not how often you fall or how many times you fall, it is how many times you get up.' Personally I'd rather keep standing and not spend so much time on the ground."

The audience erupted in laughter again. Fredrick Overall had just described himself perfectly. Fredrick Overall was masterful at staying on his feet. After the laughter finally died down again, Fredrick continued. "I know the drill for these speeches. I am supposed to stand up here and give you pious platitudes of how my class and I are going out into this mean old world and make it a better place. I certainly hope that is true, but based on what I have observed, we will leave here, some will go into the workplace, some will go to college and return as teachers and educators, some may even go into the medical profession, some may die defending our country. Some may even become ministers, and—looking at the graduating class intently—boy that would be a shock—Again laughter erupted.

"Well, you get the picture—we are going to accomplish just about the same things as those who have gone before us. Bottom line, we will all struggle to make a living, support our families and do the best we can with the abilities God has given us.

"Perhaps that is what success is all about. Doing the best you can with the skills and abilities God has given you with compassionate hearts and integrity.

"It is my hope for each of us that we will be faithful to that challenge.

"I cannot look down the road and envision where I will be ten years from now. I plan to go to college because I love learning—I love to be challenged. Well, I love to challenge also and sometimes that lands me in trouble."

Laughter erupted again. Everyone who had ever taught Fredrick in school, Sunday school, Boy Scouts, as well as his own family, had been challenged by him.

"I'm younger that most in my class. This has been problematic socially, but I doubt it would have been much different if I had been two or three years older. I would still look like Fredrick Overall, 'the Twerp'."

Laughter was somewhat subdued. Most felt somewhat guilty at the attitude, which had been so very much a part of Fredrick's high school years.

"I think I speak for all of our class when I tell you that our years here at Pressley High have been good foundational years. We have an excellent, caring, compassionate faculty and staff who drug us along, sometimes kicking and screaming, to this milestone in our academic lives. We thank you and we love you."

With that, Freddy with index finger pushed his glasses back against his face looked at the crowd, turned and walked back to his seat, sat down.

He received a standing ovation. He took less than five minutes. It was not the eloquent speech that most expected, but it was somewhat thought provoking. There was no way Fredrick Overall was going to get up in front of the town of Pressley and try to impress them with his eloquence and knowledge and he could be eloquent and had knowledge. Fredrick did not have to prove anything to anyone.

*　　*　　*

The day after graduation, Fredrick called the Austin Statesman Newspaper and placed an ad in the classified section. His ad stated, "Young nerdy college freshman desires room and board or room and kitchen privileges in a home within walking distance of UT. Call Fredrick at 254-658-1248 Pressley."

Three evenings later the phone rang around 7 PM. Luther answered. A fail little voice on the phone asked, "May I speak with Fredrick?"

"Yes Ma'am. Is this about his ad in the paper?"

"Yes it is."

"Ma'am, I am Luther Overall, Fredrick's father. Fredrick is in the shop. May I have your name and number and I will have him call you back?"

"Of Course. My name is Miss Emily Townsen. T O W N S E N. My phone number is 512-854-1508."

"Thank you Miss Townsen. I will have Fredrick call you soon."

Luther went to the shop and gave Freddy the information. He came in and called immediately.

He heard on the phone, "Hello, Townsen residence, Miss Emily speaking."

"Hello Miss Townsen, my name is Fredrick Overall. I understand that you called about my ad."

"That is correct young man."

"Great, Can you tell me what you have to offer?"

"Well, I'm not sure I have anything to offer until I find out more about you. I had some students in my home once that just wrecked it. I had not intended to rent again until I saw your ad. It intrigued me. Young man, why do you think you are a nerd. I do not know exactly what that is, but I don't think that is very flattering,"

"Oh, I am a bit different, Miss Emily. I study a lot. Let us take another approach, Miss Emily. Let's say—you know just pretending—that you and I had met and we liked each other, what kind of room and accommodations would you be offering?"

"Well now, in that case, you would have a private bedroom with a bathroom just down the hall that would almost be your private bath except in rare cases where I happen to have a guest. In that case, you would share a bath with a guest in my home."

'Now Miss Emily, this wouldn't be a male guest would it. You are not that kind of girl are you?"

"Oh heavens no young man! *Goodness gracious*!"

"Well you know when you are young and impressionable like me, you can't be too careful."

"Young man, just how old are you anyhow? I am 14, but I will be 15 September, 15th."

"Goodness! And you are starting to college. My, you must be smart."

"Oh no ma'am, I just study some. Now are you close enough for me to walk or ride my bike to the campus?"

"I am four short blocks."

"Wow! About all you can say about that is Wow. Do you think I will be able to afford it?"

"Why don't you come look at the place and let me look at you before we decide on a price. When can you come?"

"Let me ask Dad if he can bring me Saturday. He is a high school football coach, but I don't think he has anything planned for Saturday. Would that be convenient for you?"

"Yes, that would be just fine."

"Excuse me for a moment and I will ask him."

Luther was agreeable, so Fredrick came back and asked, "Miss Emily, would around eleven be okay?."

"Oh, that will be fine young man. I look forward to meeting you."

"And you, Miss Emily."

*　　*　　*

On Saturday morning early, Fredrick and his dad headed for Austin. They arrived at ten AM, and found the house, but Fredrick cautioned his Dad, "I want to ring the doorbell at eleven on the dot. I suspect that is the kind of person Miss Emily is."

At eleven AM sharp, Fredrick rang the doorbell. Miss Emily came to the door dressed in an immaculately tailored dress, complete with beads, earrings and matching shoes.

Luther was hanging back and allowing Fredrick to handle the first meeting.

Fredrick began, "Miss Emily Townsen, my name is Fredrick Lane Overall."

"How do you do, Mr. Overall?"

"Very well thank you. May I present my father, Coach Luther Overall? Dad, Miss Emily Townsen."

"How do you do, Miss Townsen? My pleasure."

"Won't you gentlemen come in?"

Luther and Fredrick entered a quaint little living room, very feminine. Miss Townsen asked, "May I offer you gentlemen coffee?"

Luther stated, "Miss Townsen, I am a coach, so I do not drink coffee because I fear it would be a bad influence on my young athletes."

"Oh my, I never thought of that."

Miss Towensen was obviously flustered. Luther continued, "Please go ahead and have coffee if you wish."

"Oh no, Oh no. I am fine. May I offer you something else?"

"Oh no, we are fine; we had a late breakfast. Fredrick is trying to get his lodging issue settled as soon as possible so he can relax and enjoy his summer before the start of the fall semester. I will sit back and let the two of you make the arrangements.

About this time, a huge tom cat walked into the room. Miss Townsen scolded, "Mortimer, I have guests why don't you go back to sleep."

It was too late. Mortimer had zeroed in on Fredrick and he was looking him over. Fredrick pushed his glasses back against his face and stared at Mortimer and then spoke, "Mortimer, how are you?"

Fredrick pretended that Mortimer had answered him. "Oh, then you think it is arthritis."

Fredrick nodded his head up and down and continued, "Yes, very painful I understand, but I'm not troubled with that yet."

Fredrick paused and continued to look at Mortimer, "Oh me—I came to interview with Miss Townsen about renting her spare bedroom."

Another pause and then, "No, I don't think I snore. At least I have never heard me, but I don't stay awake at night to listen to me. Do you snore?

"I see. Only during a full moon. Humm, must be a cat thing."

About this time Mortimer decided he had, had enough conversation, so, he got up and headed out of the room. As he walked through the door Fredrick called out, "Yes, thank you, and nice to meet you too, Mortimer."

He sat back in his chair, pushed his glasses back against his nose, crossed his arm across his chest and sat staring at Miss Emily.

She looked at him and then at Luther, and back at Fredrick. "You are weird, young man".

Fredrick took on an incensed look and asked, "Why Miss Emily, don't you talk to Mortimer?"

Miss Emily blushed, "Well, yes I do, but, but, well, it is different. He seemed to understand you and you seemed to understand him. How did you know he had arthritis?"

Fredrick answered. "He told me."

Luther could hold it no longer. Fredrick had reasoned that the old cat had arthritis from the way he walked and knew that an 'old maid' living alone would naturally talk to her cat for companionship. Luther also knew that this little 'twerp' had just secured himself a fantastic living arrangement for perhaps at least four years of college. He burst into laughter.

Miss Emily also laughed, looked at Fredrick and asked, "Do you want to look at your room?" Luther didn't miss, the 'YOUR' room.

But Fredrick wasn't through playing. "Well now Miss Emily, there are some things we need to work out before we come to an understanding. I would require there be no loud music after 9 pm, and the TV will need to be off by at least 10:30 each night. I study hard and don't like a lot of noise. No wild parties, and no guests of the opposite sex in the bedroom. Can we agree on that?"

"Young man that is my line!"

"Oh, I'm sorry. Well, go ahead and say it."

Miss Emily looked at him about to burst into laughter and began, "No loud music after 9 pm. TVs off by 10:30, No guest of the opposite sex in bedrooms. Did I get it right?"

Fredrick gave her thumbs up and replied, "I can live with that."

Fredrick looked at his new room. It was very feminine. "Miss Emily, May I bring my own bed covers and such? This is a little too girlish for me."

"Mr. Overall, you may decorate your room any way you wish as long as it is coordinated and tasteful."

Fredrick had a tape measure in his pocket. He measured a space near a dresser and determined that if he moved the dresser four inches he had room for a four-foot computer desk. "Miss Emily I have a computer that I must bring with me. I keep all of my records on it plus it is an invaluable tool for my schoolwork. I will also require a phone line for an interface to my computer. It is a simple phone jack. I will pay for the installation and have the phone in my name, with your approval of course."

"Well, I don't know anything about computers young man. They are not a fire hazard are they?"

"No Mam. It will look like a television to you, and uses about the same level of power. I do not require a television and do not watch it. I will simply need a phone jack along this wall," indicating the general area.

"I will pay for the phone instillation, and you can have the phone billed to me."

"That will be fine."

"Agreed. And now the price?"

"How does 200 per week, room and board sound. Is that too high?"

"It's a done deal, Miss Emily. Shall we shake on that?"

The old lady extended her frail hand. Fredrick took it and kissed it.

Fredrick gave her a check for $1000. There was no way he wanted to miss this opportunity.

He said, "This will give you plenty of time to cash my check before I arrive in September. That way you will know it is not made of rubber."

Miss Emily responded, "Young man, you are full of bull, but I trust you. I'm not worried about your check."

Luther was somewhat concerned about the old lady's cooking skills but before they left she informed them that she had a housekeeper who cooked one good meal per day and that she would see there was always plenty of soups and sandwich making available for snacks.

Fredrick's lodging was taken care of.

*　　*　　*

As Luther and Fredrick started to leave Fredrick asked, "Miss Emily, may we take you to lunch so we can become better acquainted." The poor little lady hadn't been invited to lunch in 20 years.

She stammered, "Well, I don't know. I have some things to do."

Fredrick pushed his glasses back against his face and stared at her for a moment before he spoke. What he did was give her his "stop them in their tracks look and it generally did."

"Miss Emily, I'll bet you do not have anything to do that will not wait."

She looked into his eyes, saw the sincerity of his invitation and melted. "You are right young man and I would be very foolish to miss this opportunity. Let me get my purse."

Miss Emily went into her bedroom for a few moments. When she came out, it was obvious that she had fixed her makeup, re-combed her hair and applied a liberal portion of cologne. Fredrick opened the door, stepped back, gave a slight bow, and invited her to exit. He took her arm and escorted her down the steps. On their way to their vehicle Freddy asked, "Miss Emily, have you ever ridden in a pickup truck?"

"Why no, young man, I haven't."

"Well, you are in for a treat."

Luther had just purchased a new F250 Club Cab Ford pickup. Fortunately, it was well apportioned and had a step. Fredrick helped Miss Emily into the front (bucket) seat and he climbed into the backseat.

Miss Emily looked around and said, "Why it's just like a car."

As Luther moved the truck onto the street, Miss Emily gasped, "My, you are up so high. You can see everything."

It was obvious she was enthralled by the truck. Luther was thinking all during the conversation, *"How in the world did this kid figure out that this old lady had never been in a pickup truck? That never even crossed my mind."*

Luther asked, "Miss Emily, do you have a recommendation for a good place to eat?"

Miss Emily thought for a few moments and then replied, "Well, we could eat here near the campus and give Fredrick a glimpse of what college life will be like. Several students are attending Summer School."

She suggested a nice little restaurant just off campus. She directed Luther to the parking lot. Fortunately, a car was just leaving and Luther squeezed into the parking space.

When they entered the restaurant, it was obvious that the entire staff knew her. The proprietor came out and spoke to her. She introduced him to Luther and Fredrick and informed him that Fredrick would be living with her at the start of the fall semester.

"Is this your nephew, Miss Emily?"

"Oh no! He placed an ad in the Statesman advertizing for a room. I responded."

The gentleman looked puzzled. "I thought you swore you would never rent to college kids again?"

She smiled, "Well, his ad intrigued me."

"Oh. What did he say?"

Miss Emily had the add memorized she repeated it word for word, even down to the telephone number. "Young nerdy college freshman desires room and board or room and kitchen privileges in a home within walking distance of UT. Call Fredrick at 254-658-1248 Pressley."

The gentleman chuckled. "Couldn't resist taking a look at him could you, Miss Emily?"

She grinned. "No, I couldn't."

The meal conversation was pleasant. Miss Emily ordered a Ruben Sandwich. Fredrick spoke up and asked, "What is that, Miss Emily? I am from the country and have never had one of those. Maybe I will try one."

"Well Fredrick, the Reuben sandwich is a grilled or toasted sandwich made with corned beef, sauerkraut, Swiss cheese, and Russian or Thousand Island dressing, generally served on dark rye bread."

Fredrick pushed his glasses back against his face stared briefly at Miss Emily and said, "Sauerkraut! I believe I'll have a hamburger."

Luther and Miss Emily laughed. During the conversation, Fredrick carefully and with precision extracted Miss Emily's life history. They learned that she was a UT professor's daughter who had lived with her father. She had been a music teacher at a local school for several years when her father contracted Lou Gehrig's disease. As his illness progressed, she gave up her job and became his primary caregiver. Her father was from a reasonably successful family and he had left her well provided for. Earlier in life she had played an oboe with the Austin symphony

Fredrick also learned that as a young 21-year-old bride to be, she was left standing at the altar when her intended decided that he could not go through with the wedding. He married her best friend instead.

Fredrick asked during the course of the meal, "Miss Emily, do you teach piano?"

"Well, I have in the past. I'm not teaching now."

"Will you teach me?"

"Will you practice?"

"Six hours per week. That is all the time I can spare and take a full load."

Miss Emily thought for a moment. "I'll accept that."

Their meal ended. Fredrick and his Dad dropped Miss Emily off at her home. She looked very frail and lonely as she stood in the door and waved as they left.

Luther looked at his son as they left Austin, "Fredrick, you never cease to amaze me. I don't know how you do it, but I believe you and Miss Emily were made for each other."

"Fredrick pushed his glasses back against his face, looked at his dad and replied, "Yep. I believe you are right. I like her. I'd just marry her if I weren't already spoken for."

With that, he sat back in his seat and pretended to go to sleep. Luther glanced at him—he felt a sudden chill and a picture of Eva Mae entered his mind. He didn't want to go there just now. His son, that had been his salvation since Mary died, was about to leave home and that was all Luther Overall could handle right now.

What Luther could not know was that Fredrick was slowly but surely preparing him for the future.

*   *   *

Fredrick and Luther had a pleasant trip from Austin back to Pressley. Both felt good about Fredrick's living arrangements. Fredrick breached the subject of a car with his dad. He was only 14, but he would be eligible for a driver's license a year from September 15th when he had his 16th birthday. Luther was not ready for this. Fredrick had been driving the farm truck all over the farm since before he could reach the pedals. To stop, he had to get down off the seat. Place his back against the seat and press the clutch and brake at the same time. During the stopping maneuver, he could not see over the dash. The first time Luther saw this he very near fainted. Mary calmed him down, but she was not here now to act as intercessor. He dropped the subject and this disturbed Luther more than open confrontation with Fredrick. He tried to reopen the discussion by asking, "Fredrick why do you need a car? You have just arranged for lodging near the Campus where you can walk or ride a bike. Why do you need a car?"

Fredrick flippantly replied, "Oh, it was just a whim; to make me look grown up."

Luther thought about this for a few moments. There was a believable element in what he said, but knowing Fredrick, seemingly looks had never been of any importance at all other than to appear different. This simply did not compute.

Luther was thinking, *"Oh Mary, how I need you here to reason with him. How in the 'H***' can I coach boys for over 30 years and not even know how to handle my own son. Velma, Mark and James all had cars when they went to college. Is he testing me? But this is different. He is still a little kid. But he has* *an adult mind. Why shouldn't he have a car? Lord have mercy, I don't have sense enough to be a parent."*

Fredrick could read his Dad's thoughts and he was sorry he had broached the subject since they were having a very pleasant trip up to this point. In order to change the subject he asked, "Dad, are you going to take the superintendent's job when they offer it to you? Dr. Weems contract is ending and they will offer you the job."

"Well, I don't know, Son. I have given it lots of thought. In some ways, it is a big headache. I suppose I should. I got my Masters for that very purpose."

"Think hard, Dad. Do you really want that job? Do you love coaching? What is your motivation to take the job? Is it money? Is it prestige? Is it to get even? Just what is the real reason you are considering it?"

Luther was quiet for a very long, very pregnant moment. "I don't know that I have an answer to your question, Son."

"Well, you had better have an answer because it is coming soon, and you had better have your ducks in a row or you are going to be miserable. Look at it this way. It's not the money. You could retire today and still be okay financially. The farm will support you. I'm not sure the prestige is there. Every person in Pressley would try to pick every decision you make to pieces. If you want prestige, run for governor. If it is to get even, just to prove that you can do a better job than Weems? Why? You don't have to prove anything. Just ask yourself one question, would I rather be a coach? Would I be miserable not coaching? If you answer those two questions honestly, I believe you will find your answer."

With that instruction, Freddy sat back in his seat, pulled his new UT cap, that he had just purchased, down over his face and pretended to go to sleep. Luther looked at his son and thought, *"How can a fourteen year old kid have that much more wisdom than his father. I have lost many, many nights sleep over this question for two months. The answer has been there all the time and I just couldn't see it. I don't want the damn superintendent's job after they have given it to Weems. I think this a personal affront to even consider taking it. I'll tell them to take it and shove it."*

They were just turning into the farm road when Luther came to his decision. He reached over and placed his hand on Freddy's shoulder and said, "Thanks, Son. When you get ready for a car, Go buy what you want."

Freddy replied, "I like the Ford Ranger or Toyota pickup."

"That is about what I figured."

*   *   *

Fredrick was dreading leaving home for college. He knew he would be coming home often on weekends, but life was changing. He and Eva were very close and were together every day. Fredrick more than anyone, influenced Eva to be a secure, self confident young lady. She was a beautiful girl by anyone's standards. Over the summer he and Eva decided to build their own computers, so, Freddy could leave the farm computer for Luther. Luther became interested in the computer and Freddy instructed him in the use of the Farm records program. By the end of the summer he was proficient at entering data, printing checks and keeping the farm records.

Fredrick studied computer magazines, and called everyone in the computer industry who would talk to him about building your own computer. He bought and read books. He experimented. By the time he started, he was quite knowledgeable—more knowledgeable than most. He didn't just scratch the surface with his research; he got into the guts of the matter and worked his way out. Eva was right beside him and he taught her as they went. Fredrick was caught up in a study of communication using computers and gained much insight into ARPANET, the forerunner of the internet. In 1983 ARPANET standardized on the TCP/IP type protocol. This was the year before Fredrick got his first computer, a Commodore 64. In his computer studies he discovered this network, struggled through and set up a communication system that would allow him to link to the major libraries around the country via modem. More importantly, at this stage, his computer communication skills allowed him a link to Eva Mae while he was in Austin. The Internet was just around the corner but Fredrick could not wait. Luther never knew how much Fredrick spent on getting three computers to talk to one another. By the time he left for his first semester Fredrick could communicate with the farm computer and Eva Mae. Luther really didn't want to know the cost. He had already learned it was best not to know, but he had grown to trust Fredrick's judgment.

On September 10, 1989, Fredrick and Luther made their way to Austin to move Fredrick. This would be Fredrick's home for the next six years. It was a bittersweet day. The excitement of starting college is always a grand experience, but leaving a home you love is always 'gut wrenching'.

Fredrick warned Luther, "Dad, just get me in the door and say goodbye. I don't want to cry, but if we string it out I know I will lose it. Luther felt the same, so, this is exactly what they did.

Arriving at Miss Emily's home about 11 AM, Luther quickly helped Fredrick unload his clothes, linens, computer, bicycle and books and they said goodbye. Luther headed back to Pressley, weeping before he got to the end of the block. There had not been a dull moment in the house when Fredrick was there. Now he faced an empty home. Both Mark and James were in the military completing an ROTC commitment. Mark was in Germany and James was in Washington DC. Velma was married, and fortunately, she was still in Pressley, but Luther was very much alone. The pain of Mary's death hit him full force again. Fredrick had reasoned this entire scenario out and knew his dad was going to be very vulnerable and had cautioned him about women. Luther was amused.

*   *   *

Miss Emily was as excited as a kid with a new toy. She engaged a contractor to come in and paint the house head to toe, inside and out. It shone like a new dollar. Fredrick looked it all over and commented on the color coordination, the excellent job by the painter, and the clean new smell.

He bragged on the color choice (pale blue) for his room. "Just exactly what I would have chosen", he commented.

Miss Emily beamed. Fredrick had people skills, but there was an undertone of appreciation for the old lady's effort to provide a pleasant home for him. He did truly appreciate what she had done and it showed. That was forever endearing to Miss Emily.

Fredrick had not been there very long before Mortimer walked in. "Hello, Mortimer."

"Very well thank you, and you?"

"Oh! She stunk up the place just because I was coming, Well don't blame me for that."

"You don't like your room. Why not?"

"Oh. I see. Well maybe you can just move in with me."

Miss Emily interrupted Fredrick's conversation with Mortimer. "What did he say? Why doesn't he like my room."

"He says it's pink."

"Oh! Well, he should have said something."

Fredrick turned back to Mortimer and asked, "Why didn't you say something?"

Mortimer had finished his conversation and he got up and started walking off.

As he left, Fredrick called after him, "That is just what I figured."

"What did he say?"

"He said he would rather be mad."

Miss Emily burst into laughter. Fredrick had just described the cantankerous old cat she knew.

*   *   *

Fredrick piled everything in his room, climbed on his bike and headed to Orientation.

Miss Emily had her housekeeper find his sheets and coverlet and make his bed. The housekeeper saw the computer and was afraid of it, so, she did not touch anything else. That suited Fredrick fine, but he was very grateful to have his bed made when he came in.

After Orientation, Fredrick came in, ate a snack and began setting up his computer. Within an hour, he was communicating with Eva, and he wrote his dad a short note.

Miss Emily was intrigued by the computer. She had the phone line installed for him before he arrived and she had thought he simply wanted his own private phone. When she learned that he wanted to tie the computer into the phone line, she could not grasp the concept of computer communication. Over the next six years she would learn a lot of 'computerese'.

Fredrick's first class at UT was an English class. There were 50 students in the class, and the first day the Professor asked each student to stand and give their name and tell where they were from. Fredrick had arrived early, so he sat near the front of the class.

Two students were before Fredrick. When it came his turn he stood and said, "I am Fredrick Lane Overall from Pressley, Texas and people call me the Twerp.

Frowning, the professor looked at him and asked, "The Twerp?"

"Yes, ma'am. A contemptible or insignificant person."

"And you don't object to this nickname?"

"No ma'am. It fits."

"Well, stop calling me ma'am, and we will not call you The Twerp in this class."

"Yes ma'am", Fredrick blinked his eyes and continued, "I mean yes sir, I mean yes Professor. But that is what my mama learned me, I mean teached me, I mean taught me." He was blinking before each correction. He then, with index finger pushed his glasses firmly back against his nose and stared at the professor.

She said, "I am Dr. Burke and you will refer to me by that name."

"Yes ma'am, I mean yes sir, I mean yes, Dr. Burke."

The class was 'in stitches'.

Fredrick looked so comical Dr. Burke could not keep from laughing. She tried hard but could not pull it off. She asked, "How old are you young man if you do not mind me asking?"

"Oh, no ma'am, I mean nosir, I mean No, Dr. Burke. I am fourteen. I'll be fifteen tomorrow."

"Young man, What are you doing in College?"

"Trying to learn something, ma'am, I mean sir, I mean Dr. Burke."

Fredrick was becoming annoying at this point, and Dr. Burke looked sternly at him. He pushed his glasses back again and stared back at her. He was such a funny looking kid, she could not look at him without laughing. "You really are a 'twerp' aren't you?"

"Yes, ma'am."

Dr. Burke just shook her head, waved her hand and said, "Just sit down."

Fredrick plunked down in his chair and looked over his glasses at her, looking very much like a puppy who had just torn up the morning paper.

Dr. Burke was thinking, "Oh!" This is going to be a very long semester."

Little did she know that she had just met her ace student.

*　　*　　*

Most of Fredrick's other classes got off to a rather unique start. In his Algebra class, he was reading a book while the professor was explaining a problem. This irritated the instructor tremendously. He put a similar problem on the board and instructed, "You, young man—the gentleman reading the book please come to the blackboard and solve this problem."

He really thought Fredrick was not listening and he would catch him off guard and embarrass him in front of the class, and nip the book reading in his class in the bud. Fredrick immediately rose from his seat, looked over his glasses, to each side, pushed his glasses back against his nose and almost sprinted to the board.

He said, "Now, let's see you could solve it in this manner," and he started factoring all the terms to solve the problem and got almost finished with that solution and promptly quit. He then began in a different direction, and got almost to the final solution and quit that direction. He looked at the problem and said, "Or you could solve in this manner," and started in another direction. Before he got to the end he turned to the professor and then explained, "Or you could just look at the problem and say that A= 26, B= 13, and C= 7. Which method do you like best?"

Professor Johnson went ahead and solved Fredrick first method and came up with A= 26, B= 13 and C= 7. He turned and looked at Fredrick. Fredrick pushed his glasses back against his face and stared back at him. Finally Professor Johnson said, "Young man you may take your seat."

Fredrick smiled at him, said, "Thank you", and took his seat. Professor Johnson stood looking at the three different approaches, solved all of them and came out with the same answer. Under his breath he said, "Well, I'll be damned."

The entire class erupted into laughter. Fredrick appeared to be absorbed in his book.

*　　*　　*

The truth of the matter was that Fredrick was 'wrung out' after his first day of classes. He had decided up front that he would put up a big bluff because of his age. It had taken all of his will power and stamina. He went to his room crashed across his bed and went promptly to sleep. Miss Emily became worried about him. She came and gently shook his arm about seven PM. He awoke with a start. Mortimer had been asleep beside him all evening, but had gotten up and gone to Miss Emily.

Miss Emily touched Fredrick's arm and stated, "Fredrick, I hate to wake you, but I know you need to eat dinner. I have kept it warm for you."

Fredrick jumped up. "Oh Miss Emily, I am so sorry. I didn't mean to sleep through dinner. I was just going to rest for a moment. My first day of classes has worn me out."

"That is OK Fredrick. Mortimer came and got me and told me you needed to get up and eat. He had been sleeping beside you."

Fredrick looked at the old cat. "Thanks Mortimer. I'm glad you were looking out for me."

"Oh really! You are one of those kind, are you."

"I see."

"What did he say?"

"He said it would cost me later."

"What else?"

"Oh Miss Emily, I would be embarrassed to tell you."

"Well, you tell me anyhow."

"Well, he said you were a tough, cantankerous old woman and he and I would have to stick together to survive, but Miss Emily I didn't believe him. I think he is just mad because you painted his room pink."

Miss Emily placed her hand on her hips looked at Mortimer and scolded, "Mortimer Townsen that was not very nice. Just for that, you get to go to the vet tomorrow."

Mortimer stretched, yawned, and started licking his paws.

Fredrick commented, "I see what you mean."

Fredrick and Mortimer looked at one another and Fredrick faked abject terror and almost screamed, "Oh no!"

"Well what did he say now?"

Pushing his glasses back against his face and staring wide eyed at Miss Emily, "He said that before too long you would have me neutered."

Miss Emily blushed but burst into laughter. For the next hour, every time she looked at Fredrick she continued to laugh. Fredrick had brought joy and laughter back to her home. While her father was alive he was a jovial sort to the very end, although a terrible disease was taking his life. Miss Emily loved her father and his death left her empty and alone. Fredrick Overall reminded her so very much of him. Brilliant, fun loving, and compassionate.

Rosa, the Latin American cook, had cooked steak smothered in gravy. Fredrick loved this kind of steak because it covered up the fact that it was steak.

He loved fried chicken, but he had to fight the fact that he was actually eating a chicken leg. He would not eat it directly off the bone, but pulled the chicken off and threw the bones away before he ate the chicken.

It did not take Miss Emily long to realize that Fredrick had problems with eating something that he knew had lived.

Thursday morning during Fredrick's and Miss Emily's breakfast of oatmeal, Fredrick asked, "Miss Emily may I have a date with you on Saturday night."

"Well, I don't know young man, what did you have in mind?"

"Oh, I thought I might take you out to dinner and maybe go dancing or something."

"Well, I will go out to dinner with you, but I'm not sure about the dancing bit. Where did you wish to go?"

"Somewhere close. Riding on the handlebars of my bike is not going to be very comfortable for you."

Miss Emily burst into laughter. "Now that would be a sight."

"We will be the talk of the town Miss Emily."

"They would lock us both up in the nut house."

Fredrick looked at Mortimer. "Now that wasn't very nice."

"What did he say?"

"He said that is where we belong."

Miss Emily burst into laughter.

For two days, Miss Emily wondered just what Fredrick had in mind, On Saturday evening, about six PM; Fredrick asked Miss Emily if she was ready. She was. The two walked down the street to the little restaurant that Miss Emily had suggested to Fredrick and his Dad when they came to look at lodging. When they walked out the door and started down the walk, she knew immediately where they were going. It suited her fine.

For the next several years, this became a ritual for Fredrick and Miss Emily. The old lady had developed a grand sense of humor from her father, and she appreciated Fredrick's humor more than most. She was a grandmother to Fredrick who had never had a grandmother, and she helped fill a very deep void left by his mother's death.

*   *   *

Fredrick underwent another growing spurt and by the end of his first year of college, he was over six feet tall. He was still skinny as a rail and his face was still thin, making his glasses stand out even more. He became known on campus as, "That weird kid with a brain too big for his body". Girls loved him. They didn't feel threatened by him and flocked around like flies on a ripe peach. He was always good for an answer to a tough problem they were working on.

He carried a Hewlett Packard scientific calculator with him at all times and he could almost make it talk. He could solve the most complex math problems with the calculator.

Fredrick took most of Dr. Johnson's math classes over the next several years, and Dr. Johnson wound up letting Freddy teach many of his classes. He discovered that he had an uncanny way of explaining math functions.

One student commented to Dr. Johnson once, "You know, he actually understands that stuff."

Dr. Johnson almost rolled on the floor laughing.

*   *   *

Just after he began his second year, Miss Emily failed to stop at a stop sign and ran out in front of a delivery truck. The truck stopped, but it was about six inches inside Miss Emily's left door. She was shaken up, but not badly injured. She was so traumatized by the accident that she decided to give up her car.

Realizing there would be no transportation; Fredrick scrambled to take his driver's test, got his license. He went to the Ford dealer and bought a new Ford Escort. He decided a pickup would be too hard for Miss Emily to get in and out. From that point on, Fredrick drove Miss Emily to the grocery when she needed to go. Because of her dependence on him, Fredrick decided from that point on to go to summer school. This did not please Eva, but she understood his reason.

*   *   *

Fredrick received a note from Eva that disturbed him. Eva warned that his dad was courting and she did not like the lady. The note came on Thursday and on Friday afternoon, after his last class, he and Miss Emily were headed for Pressley. Miss Emily had never been home with Fredrick and she was very excited. She was anxious to meet Eva, who she knew was very important in Fredrick's life.

Luther had mixed emotions about the visit. He was uneasy about Fredrick meeting his new girlfriend. She was twenty years younger, and had been married three times already. Eva had communicated that to Fredrick and this was one of the reasons she was uptight about the relationship.

Luther warned Fredrick that he would be late getting in on Friday evening because he had a game out of town. What he did not tell him was that he had a date after the ballgame, but Fredrick suspected. It was nearly one o'clock before he got home. Fredrick and Miss Emily were asleep when he got in.

Fredrick got up the next morning and made biscuits and sausage gravy. That had been a staple in his diet growing up. His biscuits were light and fluffy and

Miss Emily loved the breakfast. Luther got up in time to have breakfast with them. Eva also came over for breakfast. Miss Emily finally got an opportunity to meet her. Eva was gracious and vivacious. Miss Emily was impressed and knew immediately that this young lady held Fredrick's heart in her hand. After meeting her, she decided it was in good hands.

Fredrick kept staring at his daddy, which made him very uncomfortable. Before breakfast was over, Luther cleared his throat. "Uh, I will grill steaks tonight and I have invited a friend over to dine with us."

Fredrick pushed his glasses back against his face and just stared at his daddy a moment before he spoke. "A friend. What's his name?"

"Oh, uh, uh, it's a lady. Her name is Melanie. She is a new teacher in the district."

Fredrick pushed his glasses back against his face again and just stared at Luther for a few moments. Miss Emily grinned at this maneuver.

Luther waited for Fredrick to speak, but he just filled his plate again and started eating.

Luther could not stand it. "Well, aren't you going to say something."

Fredrick swallowed a big bite of Biscuit and gravy, looked at Luther intently and replied, "Well yes, if you wish. Something."

Eva and Miss Emily cracked up.

Luther could stand it no longer. He just got up and walked out of the dining room. He got in his truck and headed to town to buy the steaks and to go by Melanie's apartment to warn her about Fredrick. He was very uptight about her meeting Fredrick. If Fredrick did not like you, you were generally aware of that fact. Luther already had some reservations about Velma. She and Bob were invited also. Luther was stressed to say the least.

*　　*　　*

Miss Emily had never been on an operating and working farm of this size, so, Fredrick and Eva Mae got her in the old farm truck and took her on a tour. The corn had been harvested and the soybeans were ready for harvest, in fact the combine had been moved to the field to start harvesting beans on Monday. The Starnes farm was between the Overalls and the Lanes, so, now the Overalls farmed a 2,600 acre block. There was a farm road that traversed the property and it seemed to Miss Emily that they traveled miles in order to cover the entire farm. Most of the farm was in cultivation. Fredrick and Eva were peppered with hundreds of questions, and they were able and willing tour guides. Fredrick even drove her back in the woods and showed her an old coyote den that he and his mom had watched for hours just to get a glimpse of a young coyote.

Fredrick talked almost nonstop and the old lady got a glimpse into the complex and beautiful mind of this young man. For the first time he spoke openly of his mother and of the devastation her death had been for him. He even admitted his struggles with taking his own life after her death.

"I came to the creek with the thought that I might just jump in and resist the temptation to swim out, and simply end the pain. Then an image of Mom shaking her finger at me, telling me that I was not a quitter came to mind. When I finished my cry, I looked around and Eva was right behind me. She would have stopped me anyhow."

Miss Emily and Eva could not keep from weeping as Fredrick related this story. Eva had always suspected what was going on in Fredrick's mind, but they had never discussed it. Fredrick had not intended to reveal these thoughts, but verbalizing them had a cleansing effect on him. The old adage, "confession is good for the soul" certainly proved correct in this instance. It tightened a bond of friendship between these three individuals. After they left Fredrick's 'crying spot' he was back to the old joke cracking, carefree Fredrick the world saw. Miss Emily for the first time ever got a glimpse of just how deeply the current flowed underneath this brilliant young man's mind. She had only gotten snippets before, but now she had the full view.

Back at a corner of the Overall property where it joined the Starnes farm there was a hill that was not cultivated. At the edge of the hill a bluff overlooked the creek on one side and a small river. Actually, it was a stream that eventually joined the Brazos. The bluff was at the intersection of the creek and river. Fredrick drove the old truck as far up the hill as he could. He remarked to Eva, "I wonder if Cleo and Clyde are still around?"

"I don't know, I haven't been back here since you left."

"Who are Cleo and Clyde?" Miss Emily asked.

"They are a couple of black vultures that always started circling every time Eva and I climbed a tree. They were hoping we would fall. I heard Cleo tell Clyde one day, 'Patience my rear. I'm gonna kill somebody'."

Miss Emily burst into laughter and the mood was immediately drawn away from the dark side and moved back into the light. The tour had been in progress for about three hours when Fredrick remarked, "You know I'm thirsty and I am hungry. Eva, let's go see your Mom. Do you think she has any 'tater pie"?"

"If not, she will bake one for you."

Fredrick loved sweet potato pie. Mrs. Burks knew this and she generally kept one baked when Fredrick was home. It was almost noon when the tour ended at the Burks Home. Rosalie had not seen Fredrick for several weeks and she was overjoyed to see him. She hugged him just like he was her long lost son.

Miss Emily was in shock. She knew Eva was dark skinned but she thought it was because of exposure to the sun as a result of her farm life. She had no idea that she was half-black before arriving at the Burks and meeting her parents. She was unable to cover her shock very well, although she put her best foot forward. Though Miss Emily was from a very educated family, she was southern Aristocracy personified, and old traditions are very hard to break. She was struggling to cope and Fredrick read her thoughts perfectly. Duke had come in and greeted Fredrick and met Miss Emily. Rosalie invited everyone to sit down at their dining table.

Being Fredrick, and knowing that someone he cared about very much was struggling, he just opened up. "Miss Emily, "I suppose you are shocked to meet Eva's parents. Don't be. They are part of my family. Eva and I are going to marry when we are old enough and mature enough for that. You see, I look at the heart rather than outward appearances and hearts of gold live in this house."

Rosalie, Duke, and Eva were all smiling at her. All three understood her thoughts and knew that Fredrick was simply clearing the air to start her relationship with Eva. Every person in the room was very bright, and Fredrick simply realized that everyone in the room could handle the truth and work through it.

Miss Emily sat for a moment before she spoke. When she spoke, she came through like the champion she was. "Please forgive my thoughts. I know you are all reading them. I was born and bred in the South in the tradition of racial prejudice. I'm not proud of the prejudice I have held all of these years—it is simply a way of life that dies very slowly. Fredrick, I am so proud of you for breaking those bonds, and Mr. and Mrs. Burks, you are to be commended for instilling such a quiet confidence in your daughter."

Rosalie spoke up. "Oh Miss Emily, it was not me. It was Miss Mary, Fredrick's mother. She is the one who helped me give up my hate of white people. It has been such a relief for Duke and I both to give that up. Mr. Luther didn't help any, but Miss Mary was a saint, and she led us through the tough job of releasing that."

Miss Emily smiled, "I had already decided that, just knowing her son."

Eva's sister came in about this time and ran to Fredrick and hugged him. She had more black features than Eva. Fredrick introduced her to Miss Emily.

Her name was Mary, a vivacious and outgoing thirteen year old young lady. She greeted Miss Emily like a long lost friend, Miss Emily quickly warmed to this family.

Rosalie turned to Eva and Mary, "Girls, please set the table. I have lunch fixed for everyone—and Freddy, I have a sweet potato pie for you.

Fredrick got up and hugged Rosalie tightly. Miss Emily could feel the affection he had for this woman and she felt a slight tinge of jealously. She was thinking to herself, *"My goodness, what am I thinking?"*

The air was cleared for the beginning of a relationship with this strange and dynamic family. Fredrick and Duke went into a very frank discussion of farming strategy, Duke expressing displeasure with Luther for meddling.

Fredrick assured him that he was to do what he thought best and leave his daddy for him to handle. Duke agreed that was a good plan. He said, "Mr. Luther won't mess with you Fredrick. He is afraid of you just like the rest of us."

Fredrick with middle finger pushed his glasses back against his face and just stared at Duke. Duke burst into laughter. Duke turned to Miss Emily and said, "Miss Emily, this boy gets in your mind and stomps around, but I guess you know that by now."

"Yes, Mr. Burks, I have had mine tromped on quite frequently."

There was another round of laughter—all except Freddy. He simply sat looking over his glasses at everyone.

The girls had the lunch on the table almost instantly. It consisted of fresh green salad, fruit salad with whip cream, (The real thing, made with cream) Purple Hull peas, cornbread, fresh green beans, sweet potato pie, and coconut pie (with a two inch meringue). The main dish was a chicken dish with no bones and the meat covered such that it was hardly recognized as being meat.

Miss Emily took special note of this fact. She learned soon after Freddy came to live with her that he had a hang up with meat. She really had not realized just how much until this visit to his home. She also noted at breakfast that he smothered his sausage in gravy. She clearly fixed the picture in her mind of this family understanding this complex young man, loving him and accepting him as he was. Her appreciation for them was elevated two notches, because she loved him like the son she had never had.

During the course of the lunch, Duke asked Fredrick, "Mr. Fredrick, are you learning anything in school that is gonna help us here at the farm."

Fredrick had his mouth full. He had been shoveling in peas and cornbread. Perhaps more than anything else he missed peas and cornbread as part of his new diet with Miss Emily. When he finally got his mouth cleared he pushed his glasses back against his face and began a dissertation about what he was learning, He was eloquent.

"Well, Mr. Duke, all knowledge is helpful. I have to hoe some ground I have never hoed before; but I suppose that most importantly I am interacting with some different kinds of people. Some good, some bad, some smart, some think they are smart and some that are smart and don't know it. I like them the best.

Fredrick sat back from the table and got that look on his face that indicated deep thought. "You know, I have learned that you can learn something from everybody. If a fellow is digging a ditch, if that is his job and he does that day in and day out, you can learn the best and easiest way to dig ditches. This is especially true if that person is from a minority race; black or Hispanic. All of the Burks laughed.

Fredrick raised his hand as if to caution everyone. "That is not a prejudicial statement. That is a true statement. I have thought on this some and asked myself why this is. I have concluded that white folks are so lazy that all the time they are digging the ditch they are planning a way to get out of the ditch and into something else. On the other hand, poor blacks and Hispanics take a defeated attitude and think, 'It's not gonna get any better, so, I better figure out the easiest way to do this'." Now that may change with education. It is sort of like the exodus from the farm after WW II. After young men had seen the other side of life, they weren't real anxious to come back to the farm.

"At a construction project on campus, I watched an elderly Mexican man dig a trench for a sewer line. He did not seem stressed or rushed he just dug with slow continuous strokes with his shovel. He and the shovel appeared to be connected somehow. He never used a line, a level, or any kind of measuring device, but that trench looked like it had been precision dug by a machine. I marveled at the straight sides, the flat bottom and the tolerance he had held on the width. It was a work of art, and I told him so. He beamed with pride in his work. I wanted to get to know him."

Miss Emily's eyes were misted as Fredrick spoke. She was thinking, "What other brilliant young college student would have given this man and his trench a second thought. That is who Fredrick is. He is kind, compassionate and has a caring heart with an eye for the details of life. He will go far in whatever he chooses to do.

Continuing, Fredrick pushed his glasses back again and looked at Duke, "Mr. Duke, I don't know how useful my education will be here on the farm. What I am hoping for most is that it won't hurt us any."

Duke burst into laughter. He loved this kid. He had loved him all his life. His heart broke for him the day his mother was killed. Fear gripped his heart that day, gut wrenching fear that it would destroy him, but he had watched as Fredrick became the strength that held the family together. He knew very well that educating Fredrick Overall would not harm him.

*　　*　　*

Luther spent a restless day. He went by Melanie's apartment to warn her to beware of Fredrick. Melanie thought to herself, "*He is just a little old college kid. I can knock his socks off.*" Melanie knew that hormones were pumping in college age boys and she decided to dress accordingly to impress him. Big mistake!!!

Luther started his steak cooking fire and went to pick her up. Bob and Velma came while she was gone, and Fredrick introduced Miss Emily to his sister. Since Velma married Bob, she had learned some social skills and she was gracious, and she and Miss Emily had a very pleasant but brief visit. Luther rushed back with Melanie to get his steaks on the grill. He was nervous as a cat in a pen full of pit bulls. Melanie had worn a very, very short mini skirt with a blouse that left nothing to the imagination. Velma was disgusted. Miss Emily was in shock. Luther came in and putting his best foot forward and made the introductions.

When he introduced her to Fredrick, he, with middle finger pushed his glasses back against his face and just stared at her exposed breast. All he said was, "How do, ma'am", and continued to stare. Velma almost lost it. Miss Emily was horrified and Eva was livid. All evening long, Fredrick stared. He hardly spoke, he simply stared. If he wasn't looking at her breast, he was looking at her exposed legs. Melanie spent all evening trying to pull the mini down. There was nothing to pull. Luther was horrified. Melanie thought he was retarded, and he scared the life out of her. Eva finally read his thoughts and could see nothing but disgust in his face. She lightened up, and tried to pull him away as much as possible, but Fredrick was right back staring again.

Miss Emily had been studying him, and she, recognizing this was out of character, began to understand what he was doing. She and Eva went in the house to get plates to bring to the patio and they both had a huge belly laugh. They could hardly regain control to carry the plates back outside.

Luther got through his steaks cooking without burning them. Miss Emily noticed that Fredrick only ate a baked potato. Luther's steaks were good. He had bought choice cuts of meat.

The meal conversation was somewhat subdued. Several attempts were made to get Fredrick started talking but he only gave yes and no answers. Melanie asked him what he was studying in College and he answered, "Mechanical Engineering."

She answered, "Oh, I thought you just majored in engineering. I didn't know there were different types."

Fredrick opened his eyes wide and just stared at her breast. He still did not look at her face. Luther, realizing the Fredrick was not going to respond to her comment jumped in. "Oh there are several different engineering fields, mechanical, electrical, petroleum, civil—probably others I have missed."

Fredrick, still staring at Melanie's exposed breast simply said, "Industrial, Agricultural."

Melanie was embarrassed at the dumbness of her statement. The meal broke up shortly after that and Luther shuffled Melanie out as quickly as possible. Breakfast plans had been made for the following morning to meet at Ernie's for breakfast. Melanie did not think she could make it, but Bob, Velma and Bob's daughter Nelda planned to be there. After the evening, Melanie was not *real* sure she wanted to be part of this family. *That idiot kid gave her the creeps.*

Luther and Melanie did not have a real warm parting. Melanie commented to him on the way into Pressley, "That kid needs counseling. You need to do something. Take him out and show him the girls or something." The crowning blow came when she made the statement; "I would have thought that little "nigger gal" would have kept his tank empty."

That did not set well with Luther. He knew Eva's heart and his 'neck bowed'. Melanie knew she had hit a nerve and she tried her best to enact damage control, but without success. On his way back to the farm, Luther was a sea of emotions. He missed Mary more than he ever had that evening.

*   *   *

Breakfast at Ernie's the next morning was interesting. All of the servers came out and hugged Fredrick. Even the cook came out of the kitchen to speak to him. Velma could not keep her eyes off him. She knew that something was coming but she did not know what. She had seen Fredrick in this mode before and she did not expect to be disappointed. Velma could not stand Melanie. She was lazy, a poor excuse for a teacher and spent about 70 percent of her time in the lounge or the principal's office trying to 'butter up' Mr. Green. Velma was waiting and anxious for Fredrick to lower the boom.

It did not take long. Luther was an impatient sort and he too knew that something was coming, in fact Luther had already made some decisions of his own the night before. He decided to open the forum and simply asked, "Well Fredrick, what did you think of Melanie. Do you think she is pretty?" He added rather sarcastically, "You couldn't seem to take your eyes off her."

With a deliberate middle finger maneuver, Fredrick pushed his glasses back against his face and stared into Luther's eyes. Luther could not meet his gaze and looked away. Fredrick placed his chin in his hand and thoughtfully replied, "You know, Dad, I don't recall seeing her face. There was just so much other stuff to look at that I never made it to her face.—Dad, have you ever seen her face?"

Fredrick just let his statement ride. Bob and Velma cracked up. Miss Emily and Eva smiled.

Luther turned bright red. He felt that his legs were chopped out from under him. Defensively he said, "Well son, she was just trying to impress you. She wanted to make a good impression. She likes me you know."

Fredrick pushed his glasses back again and just stared at his dad for a moment and then let go with both barrels.

"Well, I have thought some on that. Just why is she, a 35 year old woman, so enamored with a 56 year old man. You are a nice guy, Dad. A very good coach, but you are still 56 years old. Looming in the back of my mind is the fact that you farm a 2600 acre farm with five oil wells on it. Do you think a woman like Melanie does not know that? She probably knows your bank account better than you do. Dad, I don't think you have looked at this rationally. I think all you have seen is a pretty face and a cute butt."

Luther's mouth dropped. Velma spoke up and enforced Fredrick's evaluation. "He's right, Dad. She is one of the shallowest people I have ever met. How in the world could that woman get a college degree and not know there were different fields of engineering."

Fredrick picked back up. "I understand she has been married three times already. Not a very good track record is it. You wouldn't pick a losing quarterback for your team would you, Dad?"

Sitting reflectively for a few moments, Fredrick had finally said something Luther could relate to and he commented. "Pretty bad isn't it. My mother had a saying, 'There is no fool like an old fool'. You know I believe she was right. I guess I had better break this off before it goes any further. Fredrick you have made this pretty easy. She thinks you are a pervert."

Fredrick looked over his glasses this time and smiled at his daddy.

Miss Emily smiled at Eva who had been watching Fredrick closely. She could read every thought. Eva and Fredrick were almost like one person. She thought, "If they don't marry, they will be miserable just like I have been all of these years. Oh, I hope they marry! They need each other so much."

Luther turned and looked at Eva. "Did you tell him?"

"Yes Sir, I couldn't sit by and let you get into trouble. You were headed into a tornado you know."

Luther sat for a few moments reflecting the events of the past months. He could plainly see how he had been drawn into a spider's web so skillfully woven. At that moment, he hated Melanie. Fredrick angered her and he had gotten a true glimpse of her heart when he brought her home the night before. He spent a sleepless night as fear of what life with her would be like gripped his heart. Luther was not the 'sharpest tack in the sack', but in reality, he had a good heart and a very strong moral ethic. He honored his commitments. He had felt somewhat committed to Melanie up until the revelation of her true character by his family.

With misted eyes Luther looked at Fredrick, Velma, and back at Eva. "Thank goodness for a family who cares."

Velma had been reasonably quiet up until now which was unusual for her. Luther looked at her and asked, "Honey, why didn't you speak up. You must have seen what was happening."

It was Velma's time to be quiet now. She thought for a long time before she spoke. "Dad, I didn't know what to do, you know how hard-headed you are. I was afraid that I would just drive you into her arms if I said anything. I am not as smart as Fredrick is. He destroyed her without even opening his mouth. He just let her self destruct right before your eyes. Bob and I discussed this last night. Bob predicted what was going to happen."

Luther smiled at Velma. "What makes you say I am hard-headed?"

No one tried to answer that question. Luther continued, "I had a long talk with your mother last night. She was pretty disgusted with me. I couldn't help comparing Mary and Melanie. I was pretty disgusted with myself by the time I got home. Mary was so very bright. Melanie is dumber that I am."

Fredrick spoke again, "I kept looking down the front of that dress to see if I could get a glimpse of the hour glass. I could almost see the abdomen. I know it is there somewhere."

Everyone laughed. Bob asked, "So that is what you were looking for?"

"Yep!"

Eva looked at Fredrick with a disgusted look. "You gonna go to hell."

Fredrick looked startled. "Why?"

"For lying."

Everyone burst into laughter. Eva continued, "You enjoyed every minute of that."

Fredrick responded, "O well, when duty calls, you may as well make the most of it."

Another round of laughter.

Luther spoke up and said, "We had better get on to church or we are going to be late. He picked up the tab and they started to leave the table. Eva got in one more shot. "Yes, and Fredrick needs to go to confession."

Another round of laughter, but other thoughts were communicated. Eva had just told Fredrick that she did not like the idea of him looking at another woman. Fredrick got her message loud and clear.

Chapter 6

Miss Emily and Fredrick had a great visit on the way from Pressley back to Austin. Miss Emily had learned much on the trip. Up until this visit to the farm she wondered why in the world one with such a brilliant mind would choose to return to the farm after graduation. In their discussions Fredrick really opened up as to his plans for his future. He had every intention of forming a corporation using the home farm as well as leased and purchased property, and building an Agri-business using sound business principles. However, on top of all of Fredrick's grandiose ideas for business, the one thing that impressed Miss Emily the most was this statement by Fredrick.

"Miss Emily, I want to have children. I love kids. I want my kids to grow up like I did—running across plowed ground with bare feet. Oh, you have no idea what that feels like. I think I absorbed a love of the land through my feet. Eva knows the feeling also. I want them to go 'skinny dippin' in the creek.

"Did you ever go 'skinny dippin' Miss Emily?"

"What is 'Skinny dipping' Fredrick?"

"Oh, you just shuck off all your clothes and go swimming in your birthday suit."

"Oh my no! I have never done that."

"Well, you will have to try that next time we go home."

"Oh my goodness, Fredrick! I don't think so, You and Eva didn't go swimming together did you?"

"Well, Mama would make us turn our backs while the other got in the creek. It was so muddy that you couldn't see anything anyhow. We had lots of fun before we started to school. We went on nature walks almost every day. Mama knew every inch of the farm."

Miss Emily was trying to picture a little boy and little girl swimming in the creek without any clothes on. Not knowing and understanding farm life, she was having trouble coming to grips with this.

Fredrick eased her mind somewhat. "Miss Emily, Eva and I played together even before we could walk. We played in the yard in the dirt. Sometimes we got so dirty that it was hard to tell if we were black or white. Mama or Mrs. Burks would simply pick us up and put us in the bathtub together. I don't know what age they stopped this, but it was after we had discovered the difference. I guess we were a little more mature than they thought we were. We both became somewhat more modest as we got older, and Eva is still embarrassed about our swimming together with no clothes on. She sometimes blushes when we are at the creek and I look at her and smile."

Fredrick smiled and continued, "I get under her skin when I do that."

"Freddy Overall, you are a little stinker. You know that don't you."

"Yes ma'am."

They both had a grand laugh over this. Miss Emily was thinking, "*Oh I hope he marries her. They will be miserable if they don't marry. If I ever saw two people born for each other, it is those two.*"

Miss Emily was picturing Fredrick's childhood in her mind and seeing a picture of a happy little boy with a mother who loved him and strived to expand his boundaries to the limit. She compared her own childhood in her mind. During her preschool years, everything was tremendously structured—dance lessons, music lessons, ballet lessons—all the things parents feel necessary to have a fruitful adulthood. Her parents sent her to preschool to learn how to relate to other people. All of that was missing from Freddy's growing up years except his mother had taught him basic piano skills, but obviously with little structure. From his dissertations it was obvious that Fredrick had gone from one serendipitous experience to another, sharing each one with Eva, and learning life skills from each one.

The miles just melted away as Fredrick drove along educating to Miss Emily. Soon, and very soon, they turned into her driveway. She really hated that the trip had ended and knew that when the opportunity to take another trip with Freddy came, she would have her bags packed.

Mortimer greeted them as they entered. He was obviously angry. Fredrick stopped to talk to him. "Hello Mortimer. How are you?"

Fredrick paused and looked at the cantankerous old cat. "Oh, surely not."

"What did he say?"

"Says he is hungry. Says Rosa tried to feed him beans on a tortilla."

"Oh Mortimer you are lying. I left plenty of food for you. What happened to it?"

Fredrick looked at the old cat, "Oh really"

What did he say?

"Said Rosa ate it."

"Oh my goodness, Mortimer. I should take you to the woodshed for lying."

Again Freddy answered for him. "That's my story and I am sticking to it." Then the old cat just turned his back to Freddy and Miss Emily.

Miss Emily burst into laughter. With Fredrick around she felt at least 10 years younger. She had a new zip in her step, her entire countenance had changed. Miss Emily had a family again.

Miss Emily and Fredrick ate a sandwich for supper and then Fredrick began studying. One thing for certain about Fredrick Overall—he was going to class prepared or not at all. He read two books, which lasted until late into the night, but the next morning he was up, bright and early, raring to face the day. His first class was an American Literature class.

Dr. Fallen had decided before the class began that today was the day she was going to put a stop to Fredrick Overall reading books during her lecture. As usual, Fredrick came in slouched down in his chair and opened an engineering book and started to read.

Dr. Fallen began her lecture, which happened to be about William Faulkner. She had just told the class how much she loved Faulkner and pointed out many of the attributes of his work. She then looked at Fredrick and asked, "Mr. Overall, what do you think of Mr. Faulkner's works? Have you read any of his work.

Fredrick immediately put his book down, pressed his glasses back against his face with his index finger and began, "Well, I have read, 'The Sound and the Fury', 'Unvanquished', and 'Absalom, Absalom'. Whee, he tires me out. I had to keep a dictionary in front of me all the time. He sure knew a lot of big words—old word in some cases that no one uses any more, but you know Dr. Fallen, they express perfectly what he wanted to say. Oh, I guess I would have to say that if you are reading simply for pleasure, you best not choose Faulkner. If you were reading to expand your boundaries, he would be a good choice.

"You know Dr. Fallen, I found one sentence in 'Absalom, Absalom', that was two and one half pages long. Dr. Fallen, If I turned in a paper to you with a two and one half page sentences you would make a eunuch out of me."

Fredrick plopped down in his seat, picked up his engineering book and started reading again. The class burst into laughter, while Dr. Fallen blushed. Not to be outdone she countered, "Mr. Overall, When you win the Pulitzer Prize, you may turn in a work with a two and one half page sentence and I will adore it."

Fredrick pushed his glasses back against his nose with his fore finger and just held them there for a long moment with his eyes scrunched up like he was in deep thought.

He looked Dr. Fallen in the eye. She was not a young woman. She was in her late sixties and in the early stages of dementia. She was known around campus as a mean old woman who would chew you up and spit you out. Fredrick realized at this point that he had never flunked a course, but this was probably going to be a first. He asked, "Well Dr. Fallen, where will you be, up or down? You see, I don't expect this to happen real soon."

"The class again burst into laughter. Dr. Fallen was livid. She screamed, Young man you are impertinent. She picked up a paper weight on her desk and threw it at Fredrick as hard as she could. He threw up his arm to block the projectile. A sharp edge of the paper weight struck him just below his hand and cut a deep gash. The blood flew. Fredrick grabbed his arm with his opposite hand and when blood began to ooze through his fingers, he fainted and was out like a light. He hit the floor with a thump. The young lady behind him jumped up and screamed, "You have killed him!!!"

Dr. Fallen panicked. "Oh! Oh! Someone run call a doctor." Fredrick began to come out of his faint, and started trying to sit up. A student ran to an adjacent classroom and she came back with another professor.

The professor from next door ran to Fredrick and asked, "What happened?"

Weekly, Fredrick stated, "Fainted. Can't stand the sight of blood."

Grinning he added, "Especially mine."

Fredrick was pale as a sheet. The professor recognized the situation and told another student standing nearby, "Lets lay him back down and get his feet elevated. We need to get some blood to his head. With his head lying on the floor, and his knees bent upward, he slowly began to regain the color back in his face.

Dr. Jones, the professor from next door asked, "What happened? Why are you bleeding?"

A student spoke up. "Dr. Fallen threw a paperweight at him and struck him on the arm."

Dr. Jones had engaged in many battles with Dr. Fallen. He looked sternly at her and responded, "This is a matter for the campus police."

Fredrick came up off the floor. "Oh no! Don't do that!"

His wit, wisdom, and mischievousness were returning. He tried pushing his glasses back against his nose but discovered they were missing. "Glasses!" Looking around he asked, "Has anyone seen my eyeballs?"

A young lady had picked his glasses up for him. She gave them to him. "Thanks,"

Looking at Dr. Fallen, Fredrick said, "Don't call the police. They might find out that I am a mass murderer who only picks on little old ladies."

Everyone in the room burst into laughter except Dr. Fallen. She put her hands to her face and gasped. Fredrick just looked at her and smiled a guileless smile.

Someone had already called security and two campus police came running in. "What happened?" exclaimed one of the officers.

Fredrick pushed his glasses back against his nose, glanced at Dr. Fallen and lied, "I scratched my arm, started bleeding, fainted and fell out of my chair."

"Do you need to go to the infirmary?"

"Oh no, I'm fine now as long as I don't look at the blood. I can't stand the sight of blood."

One of the older female students had gone to the restroom and gotten paper towels to cover the wound. She spoke up and admonished, "You are going to the infirmary and get that arm bandaged."

Fredrick took on his little boy contrite look and answered, "Yes, Mama"

This brought a laugh all around the room and lightened the mood. One of the security officers instructed, "Come with us, we will take you."

Fredrick was back in his seat and he had trouble standing. The young woman he had called "Mama", Carrie Allen, stated, "I'm going with you."

Carrie grabbed his arm and helped him up out of his seat. Another young lady spoke up. I will go along also and help you, so, between two fantastically beautiful young women, Fredrick and the security officers left for the infirmary.

The professor from next door, Dr. Ed Jones, looked at Dr. Fallen and instructed, "Dr. Fallen, this is a serious matter. The young man was very gracious, but I suggest that you report this to the Dean.

Dr, Fallen was weeping almost uncontrollably at this moment. Another student from the class, an older lady, Martha Ward, returning to college to finish her education after her children started to school, placed her arm around the poor old lady and asked, "Would you like for me to go with you?"

"Please, just dismiss the class and help me to my office."

"Let me dismiss my class and I will go with you", said Dr, Jones.

Martha picked up Dr, Fallen's briefcase and purse and with Dr. Jones on one side and Martha on the other, they escorted the poor old lady to her office. Dr. Jones knew that for some time the chairman of the English department had been encouraging Dr. Fallen to retire. In earlier years, she had been an excellent teacher, but as she had aged, she had taken on more and more quirky ways and demanded too much from students. Her classes always filled after all the other classes were full because of her reputation.

In Dr. Fallen's office Dr. Jones counseled, "Dr. Fallen, that young man was very gracious. He protected you and saved you the embarrassment of having to answer some very tough questions. Now once he has had a chance to think about what happened, he may become very angry and this could cost you your job. You were way outside the bounds of civility. If I were you, I would talk to the chairman of the department, ask to be allowed to remain in my job until the end of the semester and tender my notice of intent to retire at the end of the semester. That way you will be allowed to leave and keep your dignity."

Dr Fallen wailed, "But this is my life, Dr. Jones. This is my identity. If I give this up, I have given up a very large part of my life. Dr. Jones knew exactly what the elderly teacher meant. He was mid fifties and knew that he would be facing a similar problem in just a few short years, but hoped he had the good sense to go gracefully.

He softened just a bit, but remained firm. "Dr. Fallen, none of us wish to grow old, but if we are smart, we all desire to do it gracefully. You will simply have to find a new identity. 'There is life after teaching'. You simply have to find it."

Dr. Fallen sat at her desk, a dejected and beaten old woman. Martha placed her hand on her shoulder and in a quiet and sincere voice stated, "Dr. Fallen, there are stages in all of our lives. I have just gone through a very tough stage in my own life. I have raised three beautiful children. When I dropped my youngest off at first grade this year it tore my heart out. My baby, my last baby was gone. I started back to college to ease the pain. I know there are things that you can do to ease your pain."

Dr. Fallen, for the first time in many years, looked at a student and saw a real person with their own set of problems. For some time now, she had seen her aging as the only important issue in life, and that had consumed her thoughts and governed her attitude and behavior.

She began to recover her composure. She looked at Martha, smiled and said, "Thank you", and turning to Dr. Jones, "thank you both. You have taken the blinders off my eyes.

Dr. Jones, will you go with me to see the chairman of the department?"

"I will be happy to Dr. Fallen, but you need some time before you make this move. Let me talk to him and set up an appointment and get back to you. I will explain to him what happened and will make some suggestions. Dr. Fallen, none of us desires to see you hurt. Dr. Reeves may wish to talk to the young man."

"Thank you, Dr. Jones."

Dr. Jones and Martha left Dr. Fallen's office. Outside Dr. Jones asked Martha to describe what happened. She related everything in detail, including Fredrick's mannerisms, how he always slouched down in his chair and read, and how everyone in the class including Dr. Fallen thought that he was not listening to the lecture. By the time she got to the point of telling Dr. Jones that Fredrick asked Dr. Fallen if she would be up or down so he could turn in his paper, Dr. Jones was in stitches, just shaking his head.

"I have to get that kid in one of my classes. I have heard stories about him, but never met him.

Martha stated, "Dr. Jones, that kid is brilliant. He could probably have quoted that two and one half page sentence if asked to do so."

"Oh, no doubt, no doubt. I would like to be a fly on the wall when he comes back to class on Wednesday, if Dr. Fallen is still around. He will cook up something if he doesn't decide to get her fired."

"Oh, he won't do that. He would not give up the opportunity to pester her for the rest of this semester."

Dr. Jones burst into laughter. "You are right. By the end of the semester, he will be her favorite student, and mark my words; he is the one she will go into retirement remembering."

*　　*　　*

Dr. Fallen met with the department head, and in a stern warning, Dr. Reeves stated that she would be allowed to finish out the semester if the student did not file a complaint. He warned, "If he decides to press the issue, Dr. Fallen, we will be forced to call for your resignation."

For the first time all semester, each and every student in Dr. Fallen's English Lit 202 was anxious to go to class on Wednesday to see what was going to happen.

Fredrick came in, slouched down in his chair, opened his engineering book and started to read, but everyone noticed that he was carrying a sack. Dr. Fallen came in, walked to his desk and said, "I am so sorry for throwing the paper weight at you, Mr. Overall."

Fredrick responded, "No problem Dr. Fallen. I'm good as new."

She handed him a letter and walked to her desk. As she was walking to her desk, Fredrick simply reached into the bag, pulled out a catcher's mask and put it on. When Dr. Fallen seated herself, looked, up at the class; Fredrick was sitting in his seat and looking at her through the mask. Her mouth flew open, and a startled look came over her face. She started to cry. Fredrick put the catcher's mask back in the bag, got up went to her, blotted the tears from her cheeks then reached down and kissed her and smiled at her as if to say, all is forgiven.

Dr. Fallen felt forgiven. It was a freeing experience. Not only did she feel forgiven by Fredrick, she felt the load of guilt removed from her harsh treatment of other students.

When she regained her composure she apologized to the class and opened up. She expressed her fear of getting old, her anxieties of retiring and giving up her identity, of how much she hated to leave her teaching career. She, at that point was a totally vulnerable person.

The entire class was focused on Fredrick. He looked up and began, "Dr. Fallen, I am sure you have been a great teacher. I'm also sure that over the years you have instilled the love of literature into many, many young minds. Unfortunately for the last few years, you have let your anxiety destroy your joy of teaching. You have a terrible reputation on this campus of being a mean person. I have just formed an ad hoc committee of this entire class and I as chairman of that committee make the motion that we enter into an agreement with you that we make this the best semester of your whole career and have fun together for the rest of the semester. Do I hear a second?"

Martha Ward spoke, "I second the motion."

"All in favor please signify by stating Aye."

Every person in the room spoke, "Aye."

All opposed. "nay."

Silence

Dr. Fallen, "We unanimously agree to make this your best semester ever. Do you enter into this agreement with us, and I warn you that this is a serious gesture on our part and we expect compliance with our agreement."

Dr. Fallen sat thinking for just a moment before she spoke. She looked at Fredrick and he stared back at her. By the seriousness of his look she was well aware that Fredrick meant business—that he did not take this agreement lightly. She could tell this was no ruse. She finally answered, "Mr. Overall, if you will help me I promise to do my very best to comply."

"Our best is all that we can give Dr. Fallen. We accept that. And we are all in agreement."

From that day forward, Dr. Fallen became a different person. She and Fredrick bantered back and forth all semester. He teased her into reading the Louis L'Mour book, *Haunted Mesa*, which is loaded with Indian legion, and she actually liked it. She finally admitted to the class that it was well written and that his descriptions placed you in the scene. She and Fredrick often quoted whole segment of Shakespearean plays to one another for the class's enjoyment and related that to how Shakespeare had affected American literature. Fredrick could quote whole sections of Poe which fascinated her. Dr. Fallen and Fredrick had a ball for the rest of the semester. At the end of the semester, Fredrick arranged a banquet for the class to give Dr. Fallen a send off into retirement. He had promised for several days that he was bringing his girlfriend, and sure enough, he and Miss Emily showed up dressed as Romeo and Juliet.

*   *   *

Fredrick had completed three years of college by the time for Eva to graduate from high school. All year, Eva had top grades in the class of graduating seniors. Many in the town of Pressley were still very racially prejudiced. This segment of the town society was very vocal and influential. Leading the charge, and engaging in a campaign of slander against her was the grandmother of the young lady who was second in the class. Because of the gossip, and a result of this hate campaign, Eva's last two months of high school were devastating for her, but her grades remained high in spite of very harsh grading by two teachers.

In her American History class, where she had felt the most heat, a term paper was assigned which was due the last week of school; in fact presenting this paper in class was the last assignment for the class. Students were told that they could choose any topic they wished. Then they were to do their research, and present their paper. The instructions were presented to them in writing. They would be graded on choice of subject matter, quality of their research, and presentation of their work in class. One stipulation of the instructions was that no one, not even the teacher was to know what their chosen topic was. This was a very large project; twenty-five percent of their semester grades would hinge on the grade received on this paper.

Eva's heart sank when she saw the assignment. She could see how subjective the grading could be on a project of this nature. She raised the issue of not requiring subject approval before starting their paper. Mrs. Grimes, the History teacher was the sister of the bank president's wife, and the aunt of Andrea Turner, the young lady second in the graduating class. She stated emphatically that choosing the right subject was indicative of the student's maturity level. This was also an indicator of how well they would do in college.

As soon as Eva exited the bus that afternoon, she went straight to her room, got on her computer and poured out her heart to Fredrick. Fredrick received her texted message almost immediately on his computer but he responded by telephone. He tried to console and counsel, but he and Eva both knew what was coming. Fredrick began to rack his brains about how to head off the inevitable, but he felt powerless. He went into deep depression. Had this been something that affected only him, it would have been like "water off a duck's back", but this affected someone he loved and he could not figure out how to stop it. Fredrick Lane Overall was stumped.

Mortimer picked up Fredrick's mood shift almost immediately. He took every step Fredrick took. He clung as close to him as he could get, wanting to climb in his lap, something that Mortimer had never done. It was if to say, "I am sorry you are hurting, I wish I could help." Miss Emily became alarmed. Normally she gave Fredrick all the space he needed, but this time she could not stand idly by. She went to his room. He had his door closed. Miss Emily tapped gently and Fredrick without getting up said, "Come in."

When the old lady entered, Fredrick was sitting in his computer chair with Mortimer in his lap. Mortimer looked at Miss Emily as if to say, "What are we going to do?"

This disturbed Miss Emily more than anything up to this point. She knew the old cat sensed something she did not understand. Miss Emily in a voice that was cracking stated emphatically, "Fredrick, you have to tell us what's wrong. Mortimer and I are hurting for you."

Through tear filled eyes, Fredrick looked at Mortimer who gave him a guileless look and then at Miss Emily whose eyes were misted.

131

"Please sit down, Miss Emily." Miss Emily sat on the edge of Fredrick's spare chair. He regained his composure and outlined the problem to the old lady and the cat. Mortimer and Miss Emily both listened intently.

After he had explained the problem he stated, "I do not know how to fix this. Someone I love very dearly is going to be hurt and I can't change it. The grading can be so subjective and is based so much on opinion that I can't block the outcome. I can't even think of anything devious to head this off. The school administration will be tremendously biased and we will receive no help from them. I have left a trail of animosity there. My shenanigans have caught up with me and now Eva is going to be hurt.

Miss Emily began to pace the floor. Eva had become another of her family because of Fredrick.

As an afterthought, Fredrick added, "Eva was depending on that scholarship. Her family is definitely not destitute, but the scholarship would have helped. I can pay her way. I am sufficiently funded to do that.

Miss Emily put her hands on her hips and stated emphatically, "Well Fredrick that is not a problem. She can come here and live with us. I will pay Eva's way through school. You tell her to tell them to go jump in the lake."

Mortimer jumped down from Fredrick's lap and just sat staring at him. Fredrick looked at the old cat and sort of scrunched up his shoulders and said, "Oh really. Them that—huh?"

"What did he say?"

Fredrick cupped his hand, placed it up to his cheek and whispered, "He said, 'Tell 'em to go to hell'."

Miss Emily looked at the old cat. "You tell'em Mortimer!"

With that she left Fredrick's room. Shortly thereafter Fredrick heard her talking on the phone. He could not hear all that she was saying, but he could hear enough to know that she was very agitated and someone was getting the whole story.

Fredrick's mind went to work. He finally came to the conclusion that he could not alter the outcome of the inevitable, but he could embarrass those responsible beyond belief. From the conversation he had just overheard between Miss Emily and someone on the other end of the phone, Fredrick sensed that Eva did not have to worry very much about loss of the scholarship.

Early the next morning during Fredrick's first class there was a note delivered to the class. A note addressed to him from the office of the president of UT was handed to him. The note simply stated, "Mr. Overall, please bring this note to my office and give it to my secretary at your convenience." It was signed by the president."

Fredrick had a one hour break between classes, so, he took the note to the president's office and gave the note to his secretary. She went into the office and came back out shortly and said, "Dr. Westfield would like to speak to you, Mr. Overall."

Fredrick was ushered into the private office and Dr. Westfield came around the desk and extended his hand and introduced himself. Fredrick noticed his file in the center of the desk.

Fredrick was invited to take a seat, and Dr. Westfield sat in a chair close by in what appeared to be the setting for a casual conversation.

Dr. Westfield opened the conversation. "Mr. Overall, I have been reviewing your file, and I must say I am very impressed with your demonstrated abilities as a student here at UT. You have an excellent record in all subjects, and I must admit that stories of your exploits here on campus have reached my ears." Dr. Westfield was smiling when he said this."

Fredrick responded. "Well Dr. Westfield it was not my intent to call attention to myself. I normally like to keep my neck down in the grass. You know when they come to mow the lawn, if your head is sticking up. It is the first to get chopped off."

Dr. Westfield burst into laughter. "Yes, Mr. Overall you are right, and sometimes I feel that my neck is sticking way out."

The president started to speak again and Fredrick held up his hand. "Dr. Westfield, I'm Fredrick or Freddy, which ever. My daddy, the coach, is Mr. Overall. Dr. Westfield smiled. "Okay Fredrick." After a brief pause. Dr. Westfield began. "Miss Emily called me last night and we discussed an inequity that she says you believe to be eminent. As a courtesy to Miss Emily, I wanted to chat with you briefly and get more information. As you probably know, Miss Emily is tremendously distressed over what she thinks is about to transpire. As you may or may not know, Miss Emily's family has endowed a scholarship fund for the University. Miss Emily has oversight of this fund. She has instructed me to see that this young lady is well funded for her education here at UT.

"What can you tell me about what is about to happen?"

Fredrick began at the beginning starting with the schools desire to place him in special education classes; the bus incident where Eva was referred to as 'That little nigger gal'; the attempt to frame Velma. He discussed the attempt by the Superintendent to put him back two grades. He brought Dr. Westfield all the way to the current event.

With a pained expression on his face Fredrick pushed his glasses back against his face and remarked, "Dr. Westfield, the most influential person in the town is the grandfather of the girl in second place for the valedictory honor. Her Aunt is the History Teacher who has assigned the project and the instructions are subjective enough that the final grade can be heavily weighted by the teacher. There is no way they will allow a half-black farm worker's daughter to win that position over this girl. Because of Eva's race and the fact that she is associated with Fredrick Overall. I feel a great responsibility for what is happening to someone I love. I can't stop it from happening, but I can sure cause some embarrassment to those responsible."

Dr. Westfield sat looking at Fredrick for a brief moment, seeing the intensity of this young man. he smiled and remarked, "You know Fredrick, I sure would hate to be in their shoes.

"Do you think Eva can find a time to come talk with me? I would like very much to meet with her."

Dr. Westfield removed a cardholder from his pocket and handed a card to Fredrick with his home phone number on it. He said, "If you lose the number, Miss Emily has it. Whenever Eva can come, please give me a call and I will meet with the two of you. By the way Fredrick, just how close is your association with this young lady."

Fredrick pushed his glasses back against his face again and looked intently at Dr. Westfield. "Well, when we were four years old, we went 'skinny dippin'. Now I guess I have to marry her."

Fredrick took a chance that Miss Emily was more closely associated with Dr. Westfield than most and that she had possibly related what he had told her about him and Eva swimming in the creek in their birthday suits. He was right and Dr. Westfield burst into laughter.

*　　*　　*

Eva struggled to pick a subject. She and Fredrick discussed this at length. Earlier in the year, Fredrick had found a park bench on campus in a secluded spot by a walking trail. He met a retired history professor who took a daily walk through the campus along this trail. Fredrick often studied for his history class, looking over his notes and reading during this break sitting on this bench. The Professor stopped at the bench one day to take a breather and he and Fredrick started visiting. The professor was a wealth of information and Fredrick always went to class informed and prepared from that point forward. Fredrick breached the subject of Emma's paper with the professor and asked for a suggestion. Fredrick alluded to the fact that Eva was leaning toward the subject of "How Families Leaving the Family Farm and Moving to Industrial and Service Jobs is Reshaping Our History."

Dr. Hill thought this a great title. "Young man, this has caused some of the greatest changes in our society. It moved us from an Agrarian Society to an Urban Society. This brought along with it all of the attendant problems such as increase in crime as well as breakdowns in family values. I think that a grand idea."

Fredrick passed Dr. Hills enthusiasm on to Eva, and she decided to go with that. The next day, Dr. Hill with renewed vigor went to the UT library and photo copied article after article relating to the subject. He also provided a detailed bibliography of references that she might look at. Fredrick placed the packet of information on the Greyhound bus which passed through Pressley. Eva picked it up at the bus station three hours later. She was off and running. Fredrick also went to work instructing her how to make pie charts, grafts and etc. using Lotus 1 2 3. Eva created a very professional paper that would have stood up in any college class.

The big day came and Eva presented her paper. She had gone to Waco to a print shop and produced overhead slides of her charts and grafts. Her presentation was flawless. On Friday afternoon just before the announcement of the Valedictorian was made, Eva received her paper back with a grade of B-. A B+ would have kept her valedictorian. A B—carried a numerical grade of 80 to 83. A B+ carried a numerical grade of 84 thru 87.

In the final assembly, the announcement was made who would be Valedictorian. Andrea Turner had a grade point average of all subjects of 98.75. Eva Burks had a grade point average of 98.50.

There was a rousing cheer from about half the students and boos from the other half. The school was almost equally divided down the middle. Luther Overall was a popular coach, but over the years, there were many who thought their child was a better athlete that his abilities demonstrated. Luther had integrity and made some very unpopular choices of starting lineups. He had enemies, and poor Eva felt the full force of animosity toward the Overalls plus the fact that she was half-black in a very racially prejudiced town.

Fredrick Overall could not stop Eva from being hurt in the crossfire, but he was loading his own guns, and the first blast of the cannon was about to occur.

*   *   *

Fredrick finished the semester and signed up for the summer term, but he had a short break before the summer semester began. He went to work. First he obtained a copy of Eva's assignment and a copy of her paper with the teacher's grade and comments. He, with Miss Emma' right along beside him, took the copies to Dr. Westfield and asked him to read the paper and comment. They also took copies to Dr. Hill, the retired history professor who had enthusiastically encouraged Eva to use the topic.

Miss Emily's meeting with Dr. Hill turned out to be an interesting event. Fredrick just happened to notice that Dr. Hill and Miss Emily seemed to be somewhat enamored with one another. They had known each other some years earlier before Dr. Hill's wife died. Miss Emily had known his wife well. This raised Fredrick's eyebrows and sparked an idea that he would address as soon as the task at hand was completed.

Fredrick was thorough. He also took the paper to Dr. Jones the English professor and asked for his comments from an English perspective.

All three professors were candid in their comments. Dr. Westfield's comments were somewhat general but his praise was high and according to him, the grade on the paper was a mystery. He also added that the University was looking forward to welcoming a student of this caliber to The University of Texas for the start of the fall semester.

Dr. Hill commented on the historical accuracy of the paper, the organization of facts, and use of references. He stated that the paper would be a good start for a Master's Thesis in any History department. His comments ended the same as Dr. Weatfield's, emphatically stating that the grade was a mystery.

Dr. Jones commented on clarity, use of references and the bibliography. He stated distincly that the teacher's corrections of English usage were incorrect and that Eva was correct in her grammar.

Fredrick then got permission to use the professor's comments. No one knew, and it is still a mystery, how Fredrick obtained the Walchik County Tax office mailing list, but he wound up with it on a floppy disk. In fact, no one ever figured out where his mailing list came from, but he obtained the list. He went to work. He engaged the services of a small print shop, which printed a weekly classified ad for distribution throughout the country. He wrote a paper he called the Walchik County Reporter, Fredrick Lane Overall, Editor in Chief. In the paper he wrote a few news type items that were old news in the public domain, but his feature article was entitled, A Miscarriage of Justice—You be the Judge. He then printed Eva's term paper along with the teacher's assignment, the teacher's comments and the comments from the University Of Texas Professors along with the UT President's comments.

Using his computer skills, he and Eva printed mailing labels for every family in Walchik County and mailed each family a copy of the paper. The paper arrived the day of graduation. To use an old East Texas expression, "Lightning Hit the Outhouse." Luther was bombarded with praise, taunts, insults and verbal abuse of every form. The teacher was disgraced and many were calling for her resignation. Mr. Green the principal also felt the heat. Dr. Weems the Superintendent's contract was up and not renewed, so, he was unavailable for comment.

Dr. Elliot, the school board president was candid in his reply, "I haven't spoken with Eva or Mr. Overall. They did not bring their complaint to the board. From all appearances, it seems that the Burks simply accepted the teacher's grade and moved on. I knew nothing of what had transpired until I received the Walchik County Reporter. Reading the young lady's paper, I suspect she will do well in college and I certainly wish her the best. I suspect we will wind up having a talk with the teacher who gave the grade."

The Dallas Morning News showed up in Pressley, The NAACP was immediately on the scene, the Austin Statesman reporters were in town. Duke and Rosalie decided it would be a very good time for them to take a family vacation, so they just quickly packed and headed to Houston to take in the museums, the Zoo and also Astroworld, leaving the school administration and poor Luther to answer all of the questions. Eva was absent for graduation thus did not give the Salutatorian's address. Poor Andrea gave her Valedictory address but she was so nervous by this time that she could only stammer through it.

Fredrick decided it was time for him to go camping, so he took an old tent, a frying pan, some fatback, 14 cans of pork and beans, a stack of books and went to the creek, so he was unavailable for comment. The newspapers could not find Fredrick, Eva or any of the Burks or Overalls to interview except Luther and Velma. Luther would not comment stating that he knew nothing about what had taken place. Velma on the other hand was very angry over what had transpired. She was angry at everyone, the teacher, the school system that allowed the injustice and she was also angry at her brother for stirring up trouble. She ended her interview with the statement, "When you take on my little brother you have a tiger by the tail and someone is going to wind up chewed to bits. I have never won a battle with him and I don't intend to ever try again."

The reporters all wanted to interview Fredrick, but they simply could not find him. They learned that he was a student at UT and got his address from Velma. She knew he was on the creek camping, but she did not divulge that information. The reporters went to Miss Emily's home and she did not know where Fredrick was. They wound up interviewing her. She ended her interview with the statement, "Fredrick is the sweetest child I have ever known." The statement was carried by all three major newspapers.

*   *   *

After the flack died down, Fredrick eased back into his school routine and now he was ready to encourage a budding romance between Miss Emily and Dr. Hill. Miss Emily lost many of her old-maidish, quirky ways with Fredrick in the home with her. She attended more events and Fredrick coaxed her into buying another car. She had been so traumatized by the accident that she was afraid to drive for a while, but Fredrick one day insisted that she drive his Ford Escort, and she liked it. She had always driven Dodges, but Fredrick teased that those were "old women's cars and she needed something sporty if she was going to catch a beau.

Miss Emily countered emphatically, "Well, I don't know that I need a beau, but I'm certainly not an old woman."

"Atta boy, Miss Emily," Fredrick responded.

She wound up with a bright blue Honda Accord. She fell in love with it. On Saturday night after Fredrick's return to summer school, he invited Dr. Hill to dine with him and Miss Emily for their night on the town. Dr. Hill readily accepted his invitation.

Instead of Freddy and Miss Emily's regular hamburger spot, Fredrick took them to one of those Austin "trendy" places that had live music. On this evening, the restaurant had a two man band that played about a half dozen different instrument and they were both good vocalists. They played and sang a variety of songs—some old, some new, but Miss Emily and Dr. Hill enjoyed every minute of the band's performance. The evidence was clear that Fredrick had done his homework and chosen just the right place for this couple to become better acquainted. They liked one another tremendously. Dr. Hill had known Miss Emily's father when he first came to the University as a young professor. Professor Townesen had been his mentor as he learned the ropes of teaching in a large university, so he already felt a special fondness for this lady. By the end of the evening, both Dr. Hill and Miss Emily were thinking down the road.

Fredrick was also thinking down the road and could see that they both needed time to adjust to their new relationship and he became alarmed that they might move too quickly. After they dropped Dr. Hill off, and were headed home, Fredrick looked at Miss Emily and asked, "You like him a lot don't you, Miss Emily?"

Miss Emily's eyes misted. "I am afraid I like him too much Fredrick. I'm scared."

Fredrick reached over and took her hand. "I'm glad you are scared Miss Emily. He is a great guy—terribly lonely. You are going to have to be the strength of this relationship. You take your time, get to know him, but most of all, get to know yourself. The intimacy of marriage will be a gargantuan task for you. You need to spend lots of time with this man before you are prepared for that."

Miss Emily looked at this strange young man. "Fredrick, how did you learn so much in such a short life?"

It was a serious question and straight from the heart. Fredrick had just zeroed in on Miss Emily's greatest anxiety. "Could she allow intimacy with a man? She was a 70 year old virgin. Would marriage ever work for her?" Fredrick had read her mind.

"Miss Emily, I don't know much, but I do know people. I guess it is just a gift God has given me. Perhaps I don't always use it as I should."

It was Miss Emily's time for thought and introspection now. She finally answered, "Well son, it looks to me like you just let people outsmart themselves and then you just close the door on them."

"That's kind of the way it works, Miss Emily. Of course I sometimes help them along."

Miss Emily burst into laughter and their jovial mood was restored.

When they arrived home, Mortimer met them at the door.

Fredrick looked at Mortimer, put his hands on his hips and said, "Well, maybe so; if it is any of your business."

"What did he say?"

"He said been out courtin, ain'tche"

Miss Emily looked at Mortimer. "You mind your own business, Mr. Smarty pants."

Mortimer just turned and went to Fredrick's room and climbed up on the bed. The old cat had not slept in Miss Emily's room since she painted it pink.

Miss Emily and Dr. Hill continued to see one another over the summer. Their love and appreciation grew deeper each day. Fredrick was their major topic of discussion. Both loved this young man. At the end of the summer, Eva came to begin her college career. Miss Emily insisted that she take her spare bedroom. Dr. Hill and Miss Emily worked out an arrangement that either Fredrick or Eva could stay at his home overnight if Miss Emily had an overnight guest. In the two years that Fredrick had been with her, this had occurred only once when an elderly aunt had come to visit.

Eva fit right in. She was energetic, vivacious and easy going. She and Fredrick often studied together, but they were always very careful to leave the door open. Fredrick had gotten permission from Miss Emily for the two of them to be in a bedroom together as long as a door was open.

"Miss Emily admonished, "Fredrick Overall I trust you to behave yourself, and I certainly trust Eva to slap your face if you get out of line."

"I made an agreement with you when I moved in that I would not allow a female in my bedroom. I am asking your permission to break that agreement. Miss Emily, I honor my agreements."

"Thank you, son, and yes, I give my permission."

The fact that Fredrick and Eva loved one another was obvious. Miss Emily knew it was a horrendous task for them to deny intimacy living in such close quarters. This arrangement was stirring up emotions in her own psyche that she had kept repressed for many, many years. By mid November she was ready for marriage and was hoping that Dr. Hill would ask her soon. He did.

*   *   *

Just before the Thanksgiving holidays, Miss Emily came is from a date with Dr. Hill with her head spinning and on cloud nine. Eva and Fredrick were both studying for a very large semester test, but that all shut down. Dr. Hill had popped the question and Miss Emily said yes. Now the thought had suddenly hit her, "What to do about Fredrick and Eva living together in the same house?"

That would never do as far as she was concerned. Not in her house. She raised this issue with them. Her solution was that Eva could move into the house with her and Dr. Hill. She said, "I'll talk to him about that tomorrow."

Fredrick teased, "Oh Miss Emily. Mortimer will chaperone. Don't worry about it."

He then looked at Mortimer and said, "Oh really."

"What did he say.?"

"He said, 'I warned you that she would have you neutered'."

Miss Emily looked sternly at the old cat. "Oh Mortimer, hush your mouth. This is serious."

It never dawned on her for one moment that Mortimer had not actually spoken the words, but they had come from Fredrick's imagination. She stewed and fussed at Mortimer for the next five minutes admonishing him that this was a serious matter and that he should not take it so lightly.

Eva was amused, but Fredrick brought her out of that mode quite readily with a comment to Miss Emily.

"Miss Emily, don't worry about it. Eva and I will just go get married and solve the problem for you."

Eva came up out of her chair. "Now wait a minute. This is not something to tease about."

Fredrick turned and pushing his glasses back against his face stared at Eva for a full half minute. "I'm not kidding. I love you Eva and you and I both know that we belong together."

Eva stared back. "No I don't know that Fredrick. I have thought about that a lot lately and I don't know that at all. With that brain in your head, you can do so very much with your life. You don't need to be saddled with a half-black wife. You and I both know that to most people I am still a 'nigger'."

Tears flooded her eyes as well as Fredrick's. Miss Emily's blood ran cold. To Fredrick Overall this was the second greatest crisis he had ever faced. When he could finally speak he began, "Eva, without you life would not be worth living. Don't you ever say that to me. Are you telling me that you do not love me?"

"Oh No! No! Freddy. I am telling you that I love you too much to saddle you with a half-black wife."

"Eva, we were born to be together. I have planned for this moment all my life. I thought you felt the same."

Tears were flowing all around. "Fredrick I do love you more than life itself. I would give my life for you. I just want what is best for you."

Miss Emily had gotten her voice back. She ran to Eva and engulfed her in an embrace. "Honey, don't you see that you will destroy him if you leave him? Please don't make this terrible mistake."

"Miss Emily, don't you see how it would be if he married me. Prejudice is a destructive force. I was not valedictorian of my class because I am half-black. Everywhere we turn from now on, that fact will affect Fredrick."

Miss Emily simply stood staring at Eva for a moment and then she smiled. "Eva, do you really think that will make a 'tinkers damn' to Fredrick Overall. That is just something else for him to have fun with. Those who took that scholarship away from you are still smarting. They will never live that down and I suspect they have been taught a very good lesson. Don't try to tell me that he didn't enjoy putting them in their place. That boy has a devious streak in him."

Miss Emily looked at Fredrick. "Young man, by the back door, you have asked this girl to marry you. How are you going to support her if you get married."

"Well, when my mother was killed, all three of us kids got a very large settlement from her death. I promised her that I would make good with those funds and try to make the world a better place to live. So far with a computer program I wrote, I have tripled that money, and one little investment, unless it really goes sour is going to make me a very wealthy man Miss Emily. We are well supported from investments. I can afford a frugal wife like Eva."

Miss Emily was shocked. Eva was stunned. Miss Emily recovered and was almost thinking out loud, "Well, you are both young, but you both have good heads on your shoulders. You will probably do better in your studies if you go ahead and marry. I guess I would have to give my blessings. What do you think your parents will have to say about this.'

Fredrick grimaced and replied, "Well we might get around to telling them—sometime."

"You mean elope!"

"Exactly."

"Oh my. Oh My. Your folks will be livid with me."

"Miss Emily, you don't know anything about this. You haven't heard anything."

"Fredrick, you haven't even asked me."

Fredrick fell down in front of Eva on one knee and asked in his Shakespearian voice "Dear lady wouldest thou take this, thy humble servant to be thy lawful wedded husband."

Smiling through tears, Eva answered, "I wouldest."

Miss Emily clapped her hands together and exclaimed, Oh my goodness, I feel just like cupid."

Fredrick jumped up and grabbed his chest and exclaimed, "Right through the heart my dear.

He then turned and kissed Eva, a kiss neither would ever forget.

*   *   *

The next afternoon, Fredrick and Eva were in the county clerk's office obtaining their marriage license. Miss Emily and Dr. Hill had gone during the morning. They decided they would get married on Wednesday evening just before Thanksgiving, and, drive to Houston for Thanksgiving and then fly to California for a brief honeymoon. Miss Emily had called her pastor, an Episcopalian priest to see if he could perform a brief ceremony for them. Fredrick asked her to call him back and see if he could make it two. He agreed.

So, on Wednesday evening Miss Emily and Dr. Hill stood up in front of the pastor, with Eva as Miss Emily's attendant and Fredrick standing up with Dr. Hill and they exchanged their vows. They then swapped places and Eva and Fredrick became Mr. and Mrs. Fredrick Overall. The two couples then went out and had a grand dinner together. Fredrick was in fine form and kept them all in stitches. He was on cloud nine.

Eva and Miss Emily, now Mrs. Hill excused themselves and went to the restroom. In the restroom, Miss Emily confided to Eva. "Honey, I don't know about you, but I am scared to death. Do you think it will hurt."

Eva smiled at Miss Emily and confided, "I don't know, but I am ready to find out."

*   *   *

Dr. Hill and Fredrick were also having a serious discussion. Dr. Hill wanted to counsel Fredrick, but Fredrick also wished to counsel the good Doctor.

"Dr. Hill, this must be a tremendously stressful night for Miss Emily. Marriage is going to be very difficult in some ways for a person who has been by herself all of these years."

"Yes Fredrick, I am aware of that. We have had long discussion about this. We are both lonely for companionship. She is a marvelously clever woman and I think very flexible thinker for an 'old maid'. You have been great for her Fredrick and we so very much appreciate your bringing us together."

"Well, Dr. Hill, I am going to miss having her around to pester. She and I have had a grand time together. Eva and I will be under your feet for a few more years yet.

"I hope that you and Miss Emily will have a great marriage, and many, many happy years together. She is a fun person."

"And I wish the same for you and Eva. She is a vivacious young lady. What are you two going to tell your parents?"

Fredrick pushed his glasses back against his face, looked long and hard at Dr. Hill. "Are you trying to spoil my wedding night? We will work that out on the way to Pressley tomorrow. It is going to be tough enough getting through tonight with zero experience. Eva and I do not know anything about all this, but we love each other and I think we can manage."

Dr. Hill smiled at this strange young man that he had grown to love like a son. "You know, Fredrick, I'll just bet there are a few things that you and Eva can't handle together. She is a beautiful, intelligent and vivacious young lady. Everything is going to work out fine."

Dr. Hill signaled the waiter and asked for the check, but much to his chagrin he learned that Fredrick had already taken care of it. Fredrick was the chauffer, so he dropped Mr. and Mrs. Hill off at Dr. Hill's home and he and Eva headed to Miss Emily's house which was to be their home for the next four years.

Mortimer was asleep when they came in and he barely stirred. He did raise his head and smiled at the newlyweds, at least that is the way it looked to them. Eva and Fredrick were two people who had been in love all of their lives. This night that love reached a new dimension.

*   *   *

Miss Emily was entering into a strange new world, but she adapted like the trooper she was. She was a very happy lady. Her love had been repressed for forty-eight years, ever since being left standing at the altar by a young man she loved with all her heart. Now she transplanted that love to Dr. Hill. He felt it and reciprocated. Dr. Hill did not have a good first marriage. His first wife was a whiner and complainer. During the two years of her illness before her death, she made his life a living hell. He had no interest in remarrying until he met Miss Emily. It was Fredrick's evaluation of Miss Emily that turned his thoughts around. Fredrick often shared funny exchanges between himself and Miss Emily.

Dr. Hill and Miss Emily were driving to Houston to spend Thanksgiving with Dr. Hill's brother and his family. After that, they were flying to Los Angeles to visit Dr. Hill's daughter and spend a few days of Honeymoon in California. Miss Emily loved San Francisco and they were winding up their honeymoon there. One Item high on their honeymoon list was to see Muir Woods, the redwood forest again. Each had been there, but never together. They did that, and a walk through the serenity of the towering Red Woods together was one of the grandest moments of their lives.

*   *   *

Fredrick and Eva were not really having a honeymoon. They were going home for Thanksgiving to face parents. They were only 18, but that was old enough so an annulment was not an option for parents. Rosalie knew that

Miss Emily was getting married. She had questioned Eva about where she was spending the night on Wednesday before Thanksgiving. Eva had told her that she was staying with a friend and that they were all going out to eat and then she and Fredrick would drive home Thanksgiving morning. Rosalie was not happy about this arrangement. Eva told her by phone that they would discuss living arrangements when she got home. She had not told a lie, since Fredrick was her best friend. She also told her mother that the suggestion and an offer had been made for her to move into the house with Dr. Hill and Miss Emily. All of this was true, but it just did not ring quite true with Rosalie and she was worried.

On the way from Austin to Pressley, Eva kept saying over and over, "Mama is going to kill me. She is just going to kill me."

By the time they arrived in Pressley, Fredrick and Eva were wired. Fredrick was generally laid back, but his emotions were in overload and Eva eyes were dilated and she was pale as a sheet. Arriving at the Burks in this state did not help. When they came into the kitchen Rosalie turned and stared at them. No words were spoken for a moment.

Rosalie had been making dressing and she had a big spoon in her hand. She stood looking at Eva and Fredrick for a moment and then she pointed her spoon in their direction and gushed, "You two have been in bed together haven't you. You spent the night in that house by yourselves. Eva you lied to me. You lied to me and you have never done that."

Tears were streaming down Rosalies's cheeks. Duke was standing and looking like he had been run through a sausage grinder. Eva started crying. She gushed, "Mama, I didn't lie. He is my best friend and now he is my husband."

"Yo what!" Rosalie screamed.

Eva held out her hand to show her mother her simple gold, diamond studded wedding ring. Duke had the presence of mind to grab a chair and shove it under Rosalie before she crashed to the floor. Eva ran to her mother and cradled her head against her breast. "I'm sorry, Mama. We knew you wouldn't give us permission so we just went ahead and did it."

Rosalie was weeping out of control. Fredrick walked over and turned the heat off under the dressing. He loved dressing and he didn't want it to burn. He glanced at Duke and found a very stern look on his face. "Boy, I ought to kick your little butt."

Fredrick pushed his glasses back against the face and just stared at Duke for a very long moment. Rosalie had calmed down just a bit and she and Eva were both watching to see what transpired between Duke and Fredrick.

"Well, Mr. Duke, I guess all I can do is just stand and take it. I think she is worth a good hard kick don't you? Do you remember back when Mom and Mrs. Burks let Eva and I go 'skinny dippin' in the creek? Well I must confess, I sneaked a peek and I knew then I would have to marry her."

Eva gasped, "Fredrick, you didn't."

"Did too."

Eva placed her hand over her mouth and snickered. "So did I."

The tension was broken, but the shock still lingered. Rosalie reflectively said, "You are both so young. You should have had a chance to enjoy your college years."

"We will enjoy our college years, Mom. We will enjoy them together. Fredrick has already rented Miss Emily's house. Dr. Hill has his own housekeeper and Rosa is going to stay on with us. Who could ask for anything better. Fredrick is consulting with a computer company in Austin part time and he is making enough to support us from that. I would think that you should be proud of us."

Eva had not lived with Fredrick Overall for 18 years and learned nothing. Fredrick always believed that the best defense was a tremendously good offence and Eva had just gone on offence. She scored.

Duke walked over to Rosalie and placed his arm around her shoulders. "We are proud of both of you. This is just such a shock for us. Why didn't you tell us first?"

Fredrick had been on defense too long already. Pushing his glasses back, "We wanted to save you the trouble of having to protest. You know damn good and well that both of you are pleased as punch.

"Come on Eva, We have to go face Dad—Mama (Eva's name for her mother and one that Fredrick would use from now on), don't burn the dressing."

After Fredrick and Eva left, Duke looked at Rosalie and she stared back at him. "Well it's over. We knew it was coming sooner or later."

Rosalie simply said, "Yes, but I had hoped it would be a little later."

"Why, Mama? Do you think a little later would have changed things?"

Rosalie thought for a moment before she spoke. "Not one bit."

With that she went back to her cooking.

*   *   *

For years, the Overalls and the Dukes had enjoyed Thanksgiving together. It was served in the Duke home one year and in the Overall home the next. This year it was at the Overalls.

Velma was at her Dad's home cooking pies when Fredrick and Eva came in. Luther was in the kitchen drinking coffee and visiting with Bob. Fredrick and Eva burst in and Fredrick announced, "Well, folks, meet my bride. Eva, show them your finger."

Luther jumped up. "What are you talking about?"

"Eva and I just decided to make it a double wedding last night with Miss Emily and Dr. Hill."

Velma screamed, "You're crazy! You did not!"

"Did too."

"Eva and I are going for a drive over the farm to look things over." They turned and left the kitchen, giving everyone a chance to recover.

Velma and Bob were both staring at Luther. He was still in shock. Luther shook his head like he was trying to shake the cobwebs out. "Did he say what I thought he said or am I dreaming?"

Velma screamed. "He said it. What are you going to do about it?"

Luther thought long and hard. "There is nothing I can do. You know he has covered all the bases."

"But Daddy! Before you know it, there will be little 'niglets' all over the place.

Luther came unglued. It was as close as he had ever come to slapping Velma, as she well knew. "Don't you ever utter words like that in this house again. Eva is as nice a girl as you will find anywhere. How dare you make a statement like that."

Velma was duly chastised. She was sorry for what she had said. "Oh Daddy, please forgive me. I didn't mean it. You know that I love Eva. But the talk. I dread the talk. It is going to be pure hell at school when this is out."

"It's not about you, Velma, and I'll knock the hell out of anyone that says anything to my face. They can talk behind my back all they want to, but mark my word, before that boy is finished in Pressley, he and Eva will be the envy of the whole town. This town had better watch their step. Now I love Eva like a daughter and I expect that relationship to grow."

Luther was never eloquent but he had spoken his heart this time. Bob was level headed and he simply admonished, "This is going to take some getting used to, but I'll just bet it works out great. She is smart, vivacious and compassionate. What a team they will make."

With their tempers cooled, Luther went to his truck and started to look for Fredrick and Eva. He had a need to place his arms around his son and his new daughter.

Luther found Fredrick and Eva exactly where he knew he would, at Fredrick's 'crying spot', but today they weren't crying. They were discussing a future together. Fredrick, although he had just had his eighteenth birthday a couple of months earlier, was a man driven to succeed. Eva was very much a part of that driving force. His promise to his mother's memory was another. As he sat at this spot years earlier, after his mother's death, Fredrick promised his mother that he would stay on the farm and make it successful. She loved the farm, the woods, and the meandering creek. He and his mother spent hours roaming the woods and enjoying the marvels of nature.

Fredrick turned to face Luther as he approached and he was not in any mood to be challenged about his decision to marry Eva. However, Luther did not come to challenge. He walked up and seeing the look on Fredrick's face and the set of his jaw, Luther sensed that the marriage was not open for discussion. Fredrick pushed his glasses back against his face and he was ready for battle. Luther held up his hand as a symbol of peace. Fredrick's features softened slightly.

Luther began, "I just wanted to tell both of you that I admire your determination to 'hoe your own row'. You know what you want, where you are headed with your life and you go after it. Son, I am proud of you, and I know your mother would be very proud. I am sorry that she isn't here to congratulate you, so, I will do it for her. Congratulations. Mary told me all along that the two of you would marry. I have known it for a long time. I'm not surprised and I think your being married will make things a lot easier for you. The only bit of fatherly wisdom I can give you is, don't get pregnant until you finish school. A little one takes more than all of your time, and I know you will be good parents."

Luther's eyes were misted. He simply turned, walked back to his truck, got in and drove away. Fredrick and Eva looked at one another. "That was a surprise", Eva said.

"My daddy is full of surprises. We understand one another a lot better now that we once did. He hated my guts when I was little. He didn't want me you know."

"I know, but your mother sure did. We had so much fun when we were little."

"Last night wasn't too bad either was it."

"Hush your mouth, boy. You embarrassing me."

"Sho nuff."

Fredrick grabbed Eva and kissed her passionately. When she came up for air, she gasped, "Watch out now. You 'bout to light my fuse."

They both laughed. Fredrick began to lay out plans for Eva. His plans were to stay in school and while Eva was finishing her degree, he would work on advanced degrees. Eva was majoring in Accounting and Fredrick insisted that she become a CPA. She questioned this because they were intending to farm, but Fredrick countered, "Education and the status that comes with it are important in all aspects of life. You can never tell when that CPA hung on the end of your name will make all the difference in the world. We just cannot see that far down the road."

Eva set her face toward a CPA that day. Fredrick then pointed out that he had his eye on 400 acres down the road from the family farm. It was not particularly good for cultivation, but it had a beautiful hill in a wooded area. It was great for beef cattle production. Behind the hill, the property dropped off sharply with a bluff overlooking the river. It was an ideal home site.

"What do you want that place for, Fredrick? You can't cultivate it."

I want it to build our home. I also have some other ideas that I am not ready to talk about just yet. I will spring that on you later."

"Where will we get the money?"

"Well, I have a confession. I gambled earlier this year."

"Gambled?"

"Yep. In the stock market. I had been talking to a couple of guys that started a little computer company. They were struggling for capital and their stock was down to five cents per share. I thought they had a good idea, so I gambled $10,000 and invested. Their stock went to a dollar. I sold, but then put all of my earnings back into the company and it jumped to ten dollars per share. I sold. I made two million dollars. I need some place to put some money. Taxes will take a heavy bite, but I need some kind of tax shelter. Something secure."

Eva was stunned. She knew that Fredrick played around in the stock market but she had no idea that he made or had this kind of money. She became very quiet.

She finally looked at him and with tears in her eyes she said, "Freddy, you could have had any girl that you wanted. Why did you choose a half breed like me. I won't do anything but hold you back."

This was the closest Fredrick had ever come to being angry with Eva. He bristled, "What do you mean have any girl I wanted. I have the girl I wanted, and don't you ever call yourself a half breed to me again."

Eva was not intimidated; "Fredrick, I am half-black. It is a white man's world. Half means all to most people in Pressley. You had better get that through your thick skull. Our children will feel the hot breath of prejudice just like I have felt it. How are you going to deal with that?"

Fredrick got that far away look in his eyes that Eva had seen before. It was as though he was looking into a crystal ball and observing the future. Commenting almost as though to himself, "When I get finished with Pressley, they won't even notice. That will be the least of their worries."

Eva was chilled by this statement. She had been taught all her life the dangers of holding grudges and un-forgiving heart. She had seen little snippets of Fredrick's hostilities toward the town for what happened to his mother, father, Velma and last of all to her. She admonished, "Fredrick, we can't live with hate in our hearts."

"Oh, I don't hate, Eva. I just sort of loathe."

"Now wait a minute, What's the difference?"

Fredrick just shrugged his shoulders, "I don't know. There must be some difference though."

"Well, I think they are the same."

"Don't think so. For instance, the dictionary uses the example, 'I loathe people who spread malicious gossip.' I do not think that actually means you hate them. I think it means you do not like what they do. In that case, your feelings are directed more at the action rather than the person."

"You are full of bull; do you know that?"

"But Eva, it is a good kind of bull. A beefy sort. Not excrement."

Eva just shook her head. She was not going to change Fredrick and she certainly was not going to out argue him. She just looked at him and grinned.

*   *   *

Luther went to talk to Duke and Rosalie. Duke asked, "Mr. Luther what do you think about those kids getting married?"

"Well, I knew it was coming, I just didn't know when. It actually occurred to me that it might happen now. I didn't expect Fredrick to ask my permission. If his mind is made up, that is all the permission he needs. I am a little surprised at Eva. She is a sweet obedient girl. I suspect she thought you would not approve and that would complicate matters. Who knows how those kid's mind works, and I use the term mind because they seem to think with one mind. I cannot fault them for what they did. It certainly simplifies matters as far as housing. Fredrick can support her. He is a whole lot better off than I am. He has done well with investments, and he makes lots of money consulting with computer companies.

Duke and Rosalie were relieved by Luther's encouraging words. They did not know what to expect from him. He was their employer and their financial security depended on him to some extent. Mary before her death, and then Fredrick, always insisted that their wages reflected a cost of living increase each year. Luther finally got out of the way and just let Fredrick handle that part of the business.

The farms produced a good harvest this year. Fredrick, at planting time had insisted that much of the land be planted in corn. Almost everyone was against this decision, but corn had done well. The price was up considerably over previous years, which made their profits very high. No one could figure out how in the world he had made this correct guess. What no one knew was that he studied the weather forecast and had learned that excessive rain was predicted for the early part of the year during the corn growing season and drought was predicted during the later part of the growing season when the soybeans needed rain. The predictions were correct. Fredrick also learned several small companies were attempting to manufacturer Gasohol to replace gasoline and that was driving the price of corn upward. It was a good, well thought out business strategy—not a guess as most had thought.

After the harvest was in, Duke told Rosalie, "I ain't never gonna argue with that boy again."

*   *   *

Mark, Fredrick's brother was just back from his tour of duty in Germany. He brought a German wife home with him. He and his wife Gretchen were stationed at Ft Hood. They had only been back in the states for two weeks and were coming for Thanksgiving. This would be Gretchen's first Thanksgiving celebration. Mark had not been home for three years and this was an exciting time. He lacked six months of his enlistment and he and Gretchen were considering returning to the area after his tour of duty was over. Luther had his feelers out for coaching jobs in the area, and he was hoping the job at Markel would open up again.

Velma was in overload. Two new sisters in law at once were just about more than she could handle. Velma had been trying to bake pies all morning and she was having a difficult time with that. Fredrick and Eva came in and Eva jumped in and started helping her. Velma had one pie that crashed and burned which she tossed out. Eva grabbed the flour and margarine and started making a new pie crust. Velma purchased two readymade crusts but she ruined them. As quick as a wink, Eva had two pecan pies in the oven, much to Velma's relief. Eva peeled sweet potatoes, chopped them up and started them cooking for sweet potato pie. Fredrick started peeling oranges for fruit salad. Velma prepared the salad. Fruit Salad with real "whupped" cream as everyone called it, was a family tradition. It was one of Fredrick's favorite parts of the meal. Cooking was not Velma's strong suit. Eva was so gracious and so much help that Velma was in situational depression over her earlier comment about the little "niglets". She had wished a thousand times already that she had never made that comment and hoped above hope that her daddy would never tell Fredrick and Eva what she had said, but knowing Luther she could not depend on that. She struggled with whether to go ahead and tell them and apologize or to risk her dad not telling. She simply could not bring herself around to telling them what she had said.

Mark and Gretchen came in. Fredrick was excited since he was in his first semester of German. When he learned that Mark was marrying a German girl, he was prompted to take German. This was his first opportunity to practice his new skill. He and Gretchen were able to communicate and they quickly formed a bond of friendship. She immediately began to teach him new German words and he was like a sponge soaking up all she threw at him.

At one o'clock, Fredrick and Eva went to Fredrick's grandfather's house to pick him up. He had a nurse who came each day to help him. She had him ready to go. Fredrick went in and with some apprehension said, "Granddad, Eva and I came to get you to go eat Thanksgiving dinner with us."

"OK, I'm ready to go. Who'ed you say was with you."

"Eva, Dukes daughter."

"What's she doing with you. She's my wife Granddad."

"Yore what."

"My wife, W I F E, as in married."

The old fellow looked stunned and addled.

"Naw!"

"Yes!"

"Naw! You didn't marry that little 'nigger gal'."

Fredrick stood up to his full height which was about six feet two inches now, pushed his glasses back against his face and looked directly into his grandfather's eyes. "Granddad, you listen to me. And you listen well. Eva and I are married. I love her very much and I will not let you talk about her like that. If you ever want to have a relationship with your grandson, I had better never hear you use that word again."

The old man could not stand to look in Fredrick's eyes through his thick glasses. If gave him what he called the "Hebe Jebes". He looked away. Fredrick took him by the chin and turned his face back toward his. The old fellow would not look at him.

"Granddad, do we understand one another."

Just as Fredrick thought, the old man was not as senile as he wanted people to think he was. He was physically impaired because of his stroke, but his mind was reasonably clear.

The old man looked again into his grandson's eyes and said, "I understand son, and I'm sorry."

"Well, it is Eva you need to apologize to, not me. He looked at Eva—just stared for a long moment. "She shore is pretty, son. Eva, I apologize fer what I said. I'm just an old fool."

Eva smiled a disarming smile, came over and put her arm around his shoulders. "It's alright, granddad. It doesn't bother me as much as it does Fredrick. He is very protective."

The old man puffed up and retorted, "Well he damn well better be or I'll kick his butt."

Eva laughed and reached down and kissed him on the cheek.

They helped him to the car and drove back to the Overall home.

When they arrived, there was a strange car in the driveway. Eva asked, "Who is that?"

"Well I hope it is who I think it is."

Eva and Fredrick helped Mr. Lane to the back door. The front of the house was much higher than the back so they helped him to the back steps. Inside the house, they found that Fredrick's Aunt Evelyn had finally given in and come home.

Fredrick called her earlier in the week and pleaded with her to come see her father before it was too late. He made a convincing case for reconciliation. When Mr. Lane saw her, he began weeping. Evelyn upon seeing an old broken man, nothing like the man she had run away from years earlier, was also touched and her emotions overcame her hard exterior and she too began to weep. Fredrick shuffled the two off into a bedroom and closed the door to allow them to have their time together.

Luther looked at Fredrick. "How did you do it? How did you get her to agree to come?"

"I made her an offer she couldn't refuse. I told her I was gonna kick her butt if she didn't come."

Luther smiled at Fredrick. "Son, you never cease to amaze me. I am so glad she came. They both needed this. You know I didn't realize just how much she looked like your mother until she walked through that door."

Fredrick pushed his glasses back against his face and just stared at his dad for a moment and then broke into a big smile. It was a smile that Luther could not get out of his mind. It lingered for the rest of the day. It woke him up during the night.

* * *

Two PM the appointed dinner hour was approaching fast. Duke and Rosalie brought in the turkey and dressing along with a green bean casserole, potato salad and candied sweet potatoes. Eva and Fredrick had the whipped cream prepared and ready for the fruit salad. Velma had made her specialty, an English pea salad. It was one of the few things that Velma made that was really good. Next to that, picking up Kentucky fried chicken was her next best dish. By the time dinner rolled around, she *was worn out.*

James was stationed in Washington DC. He did not come home for Thanksgiving but was planning to come Christmas. He called about 1:30 to wish everyone Happy Thanksgiving. He learned that Fredrick was married from Velma, who had answered the phone. He went through the roof. Velma finally called Luther to the phone and let him deal with James.

He was quiet for a few moments and then he exploded, "Well what in the hell do you want me to do about it. He is of age and there is nothing you or I can do. You just better suck it up and get used to it because that is the way it is gonna be. It is none of your damn business what he does. He is smarter than the rest of us all put together and if he wants to get married, so be it."

Luther slammed the phone down and walked away, red in the face. Luther had become a believer. Fredrick's handling of his romance with Melissa and saving him from a very bad mistake had endeared Luther to his 'strange' son.

The phone rang again and it was James calling back. Velma answered again. She looked at Fredrick and said, "James wants to talk to you."

Fredrick picked up the phone. Luther was listening and ready to grab the phone and give James another piece of his mind when he heard, "Well thanks. She is a great girl and we are excited about starting our life together."

To Luther's amazement, they seemed to be having a pleasant conversation. James had always despised Fredrick. There was always animosity between them. Fredrick was one of the reasons that James seldom came home. The truth of the matter was that Velma, James, and Mark were afraid of Fredrick. Luther could also be included in that list. Duke understood Fredrick better than his father and he and Duke had a very close relationship which would only grow in years to come.

Gretchen was intrigued by Duke and Rosalie. She knew of racial prejudice in America and this did not fit her mold. The fact that Fredrick was married to their daughter simply added to her confusion.

Evelyn and her dad finished their reconciliation. No one knew what was said except the two of them. Their discussion was frank and honest. Mr. Lane had grieved for years over the mistake he had made and needed to tell his daughter this. She very much needed to hear that from him. It was a healing moment with each regretting that it was so long in coming. Evelyn would be eternally grateful for her nephew's persistence in arranging this, much needed, event.

At the table, Luther's prayer was straight from the heart and eloquent for Luther. He did not pull any punches but gave thanks for the reconciliation between Evelyn and her father. Somehow, Fredrick had arranged to get Luther seated by Evelyn and he had placed his arm around her shoulder as he prayed. He had felt her tremble as he gave thanks for their reconciliation and he squeezed her shoulder. It felt good to both of them.

Evelyn was two years younger than her sister Mary. Luther had been the grandest thing she had ever known while he and Mary were dating. She had a big crush on him back then; and some of those old feeling came flooding back. Evelyn had a brief marriage just after she first went to Houston but she was carrying too much baggage back then and her marriage lasted only two years. She had been single for over 25 years.

Luther felt a revival of his love for Mary in her sister. Evelyn had developed a very hard shell, but it was beginning to crack. Being together with family again brought back many good memories. She could see the pain in her father's face each time she looked at him and it crushed her heart. She had been so very cold, so harsh in her judgment of him and now that she saw him face to face, she discovered a beaten and broken old man just as Fredrick had described him to her in a letter and on the phone.

One phase of his letter was still ringing in her mind, "Aunt Evelyn, your father is and old man now, crushed by the harshness of life and an unforgiving daughter. My mother's death was a crushing blow to him and one that he has not dealt with very well. He has admitted to me that he made a terrible mistake with you. He is heartsick over that. I do not know if he has asked your forgiveness for what he did, but you need to give him opportunity to do that before it is too late. Time is running out. None of us know when our time will come, but common sense tells us that one who has had a debilitating stroke is certainly more likely to pass from this life than one who is still young and healthy. Please come home for Thanksgiving and give your father a chance to say 'I am sorry'. I am young and don't know much, but I think this will be a release for both of you, and besides that, I need my Aunt. I need your love."

Mary and Evelyn had been very close at one time. After Evelyn moved to Houston, Mary still called her weekly. Evelyn simply shut the family out after Mary died. She felt an intense guilt for not staying in contact with Fredrick; A feeling that she neglected a responsibility to Mary.

Evelyn could not resist the plea that Fredrick made. She would be eternally grateful to him for caring enough to make this move. Everyone else was afraid to approach her. One thing his aunt was to learn very quickly about her nephew was that he did not shy away from any problem, but met it head on.

Mark did lots of talking during the meal. He was outgoing and reasonably proud of himself. Evelyn listened to the conversation, but the thing that she wanted most right now was to get to know Fredrick. She was extremely shocked to learn that he was married. Even more shocked to learn that he was a junior at UT and an Engineering major. She came home only once since she left and that was for Mary's funeral. She had simply come for the service and left without even speaking to the rest of the family. Mary kept her up to date on Fredrick's progress before her death. She had thought that Mary's evaluation of her son was simply a mother's boasting.

Gretchen was seated next to Fredrick. She was very shy and self conscious about her command of the English language. Fredrick kept up a conversation with her in German. This endeared him to her. Duke and Rosalie were shy at the table with all the guests, but Fredrick also engaged them in the conversation when he could wrestle it away from Mark. Evelyn quickly picked up what Fredrick was doing. It was soon evident that he was the de facto leader of this family. It took a while for Mark to discover that, but it even sunk in with him after a while.

Evelyn loved Eva from the onset of their first meeting. Eva was a vibrant, energetic and intelligent young lady. She and Fredrick kept up a banter all through the meal. Eva related an account of a three way conversation between Fredrick, Mortimer the cat and Miss Emily. Laughingly Eva said, "Every time Fredrick would pretend that Mortimer said something to him Miss Emily would ask, 'What did he say?', Freddy would tell her some outlandish tale that Mortimer had uttered. It cracked me up and I almost started believing it myself."

This brought a laugh all around the table. Evelyn asked, "How old is Miss Emily?"

Fredrick answered. "She had her seventieth birthday in October. Eva and I baked her cake and put seventy candles on it."

"Yeah, and Miss Emily got all excited when we started lighting the candles and said, 'You kids are going to burn the house down'," Eva added.

Evelyn asked, "And this is her first marriage?"

"Yep, I had a hard time convincing her that she could manage, but I think she and Dr. Hill will be very happy", Fredrick answered.

Evelyn thoughtfully replied, "Well maybe there is hope for me," and then she added, "But I had a trial run and I didn't do very well."

Fredrick never at a loss for words, expostulated, "Well you will do better next time Aunt Evelyn. You will have your family behind you. That is important you know."

Evelyn looked intently at Fredrick and asked, "Oh, did you have someone in mind?"

"Maybe."

"Fredrick is a good match maker Aunt Evelyn," Eva added.

Under his breath Luther added, "And match squishier."

There was laughter all around the table.

"Is this a private joke?" Evelyn asked.

Velma spoke up, "Daddy had a little fling until Freddy put an end to it."

Evelyn looked at Fredrick, "How did you do that?"

Fredrick smiled, pushed his glasses back against his face and replied, "Oh, just by looking."

Laughter erupted around the table. Evelyn looked at Fredrick. "I need to hear this story."

Luther spoke, "I'll tell you later. We don't want Gretchen to learn too much about this family. She will swim back to Germany."

Another laugh around the table. The meal broke up soon after. Evelyn commented that she had brought flowers to go on Mary's grave and commented that she would like to take them to the cemetery before it got too late. Luther asked, "You are not going home tonight are you?"

"Well, I have not decided. I came prepared to stay."

"Please do."

There was a warmth and pleading in Luther's voice that touched her heart.

"OK, I'll stay. I need to spend some time with Dad. I have been mean. I hate myself sometimes."

Luther got a far away look in his eyes. "That is a common problem. I have made some huge mistakes. I have wished a thousand times that I had told Mary more often that I loved her. Sometime you just can't get it said. Evelyn, I miss her so much and it has been twelve years now.

"I'll go with you to the cemetery. I haven't been in a couple of weeks. I go there and talk to her sometimes, although I know she is not there."

"Thanks Luther. I don't think I could go alone. I was going to ask Freddy and Eva to go with me, but I would really rather have you."

There was warmth in Evelyn's voice that reminded him of Mary. Luther knew the danger signs but he plunged head on.

Once in the car, Evelyn asked, "You want to tell me what happened to your romance."

Luther began at the beginning, relating his loneliness after Freddy went off to college. He said, "We had a young teacher that came in last year and she recognized my vanity and worked on it. He left out no details of how she had enticed him.

Continuing, "But then, it came time for her to meet Freddy. I was uptight about that meeting, because deep down, I feared disaster out of this relationship, but seemed powerless to stop it. When I went to pick her up, she had on a very provocative outfit, cut all the way to the waist and a very short skirt. All during the meal, Fredrick kept his glasses pushed back against his face so that his eyes would look huge and he just stared at her breast. He didn't say a word. He just stared. By the end of the evening she was simply strung out. When I took her home she called him a pervert and every other bad name in the book. Our little fling was over. He didn't open his mouth, he just stared."

Evelyn laughed so hard she almost fell out of her car. "Oh, I wish I could have seen that."

"Well it was a performance I can assure you."

They were at the cemetery by the time Luther finished his story. Their mood changed. Luther took Evelyn's arm as they made their way to Mary's gravesite. Before they arrived. Evelyn was crying. Twelve years of pent up emotions came pouring out. She said over and over. "I am so sorry. I'm sorry I neglected your family."

Luther embraced her and held her tight. She felt good in his arms.

Evelyn spent the rest of the long weekend at the farm. She and her dad completed their reconciliation. It was obvious there was a budding romance beginning between her and Luther. This was one that had Fredrick's approval. Before she left to return to Houston, much of the harshness was gone from her face, and she was already looking ten years younger. The transformation was noticeable to even the casual observer.

*   *   *

Fredrick and Eva met the Real Estate agent at the farm they were interested in purchasing. Fredrick introduced Eva as his wife and the poor little agent almost fell out. Fredrick had already been all over the place, but he had the agent show him around. The realtor figured this was a waste of his time and just a lark of young dreamers. He came across as if to say, "Have your look and let me get out of here."

At the end of the tour, Fredrick stated, "I won't pay what they are asking. The property is rougher than I had expected, with very little cultivatable land. The timber is not worth anything without destroying the rest of the property. You cut that timber and the whole hillside will be full of gullies in two years. (The agent had already been talking about all of the timber on the place) I am prepared to make you and offer—what I think is a good offer if you are interested."

"Well, Mr. Overall, we are always interested in a good offer."

Fredrick was carrying a small valise. He opened it up and pulled out a cashiers check for $300,000 made out to the realtor. "Just to prove that this is a good faith offer, I am presenting this to you with the understanding that it is an offer on the described property, Will you accept this?"

The agent looked at the check and then back at Fredrick. It was obvious that he was stunned. "Well yes, I will accept it and present your offer to the owners."

"Please sign here."

Fredrick had the property description and a receipt for the transaction all typed up and ready for the realtor signature. He signed.

The owners were asking $1,300 per acre for the property. Fredrick's offer was for $750. A bitter divorce and custody battle was raging between the owners, and Fredrick figured they would take his cash offer. It was a fair offer, but not outstanding. The property was not going to be easy to sell, unless someone from the city was simply looking for a weekend getaway.

Fredrick and Eva went to their car, got in and drove away leaving the little agent alone with his thoughts.

As they left, Eva asked, "Freddy, do you think they will take the offer?

Fredrick was quiet for a moment before he spoke. Eva could see the wheels turning in his head. "Well, I don't know. I am inexperienced at buying property, but one thing I have learned already is that when you dangle money in front of people, They seem to lose their sense of reason. I started to offer less, but I think what I offered was fair. Eva, we are going to wrestle the strangle hold on the town of Pressley away from the Turners and Gipsons. That is going to give lots of folks heartburn. One thing that I want our reputation to reflect is that we are fair.

"The farm is close to our home and that makes it nice. It has a wonderful view. I worry a little about the river behind the homesite. I know we will have trouble keeping our kids out of it. If they don't take the offer, we will look someplace else."

"Freddy, I don't know what you can do with that old hill. The place is awfully rough."

"Well, a good bulldozer can change the shape of things. One thing I plan is to contour it and place very large chicken houses on each level. If we get it, I plan to have a million chickens on feed within two years."

"Chickens! Why chickens?"

"Eva, folks are becoming more and more aware of the health issues related to red meat. True or false, it is an issue and it is changing the diet in this country. Chickens are very efficient meat producers. The waste products from chicken production are a resource that has not been tapped by most farmers. I want to give that a try."

"You are going to have to explain that to me, Freddy."

"The litter taken out of the chicken houses after a flock of chickens has been raised is very high in nitrogen and other nutrients. Can you imagine the waste from producing one million broilers every 10 weeks? Most Broiler producers are selling that off to beef cattle producers for pasture fertilizer. I think we can come up with a better use. Beef Cattle are very inefficient."

Eva became very quiet, in deep thought. Being married to Fredrick Overall was going to be an interesting ride. She wondered just how long that had been rambling around in his head, and she knew very well that he had researched the issue well before it surfaced.

Freddy warned, "Eva, keep this to yourself. We do not want to expose our hand. Business matters that you and I discuss need to be kept between you and I."

Eva looked at Fredrick and asked, "Freddy, are we gonna have a honeymoon?"

This stunned him. "Well yes. What did you want to do, sweetheart?"

Eva thought for a moment and then answered, "Just to be with you."

Fredrick reached over and placed his arm around her. The console between the seats kept them apart.

Fredrick fumed, "I hate that darn console. We need a pickup."

Eva laughed. In the old farm truck, Eva could sit close to Fredrick. She knew exactly what he meant.

Rosalie was waiting for them when they drove up. The first words out of her mouth were, "Can you two be at the photographers at 2 pm? I want you to have your picture taken for the newspaper."

They acquiesced to her request. She told them to come in and have lunch—she and Duke were waiting for them. Fredrick and Eva ate a quick lunch, dressed quickly and went to the photographer. He suggested that Fredrick remove his glasses for the photo shoot. Fredrick gave in and allowed the picture without his glasses.

Rosalie paid a premium to have the photos developed right away and passed off to the newspaper. She very much wanted the article in the Sunday Newspaper. It made it, and by the time Fredrick and Eva were ready to go back to Austin, the town was abuzz.

The headlines of the paper read, "Fredrick Overall and Eva Burks Marry."

Rosalie had written a brief synopsis about Freddy and Eva's plans to finish school and then return to Pressley to live. Her article stated that Fredrick was a Mechanical Engineering major and that Eva was majoring in Accounting. The prevailing rumor, started by the Turners and Gipsons, was that Eva was pregnant.

The town of Pressley had never seen Fredrick Overall without glasses. Most had not seen him since he went to college two years earlier, and he had grown almost four inches in two years and now stood at six feet two inches tall. He, by anyone's standards, had become a very handsome young man, tall, slender, with a pleasing smile. Even his detractors were impressed. Eva's looks spoke for themselves. She too was tall and slender, standing at five feet eleven inches. They had chosen to wear their University of Texas sweatshirts. This choice was made primarily because Pressley was a Texas A&M town. Luther Overall, head Coach at Pressley High School and Velma Overall, head Girls Basketball Coach had wielded great influence in that regard.

* * *

On Sunday before Freddy and Eva went back to Austin, Velma cornered Freddy and asked, "What do you think about Dad and Aunt Evelyn?"

Fredrick pushed his glasses back against his face and stared at her for a moment. This was always disquieting to Velma, but he smiled and gave her a "thumbs up" sign. He didn't say a word. He just stared.

Velma smiled. Fredrick commented, "Velma, you are pretty when you smile. I wish you would do it more often."

Velma was stunned. Freddy had never told her that she was pretty. In fact, she always felt inferior to Fredrick and resented him and now that he had grown up to be a handsome young man, her feelings of inferiority were only intensified. The fact that he saw her as a person—a pretty person shocked her. Bob had overheard the exchange. He smiled at her and added, "He's right as usual. I do wish you would learn to smile more. You have a beautiful smile."

Velma buried her face on his chest and wept. Freddy winked at Bob and walked away, leaving his brother in law thinking, "How in the world did he know how badly she needed that?"

Chapter 7

Fredrick and Eva went back to school an excited and happy couple. Basically, they were happy, compassionate, and warm by nature, and they were very much in love. Mortimer met them at the door. It was obvious that he was lonesome. Fredrick greeted him, "Hello Mortimer. Did you enjoy your vacation, having the house to yourself?"

With chin in hand, Fredrick mumbled. "Um huh, I see."

Eva couldn't resist, although she and Fredrick had been amused at Miss Emily asking the same question. "What did he say?"

"He said that Jack and Tony and Spooky came over and they all got drunk. Said he had a hangover for two days."

Eva picked right up and admonished, "Well Mortimer, serves you right. We turn our back for one minute and you engage in all of this debauchery."

Again, Fredrick went into his listening mode, "Um huh. Really."

"What did he say?"

"Neighbors called the cops. They will be back looking for us."

Eva burst into laughter. "Mortimer, you are too much." She sat down on the floor in front of him and motioned for him to come; the old cat got up and went to Eva. He rubbed and purred and tried to climb in her lap. She got up and picked him up and went to a big stuffed chair and sat down to give him the attention he needed. He rubbed his face against her chin and you could hear his purrs all the way across the room. It was obvious that he had been lonesome.

Fredrick watched the scene in amusement. Mortimer was an independent 'cuss', and had little to do with anyone except on rare occasions. Fredrick walked over and bent down and kissed Eva on the cheek. He then looked at Mortimer and commented, "Oh yeah, well we will see about that."

"What did he say?"

He said, "Back off buster; she's mine."

Eva burst into laughter and reached down and kissed Mortimer on top of the head. He enjoyed every minute of the affection.

With that exchange, Mortimer, Fredrick and Eva became a family.

*   *   *

Fredrick and Eva were somewhat surprised that Miss Emily left Mortimer with them, but she explained, "This has been Mortimer's home since he was a baby kitten. I am afraid that he would be traumatized if I tried to take him. I will come to visit him often. It will give me a good excuse to come see you two."

That arrangement worked out well. Dr. Hill changed his walking route and the six blocks, somewhat uphill was great exercise for him and his bride. They usually wound up in Miss Emily's kitchen. They arranged their walking routine such that Eva or Fredrick was out of class and would be home. With the new exercise regimen, Miss Emily began to slim down. The weight loss looked good on her and soon she became more vibrant and looked ten years younger. She had traveled extensively in earlier life and she and Dr. Hill were excited about travelling again, but this time with a companion to share the excitement and joy. There was one problem in their marriage. She had been Miss Emily too long and the handle was hard to break off, but it was loosening.

*   *   *

On Monday evening after Thanksgiving, The Pressley realtor called Fredrick. On the phone Fredrick heard, in a most official voice, "Mr. Overall, my clients have refused your offer and they have made a counter offer. They have dropped their price, as I have advised them, to $975 per acre. Would you consider this offer?"

"Sure, I will consider it."

There was a brief pause and then Fredrick came back with, "Okay, I have considered it and the answer is no. I will ask Dad to come by your office and pick up the cashier's check."

"Well now, Mr. Overall, the way real estate deals normally work is that you make an offer and then the other party makes a counter offer, and then you come to some compromise agreement on the price."

"Not my deals, sir. I made a fair and well thought out offer of what I thought the property was worth. I did not low-ball that offer. It is a rough property; it has only one redeeming feature about it. It has one nice home site on it that does not require a tremendous outlay of cash to make tenable. I will see if Dad can pick up the check. If not, please mail it to me by certified mail."

"Well, Mr. Overall, we have another interested party."

"Then, I suggest you sell the property to that party and I will look for something else. I too have other sites in mind.

"Thanks for your time, Mr. Bass."

"Mr. Bass was looking at $18,000 going down the tube. $18,000 that he had done little work to earn. He gushed, "Mr. Overall, Can you give me a couple of days to work on this?"

"Why yes, I can do that."

"Thank you, I will get back to you."

"Thank you, Mr. Bass, and goodbye."

Fredrick got off the phone and looked at Eva. She asked, "You didn't get the farm?"

"Not yet, but it is coming."

"How do you know, Freddy?"

"Let's just call it a sixth sense, sweetheart. I know people. I have studied them and they all follow the same pattern. They are greedy and selfish. All of us are to some extent. If we are successful, we simply have to keep that in check. If we don't, it will destroy us. It is one of my biggest faults. That cashier's check had Edward Bass' eyes bugged out like a 'stomped on toad frog'."

Two days later, Ed Bass called Fredrick back and told him the client had accepted his offer if Freddy would pay for the title insurance. Freddy thought this reasonable, so he accepted the offer. The title search took two weeks, so, by mid December the transfer of title documents were ready to sign; however since Fredrick and Eva were both involved in semester finals, signing was delayed until the Christmas Holidays.

Once Fredrick knew that he had the property, he began studying the broiler production business in earnest. He called feed companies to see what arrangement they would make with him to produce chickens for the market, and he also called processors. Within a week, he had a tentative agreement with a processor in Waco to enter into a contractual agreement with him once he was ready to start production.

By the time the Christmas holidays and semester break rolled around, Fredrick was in "high gear". Eva admonished, "Freddy, I thought you would at least wait until we got out of college to start on the place."

Fredrick pushed his glasses back against his face and just looked at her for a pregnant moment, "Why waste all that time? We could be making money while we are in school."

"Well, for one thing, I just can't process all of this, Freddy. It is too much for me. I'm afraid you gonna mess up and we gonna lose everything."

Eva, like her mother Rosalie, had a tendency to somehow revert to black dialect when she got excited. Fredrick loved it and thought it cute. He smiled at her and replied, "Sweetheart, as long as we pay cash for everything, how can we lose it?"

Still, Eva had trouble grasping the concept. Duke and Rosalie were both very frugal and spent their money wisely, maintaining a saving account that was their insurance for the future. They guarded it meticulously. This was ingrained into Eva.

But Fredrick won out. He and Eva went home for the holidays and signed the papers on Monday before Christmas. Fredrick immediately began to study the property intently. He concluded that it needed lots of bulldozer work. This conclusion came just before he and Eva went into Pressley to purchase a couple of items for Christmas. They were in the drugstore when Thomas DeVaney came into the store with his wife and tiny young daughter. Thomas was a very shy, young man. He had been one year ahead of Fredrick in school. Thomas was not a good student, but Fredrick helped and Thomas squeaked by and graduated with Fredrick's help. Fredrick went to greet him, shook his hand and commented on the beautiful baby. Thomas' wife was a mousey little lady, so oppressively shy that she could hardly speak. Freddy and Eva greeted her warmly.

In the course of their conversation, Fredrick learned that they had just come from Dr. Elliot's office with their baby who had a serious ear infection and was running a high fever. He also told Fredrick that he was going to see if the druggist would let him have medication on credit since he had lost his job.

Fredrick pushed his glasses back against his face, looked at the baby, at Thomas and his wife and asked, "May I see your prescriptions?"

Thomas handed them to him wondering why he wanted to see them. Fredrick looked at the prescriptions, walked to the counter and handed them to the clerk. The clerk took them and went back and gave them to the pharmacist. He immediately came forward. "I can't fill these without cash. They already owe me $140. I can't risk anymore."

Fredrick pushed his glasses back against his face, looked the pharmacist over closely and asked, "How much are these?"

He went to the calculator, entered some numbers and came back and informed, "They are $70.00."

Fredrick pushed his glasses back and commented, "Well, that is highway robbery, but you fill the prescriptions and I will bring their account up to date."

He reached in his wallet, and pulled out an American Express Card. He started to hand it to the pharmacist.

"I am sorry, Freddy, but we don't take that card here."

Fredrick took it back and pulled out a Visa card. The pharmacist took it and scanned it to see if it would clear. It did and he filled the prescriptions. The baby had started to cry from the ear pain. Thomas' wife Lucy was trying to quiet it. Thomas was simply numb. He struggled to make a living, and felt very inadequate.

"Freddy, I don't know how we can ever repay you. We just ain't got no money. I been out of work for several weeks and we are just flat broke. We tried to get the baby on Medicaid, but that takes time."

When the prescriptions were filled, Freddy asked, "Will you and Lucy have lunch with Eva and I, my treat?"

Thomas responded, "But you have already done enough, Freddy."

"We would like for you to have lunch with us."

Tommy finally acquiesced.

Fredrick and Eva had planned to simply have a snack at the Dairy Queen, but Fredrick drove to the Holiday Inn Restaurant, the nicest Restaurant in town. Eva was crying by the time they got in the car. Her heart broke for the young couple and Fredrick's compassion pushed her over the edge.

She looked at him with adoring eyes as they drove toward the restaurant. "Thanks, honey."

"For what?"

"For caring about Thomas and Lucy and their little baby."

Fredrick smiled, "Well, God has been good to me. I care about people, Eva. I can't solve all the problems in the world, but I hope He gives me the good sense to recognize when I can solve a problem for someone. Can you just imagine what it would be like to have a sick child and not have enough money to buy medicine? We are going to do more for this couple. I know Tommy tries, but everyone he comes in contact with tries to use him. He is such an easy target. I am going to hire him to work on our new farm. There is lots of work that needs to be done. I will hire him to work until he can find a permanent job."

They were at the restaurant when this conversation ended. Fredrick learned during their meal that Tommy was working for a light construction company that went into receivership. They became over extended with equipment and could not make payments. Two months of wet weather killed them since they were already over extended. From Tommy he learned that the company had a bulldozer, a large front-end loader with backhoe, and a tractor with a box blade. This raised Fredrick's eyelids. He decided at that point to make the lender an offer on all of the equipment. Fredrick became aware that Tommy knew the equipment well and could tell you how many hours each piece of equipment had on it. It was not new equipment, but according to Tommy, each piece of equipment was in good operating condition except the front-end loader needed new hydraulic hoses.

The lunch conversation was mainly about the equipment, which turned out to be a good thing because it relieved much of Tommy and Lucy's anxiety over being in a very nice restaurant—a first for them. Tommy rattled on and on about the equipment and how he hated that the company lost it. Their baby's ear pain had subsided and she was quiet all through the meal. Eva knew at once that she and Fredrick were going to become the proud owners of construction equipment. She had mixed emotions about this fact and feared that Fredrick was going to spend himself into a hole. On the other hand, she trusted his judgment. She was a little stressed.

Fredrick learned from Tommy that First National Bank of Pressley carried the note for the equipment and he feared that might be a showstopper. Since Freddy's one addition newspaper had been a humiliating embarrassment to the granddaughter of the bank's CEO, hearing Fredrick Overall's name was similar to pouring fire ants into this man's britches.

When the meal was over, Fredrick asked Tommy point blank if they had food in their house. It was embarrassing for this proud young man, but Fredrick was not leaving until he knew their status.

Tommy stammered, "We got some stuff that Lucy canned from the garden, and I made lots of potatoes in my garden."

Fredrick knew immediately this was a smokescreen to keep him from knowing they were destitute. Tommy and Lucy had devoured their food, which did not go un-noticed by Eva.

Fredrick pushed his glasses back against his face and stared at Tommy. The poor little guy felt that his soul had been undressed. What he did not realize was that Fredrick Overall was looking at him, but he was also looking into the future. Freddy knew Tommy well from High School. He knew he was honest, hard working and diligent. He was a slow learner, but what he learned he kept. Fredrick was also considering, "Do I have time for this next move?"

Once he had weighed the issues he asked, "Tommy, how would you like to work for me?"

Stunned, Tommy gushed, "Doing what Freddy?"

"Eva and I just bought the old Grimes place out on the river. It needs lots of work. I am going to put chicken houses on it. I will need someone to oversee and run the place."

Tommy was stunned to say the least. "But, but Freddy, I don't know nuthin about runnin no farm."

"There is lots of work to be done before we get to running a farm. Lots of construction and dirt work. You know dirt don't you?"

"Yeah, I've spent lots of time down in the dirt."

"Well Tommy, you have to get down in the dirt before you can build. That is the foundation for everything."

Fredrick pulled out his checkbook and wrote a check for $500. "I am going to give you an advance and after Christmas, please call me and we will get together to discuss details. Eva and I have to get back home or they will send a search party after us. We had only planned to be gone for a few minutes."

With that, the meal ended. Tommy and Lucy looked like two different individuals from the two that Eva and Fredrick met in the drug store. They were both smiling. What no one knew, except Tommy, was that Fredrick Overall's help and interest in him was the only reason he finished school. Without Freddy's help he would not have graduated.

Once in their car alone, Eva asked the question she had wanted to ask. "Do you know what you are doing?"

Fredrick pushed his glasses back against his face and looked at Eva for a long moment before he answered. He was very much aware that she should have been in this decision, but he felt that it was so much the thing that needed to be done that he had simply plunged ahead. He gave a soul searching answer. "No sweetheart, I don't. If I did, it wouldn't be worth doing would it? Life is about learning, but it is also about helping people who need help and sharing resources with those less fortunate. Tommy is a good guy. I do not know Lucy very well, but they seem to be similar in nature. My gut tells me this is the right thing to do."

Eva had gotten another of those brief glimpses into the heart of her husband. Over the years, those glimpses would be serendipitous moments that she would cherish. At this moment, she would follow him to the gates of hell.

*   *   *

Fredrick and Eva drove to the lot where the equipment was stored. The gate was locked and they could not get in to take a close look. Fredrick mentally calculated what he felt each piece of equipment was worth. He did not even bother to go to the bank and make an offer. That afternoon he drove to Markel and talked to the Case International dealer there and worked out a deal for him to attempt to purchase the equipment for him. He told the dealer what he would pay for all of the equipment. He suggested that whatever deal he could make for the equipment would determine his profit. He suggested that if he could purchase the equipment for less, then he could keep the profit.

Fredrick pointed out, "If you move quickly, I think they may wish to sell before the end of the year and clear their books."

The Markel dealer called the bank in Pressley immediately, asked about the equipment, and made an appointment to look at it the next day. After the look, The Case dealer offered the bank a price that would allow him a $5,000.00 profit. The bank countered and then they agreed on a price that gave him $3,000.00. Not a bad day's work.

Fredrick became the proud owner of a bulldozer, front-end loader, tractor with box blade, an old dump truck and a heavy-duty trailer. The trailer would actually haul the bulldozer. Fredrick got all of that equipment for $40,000.

Fredrick sent Tommy to pick up the equipment, but admonished him not to tell the bank who had bought the equipment. The bank officer was surprised when Tommy showed up to receive the equipment, but Tommy would not tell him who he was working for. All of the equipment was gone and on Fredrick's farm before word got around that Tommy was working for Fredrick. When Jim

Turner learned this, he went into a tirade. He called the Markel dealer and gave him a first class 'cussin'. He ranted, and raved for two days.

On Tuesday after Christmas, Freddy went into Pressley to the post office. Just as he was walking in, he came face to face with Jim Turner coming out.

"Oh hello, Mr. Turner. Nice to see you."

Jim was startled beyond speech. He had not seen Fredrick for almost two years. Fredrick had filled out and grown almost four inches in height during that time. He stood head and shoulder over Jim Turner.

"Hello, Mr. Overall."

The two men stood staring at each other for a long uncomfortable moment. Jim Turner despised Fredrick. Jim was proud of himself and Fredrick made him feel inferior. Every time they had a confrontation, Jim lost.

Jim could not resist. "Fredrick, what in the world are you gonna do with all that old junk equipment?"

"Well, I am going to play tractors, Mr. Turner. You know I am still a kid at heart."

Jim stood waiting for Fredrick to continue, but Fredrick was finished. They stood looking at one another for a moment and then Jim just turned and walked away. He had a very uneasy feeling that he had, although indirectly, just aided and abetted the enemy by selling the equipment to him. What no one in Pressley knew was that the bank had made numerous bad decisions and was very close to going under. The equipment loan to the construction company was just one of many such transactions. Having Fredrick Overall wind up with the equipment was salt in a very deep wound.

Fredrick had a warm fuzzy feeling after leaving Jim Turner as he entered the Post Office.

*   *   *

Christmas was an interesting experience. All of the Overalls were at home. Fredrick and Eva bunked at the Burks. Mark and Gretchen were home, and James came bringing with him his fiancé. She took Fredrick's old room. Evelyn was at home with her dad. His health was deteriorating fast, and he could hardly get out of bed. Home Health came three times per week and a full time live in nurse was with him except on weekends. Luther and Velma were alternating staying with him on weekends. Luther really had shown what he was made of during this time. He cared for the old fellow just as though he was his own father. Mr. Lane had always worshiped Luther Overall. Fredrick and Eva also helped out during the holidays and Rosalie offered to share weekend duty with Velma and Luther. It was a difficult time for everyone, but this family was pulling together.

Luther and Evelyn's romance was beyond bloom stage and was just about ready for harvest. Fredrick took his dad on a little drive one day to look at his new farm. Showing off the farm was not the real reason for the outing. Fredrick wanted to counsel his dad. He began, "Dad, you know Aunt Evelyn looks like Mom, but she is not Mom. You do have that straight in your mind, don't you?"

"Yes, son, I have it straight. I have lain awake at night and worried about that."

Fredrick knew that to ease his pain, his dad often went to the cemetery and talked to Mary. He knew it was irrational, but it seemed to ease some of the pain and loneliness that he felt. It had been eight years since Mary's death, but Luther was still hurting.

Fredrick asked, "Have you talked to Mom?"

Luther was quiet for a moment and then he answered, "Yes I have."

"What does she say?"

Again Luther was slow to speak. "Well, she has been silent on this one so far."

Fredrick understood this to mean that Luther still was not sure just how this would work out.

"I think you and Aunt Evelyn need to spend some time together until you are both at peace with this. Moving back to Pressley is going to be a horrendous move for her. On the other hand, Dad, having Aunt Evelyn move into a house that was Mom's will be easier than having someone else move in. She will cherish Mom's things. Someone else would want to toss them out. Now that would be difficult. I believe Aunt Evelyn has whipped her anger problem. She and her dad seem to be getting along well. If I were arranging a marriage for you, she would be the one I would pick. Just one last caution, remember she is her own person. You need to love her for who she is, not simply because she is Mom's sister. You cannot have Mom's ghost between you all the time."

It was as though Fredrick had taken a rifle with a scope and zeroed in on a target and hit it dead center. Every time Luther was with Evelyn, he saw Mary. He subconsciously knew this was a problem. Fredrick simply made him face it. He did not know how Freddy knew, but he knew that he knew.

"Son, I'm afraid you have scored a direct hit. I do not know how I am going to overcome that, but somehow if this is ever going to work, I have to come to grips with it."

"Time together, Dad. Time."

"That is difficult when she is 150 miles away."

"Well, somehow you must find a way."

Each was quiet for several moments and then Fredrick began to show his dad what he had in mind for the farm. It was an intricate plan using the refuse from the chicken raising operation to fullest advantage. Fredrick's plans were to reshape the hills to provide flat areas for the chicken houses. Within the property there was about 100 acres of cultivatable land, or land that could be reclaimed for cultivation. Fredrick's plan was to cut strips through the wooded hills and to flatten the areas for broiler houses. His idea was that the channel formed by the strips cut through the wooded areas would form natural convective airflow channels which would aid in cooling the chicken houses. His greatest concern was soil erosion and how to stem that when he cut part of the timber out.

Luther could see the cash outlay required for all of this piling up. He stopped Fredrick and asked, "Son, you are talking about a mint of money. How in the world do you plan to pay for this?"

"Cash"

"But where is the cash coming from? Surely you haven't made that kind of money from the funds you received."

Fredrick finally told his dad of his windfall profit from the "penny stock".

"But Fredrick, no one makes money from that kind of stock."

"Well, I did. It felt right at the time and I went with it. I didn't dream it would do what it did. If I had held it a little longer I would have made even more. The company sold to Digital Equipment just after I sold my shares. The guys that started the company did pretty well. I am glad for them."

Luther was stunned. He knew nothing of finances. Mary had taken care of all their financial matters and had him on an allowance. Fredrick took over the family budget after she was killed and kept his dad's feet to the fire and kept him from over spending. He had been his dad's advisor for his investment and done very well.

"Son, I don't know how you do it. How do you know what moves to make?"

Fredrick pushed his glasses back against his face and looked at his dad for an extended moment before he answered. "The same way you coach football. I listen a lot. I study the other parties involved in the transactions I am about to make. I read trade magazines and look at companies I am interested in. I listen to other people and get ideas about what they like and dislike. We are becoming a culture that has to have every whim satisfied. I have invested in companies that cater to those whims. I take some risk when the returns appear to be great if I win.

"You do the same when you are coaching. You watch the opposing safety back and see if he is lethargic. If you catch him napping you call for a long pass even though you may be deep in your own territory.

"This venture is one of those. The parties who owned this property are involved in a nasty divorce. That is consuming all of their energy. They wanted to sell the property, get out and move on. I took advantage of that and bought at a good price. I had to get the property reasonable because I am going to have a huge outlay of cash to make it profitable, but it has real property involved, which has a cash value. Much of the stock market is paper. That frightens me a bit, and is one reason I have looked for something with tangible assets. I try to look for companies that are well managed and there are few of those. Most companies in this country appear to be managed, not by the most qualified, but by the people with the strongest political base. That is not good."

"Freddy, how did you know about the divorce and the property?"

"One weekend when I was at home I overheard a conversation in the Dairy Queen. It was quite by accident, but Mrs. Groth was hyper talking to one of her friends and she was very loud. She was announcing to the world how she hated this place and wanted to get rid of it. I just filed that information away in my mind and decided to try to buy it."

*　　*　　*

An old house on the farm was riddled with termites. Fredrick's first move was going to be to burn that and move in a double wide mobile home for a farm manager. He revealed to his dad that he was going to take a look at Tommy Devaney and Lucy before he offered this job to them, but he thought Tommy would be good.

"Tommy is not the sharpest 'tack in the sack', but I think he will be very stable. He is no Duke Burks, but he is conscientious, honest and a hard worker. That makes up for a lot."

"Right you are son. Persistence generally wins."

Luther began to catch Fredrick's vision for the farm. He commented, "Son, it is going to take a ton of dozer work to get this place in shape. You know that is expensive."

"That's why I bought my own Bulldozer and hired an operator."

"You did what?"

"McKenzie Construction Company went broke. First National Bank wound up with all of their equipment. I went to the Case Dealer in Markel and had him purchase that for me for a commission. I knew old man Turner wouldn't let me have it."

Luther burst into laughter. "Now that is going to chap Mr. Turner. I wonder if he knows that you wound up with it."

"Oh, he knows. He is not a happy camper."

Luther laughed again. "I wish I could have seen his face when he got that bit of information."

When the tour was over, Luther's mind was at ease. Many of the questions, which were looming in his mind had been answered. He now knew that Fredrick was well funded, that his plans had been carefully laid and he fully expected success. By the time, he got back to the house he was on cloud nine. Strangely, the first person he wanted to share this new information with was Evelyn. He immediately got in his truck and went to see her at the Lane home.

Evelyn was dressed in jeans and she was working in the flowerbed at the front of the house setting out some flower bulbs. This was a throw back from her childhood; her mother always grew gladiolas in the front flowerbed. It was one of those warm, sunny December days and she had gotten cabin fever. She needed to work off some steam and the flowerbed afforded a good opportunity for that. Mr. Lane was asleep.

When Luther drove up and got out of his truck, she immediately sensed a change in him. He walked up and kissed her on the forehead. She pulled off her gloves and invited him to come in.

"I'll make a pot of coffee."

"Sounds good to me. I've been out with Fredrick looking over his new farm."

"What is that scamp up to now?"

"Well, let's sit down and I will tell you."

"Let me wash up first."

Evelyn went to the bathroom to freshen up and Luther made the coffee. When she came back, she had changed shirts and put on a very nice sweater which was somewhat revealing of her full figure. Luther grabbed her and kissed her with abandon. She lingered in his arms and his hands dropped below her belt squeezing her backside. Evelyn knew she should stop him, but she was powerless to do so. She finally regained her composure and slipped from his arms, but held on to his hand. They looked into each other's eyes, and could clearly envision the desire displayed there.

For once, Luther clearly saw Evelyn. She could sense a change.

"What has happened, Luther? You are different. You are not the same person I was with last night."

"I guess I have had my blinders removed."

"Fredrick."

"Yep."

"He is good at that."

"I guess he is. I will never understand my son, Evelyn. Just when I think I have him figured out, he comes out with something new. He is going into the chicken raising business. Can you imagine that? He is becoming a mechanical engineer and going into the chicken raising business. How in the world does that make any sense?"

"I don't know, but I'll bet it does to Fredrick."

For the next hour, Luther unloaded on Evelyn, relating his concern for Fredrick and his fear that he was getting into something that he should not until the tour. He related how well thought out Fredrick's plans were, even down to the details of raising a family on the farm.

Luther ended with the comment, "Evelyn, I so very much want you to be a part of our lives again. If our relationship grows to the point that you and I were to marry, do you think you could ever be happy back here in Pressley. That is going to be a gigantic move for you and I know you have your career in Houston."

"Luther, my career is that of an executive secretary. That is as high as I will ever go. I have been with the company for almost 30 years now, so I am vested in the pension plan. I really won't be giving up much there. As far as moving back to Pressley—that is another story and one I will have to wrestle with."

Luther looked into her eyes and with emotion gushed, "You wrestle that monster to the ground and when you have him whipped, you let me know."

Evelyn looked at him long and hard, "Luther, are you asking me, or are you asking Mary?"

This question, one that loomed in Evelyn's mind, finally surfaced.

"Up until today, Mary has been standing between us. Fredrick has helped me move her off to the side. Evelyn, I love you."

Evelyn burst into tears. She had never thought she would hear that from any man again.

Human emotion is the strangest of all behavior. Luther's and Evelyn's relationship took an upward turn that day and began to blossom. After the Christmas holidays, Evelyn began to take stock of her life. She got up every morning at six, jogged and then prepared for work. At work, she pampered a boss for four hours, ate lunch, and pampered her boss for another four hours. At home, she watched TV until she was sick of that, ate a snack while she read, and then went to bed. The next day she started this routine all over again. This had gone on for 30 years, and she was tired of it.

She walked in Monday morning and announced her intentions to retire. She gave the company a two weeks' notice and began packing the things she wanted to keep. She called a real estate agent and then listed her home for sale. She next contacted a used furniture broker and agreed to a price for everything she did not wish to keep. Evelyn discovered that she had little attachment for anything she owned. In her self analysis, Evelyn Lane discovered that she did not think very highly of herself; however, she decided that win lose or draw she was going back to Pressley to start a new life, with or without Luther Overall. The one thing she could do was make up for many lost years of bitter neglect of her father. She was depressed by the fact that her mother grieved because of her anger at her father and this had contributed to her death.

Evelyn was a strong willed woman, but she was very smart. She had been an excellent secretary and her salary reflected that, thus she would have no financial difficulties in her retirement years. She took a small penalty for retiring before the age of 60, but it was minimal.

Luther was calling her every day and just a few days before she was to return to Pressley she told him of her plans. On the phone he heard, "Luther, Are you sitting down?"

"Well. No. Why?"

"I have something to tell you. Perhaps you had better sit down."

Luther's blood ran cold. The first thing he could think of was that she had gone back to Houston and decided that she did not want to continue a relationship with him.

"What is it Evelyn?"

Evelyn did not miss the anxiety in his voice. "Well, I don't want you to get the wrong impression, and I do not want you to feel any obligation, but I have quit my job. I am coming back to Pressley to take care of Dad. I have neglected my responsibility long enough. You and I can get to know one another better, but please do not feel that this places you under any obligation to me."

Evelyn did not really like the way that had been voiced. It left the impression that she was considering a long-term relationship with him. To put it bluntly, she thought, he will think I expect him to ask me to marry him. She was smarting a bit over that when she heard. "Oh Evie, I am thrilled. Freddy told me we needed to spend time together to see where we stood. I couldn't figure out a way to do this with you 150 miles away. Are you sure this is what you want?"

"Luther, 'the axe is already at the foot of the tree'. I have packed, I have sold my furniture, my house is on the market. Just as soon as I can figure out a way to move a few things I will be home."

"I will be after you on Saturday with my truck. Do we need help loading anything?"

"No. I am not moving anything large, but I do not think everything will fit in your pickup."

"Call U Haul and rent a trailer one way to Pressley. I will be there by 8. Evie, I am so happy about this I am about to pop."

"Me too, Luther. I think it is the right decision."

*　　*　　*

Fredrick and Eva were busy after Christmas. They borrowed an old transit from Mr. Lane's stash of equipment and after figuring out how to use it, they staked out the location of the first broiler house. Each house was to be 40 feet by 300 feet and would house 15,000 birds. Fredrick planned to build 12 houses on this piece of property. The houses would be at three different levels on the hillside. Eva began to get caught up in the project and was anxiously anticipating her graduation (still at least three years away) and their return to the farm.

As she and Fredrick began to work side by side, he started relating information to her that he had learned. She became aware that he had researched every aspect of broiler production. He spoke of liter management, dead bird disposal, environmental impact, waste management, ventilation, automatic watering and feeding options. He related how he had chosen what construction would be used. He wrestled whether to use concrete for the floors or not, but decided to start with dirt floors. Eva finally stopped working and looked at him.

"Freddy, you tellin' me mo' 'bout chickens rasin' than I really want to know."

Fredrick was startled by this statement. He pushed his glasses back against his face and looked at her. She was smiling and he realized she was teasing.

"I'm sorry sweetheart. You know I get caught up in these projects. She laughed, "You know that I am teasing. I love to hear your plans."

"Well, I have been thinking about this for a long time. It is lots of work and we will have to find the right labor force. I think I will talk to Rosa when we get back to Austin and see if she knows a family that might be interested in moving here and operating the farm. We will need housing for them, so I better start thinking about that. We will need a well for the broiler houses. The well can also supply the living quarters and later our home."

"What about Tommy and Mattie? I thought that was what you had in mind for them."

"Oh, Tommy will be busy building and with other things. We need a little family to provide the labor for actually caring for the flocks."

Eva was amused by Freddy's statement that he had been thinking about the project for a long time. She knew that six months was a long time to Freddy, a young man in a hurry to make his mark.

New Years Eve turned bitter cold, so Freddy and Eva decided to give up their quest to get everything laid out before returning to school. They would be leaving New Years day. Freddy was pleased at their progress. He had enough work laid out for Tommy for the next six months. His first assignment was to get rid of the old house. Just before he left, he instructed Tommy, "You know, I wouldn't mind if that old house just happened to catch on fire as long as the fire was contained and did not damage the trees. I don't think there is material in it worth the trouble of salvaging it.

Tommy was still mulling that over in his head when Freddy left, and a few days later the old house just mysteriously caught on fire and burned to the ground.

*   *   *

Freddy and Eva were back in Austin when Tommy called to inform them of their loss of the house. Eva heard Fredrick on the phone. "Really! Burned to the ground. Well my goodness, what a shame. Well, we will just have to suck it up and go on. Why don't you move the dozier over there and clear off the spot for a house. I hope the fire didn't hurt the trees too bad."

There was a pause and then, "Oh, the wind was in the right direction."

"Well that was a break. Thanks, Tommy."

When Fredrick got off the phone Eva asked, "What happened."

"Oh, that old house on the farm caught fire and burned to the ground." Smiling Freddy continued, "What a shame."

"Fredrick, you gonna go to hell."

"Why:"

"For lying."

Fredrick and Eva had a good laugh. Eva speculated, "Sounds like Tommy puts legs to his prayers."

*   *   *

For the next several weeks, Freddy and Eva divided their time between study and running back and forth to Pressley to see that things were moving along. By the end of the spring semester, one broiler house was complete and ready for operation. Two doublewide manufactured homes were on sight, and Tommy and his wife were living in one. It was located at the old home site where the house had burned.

As Fredrick had planned, he talked to Rosa and found that she had a sister with a family who were working in Texas. They were struggling to make a living. Raul, the husband worked as a day laborer, Juanita, Rosa's sister worked for a hotel as a housemaid. They had one fourteen year old daughter, a son twelve years old and a six-year-old daughter. Juanita was six months pregnant and struggling to continue to work. Freddy made sure that they all had green cards to make them legal and then he and Eva interviewed them. They spoke little English, but Freddy and Eva both spoke Spanish reasonably well. At a very early age, Freddy learned to cuss in Spanish from workers on the farm. This got him in trouble with his Mom on more than one occasion.

The Garcia's jumped at the chance to move to the farm. This move would be a step up the ladder for them. Fredrick and Eva felt good about the arrangement made with this family. They were humble people, with a warm friendly air about them, which communicated, "We want to be your friend—please like us." Freddy and Eva did like them.

Little did this family know just what a giant step they had taken. The same had been true for Tommy and Mattie. Freddy Lane Overall was a master motivator, and seemed to have a sixth sense, which allowed him to look into a person's psyche and see the potential of each one he met. These two families would become a key part of the Agra Business Freddy envisioned.

Most of the town of Pressley was laughing at the fact that Freddy Overall was going into the chicken business. Velma and Luther were taunted about the fact that Freddy was majoring in Mechanical Engineering so he could raise chickens. Luther's old flame, Melissa asked Velma in the teacher's lounge one day if Freddy planned to raise mechanical chickens. Velma became livid, but fortunately, she controlled her anger. She had not lived in Freddy's presence all of those years and learned nothing.

"Oh no. He is developing a three legged chicken so they will have more drumsticks. He has to design something to catch them. They will be very fast you know, with that extra leg."

Melissa was dumb enough to believe her. Velma walked out and left her to her thoughts. The incident occurred during the lunch period. Melissa was attempting to find a time when she could use her comments to greatest advantage and maximize Velma's embarrassment.

After Velma left, Melissa turned to Velma's husband Bob, the Biology teacher and asked him, "How in the world do you develop a three legged chicken?"

Bob looked at her for a moment and then replied, "I think he plans to use genetic doping."

"Oh. Well, I guess that is possible."

After that comment, Melissa just seemed to disappear out of the lounge. Bob looked at Miss Hartman, the Chemistry teacher and remarked, "I sure hope she never marries again. She just might reproduce."

*   *   *

Pressley gossip was nasty. The Turners and Gipsons could not figure how in the world Freddy Overall was financing his broiler production operation. They even suggested that he was selling drugs in Austin, but for the most part this fell on deaf ears. Although some did not like Fredrick, they still respected him. He was different and people did not understand him, therefore he made them uncomfortable. His marriage to Eva was outside their social norms and this too added to their confusion. By the time the fourth broiler house was complete, the farm really began to take shape, and then the money started rolling in. A profit from each house was about $25,000 per house per year. Since Freddy and Eva studied most of the time, their needs were few and they lived very frugally. Rosa was still their housekeeper and cook and she was a master at conservation. Freddy's other investments were doing extremely well, so this left lots of money to put back into the business. Freddy's biggest problem was time, and he became masterful at time management.

Engineering Drawing was the only class that Freddy had trouble in. The problem with it was that it required time. Freddy mastered it, and then they came to computer aided design. Once he reached that point, everything lined out. Freddy was far ahead of anyone including the instructor when computers were involved. He had "bugged" Microsoft almost weekly about some problem that needed addressing. Through his contacts he was far up the ladder with names of people he could call. He was selected as a test site for Windows in the developmental stages. His detailed weekly reports outlining problems he encountered, suggesting changes and corrections resulted in a job offer that was hard to turn down. It was fortunate for him that he had already begun putting his business together or he would have taken the job. The job would have required a move to Washington State, and that too was very tempting to him. It was less tempting for Eva. Eva's face was already set toward a home on the hill overlooking the river.

Chapter 8

Evelyn moved in with her dad and began caring for him. Mr. Lane had mellowed over the years, and his infirmity had taken the edge off his old crusty nature. He was very docile and easy to manage; totally, different from his former self. This was a godsend for caregivers.

He and Evelyn were actually enjoying one another's company and Luther became a frequent guest. Luther and Mr. Lane were very close. Luther's patience and understanding of her dad simply enhanced the love that was maturing between them.

Evelyn was back in Pressley one month when Luther asked her to marry him. She said yes. They were planning a simple ceremony at the farm on Saturday night just before Easter. Two days before the wedding, Mr. Lane was sitting in his favorite recliner leaning back sleeping. Luther had come over for dinner and when Evelyn went to wake Mr. Lane for dinner, she discovered that he had died quietly in his sleep. It was a stunning moment. Questions surfaced immediately, "What to do about the wedding was number one?"

Luther called 911 who sent a sheriff's deputy and an ambulance. Mr. Lane was pronounced dead and the deputy wrote the death certificate, and all the paper work listing death by natural causes. Mr. Lane's body was transported to the funeral home. Luther and Evelyn were alone in the house. It was a difficult moment for each. Luther had lost a friend; Evelyn had lost a dad she had just rediscovered. *"What are we going to do about the wedding?"* was running through their minds.

Luther called Velma and asked her to call James and Mark. Luther then called Fredrick. Fredrick was not surprised. He had noted subtitle changes in Mr. Lane each time he had been home on the weekend, which was about every two weeks. He observed in steps, where those at home could only see small changes. The slow deterioration of Mr. Lane's condition was more obvious to Fredrick. He had never been close to his grandfather, but he still loved him. With his sensitive nature, Fredrick understood the old man better than any of the rest of the family. He was saddened by his passing. Eva, on the other hand was having trouble feeling sad. Mr. Lane hated her because of her color. He could never overcome his ingrained prejudice, and it showed. Fredrick observed and processed all of this and simply decided it was the nature of things and vowed that he would fight against prejudice in any form. Fortunately, it was a battle he won throughout his life.

What to do about the wedding surfaced when Luther called Fredrick. Fredrick was quiet for a moment on the phone and then he asked, "Dad, do you have your license already?"

"Yes we do."

"Call Brother Dan and see if he will marry you tonight."

"Why Freddy? Why tonight?"

"This is going to be a devastating blow for Aunt Evelyn. She needs you, and she needs you now. She does not need to be alone."

Luther ended the conversation with Fredrick and turned to Evelyn. "Fredrick told me for us to get married tonight so we wouldn't have to be alone. Are you game?"

"Tonight? Right now?"

Evelyn was stunned. "Well I guess so!"

Luther simply picked up the phone and called his Pastor. "Brother Dan, Mr. Lane passed away a few minutes ago. We will be talking to you about the service."

Brother Dan offered his condolences and offered to come over. Luther then dropped the bomb. "Brother Dan, you know that Evelyn and I were planning to get married on Saturday night. We have decided to go ahead and do it tonight, so, Evelyn and I would not have to be alone. Will you perform the ceremony for us. I have the license."

"Tu—Tonight???"

"Right now."

"Uh, Uh, Well, yes, I guess so."

"Will you meet us at my place?"

"Well, yes, I will be there in about 45 minutes."

"Great!!"

"Come on, Evelyn, We are going to get married."

"Luther, are you sure about this? What will people think?"

"Hell, I don't know and I don't care. Let me call Velma and Bob to come out and witness this."

Velma came as close to fainting as she had ever been. "Daddy, are you sure this is a good idea?"

"No, but Freddy told us to do it, so that is what we're doing. He arranged all of this anyhow, and we will be eternally grateful for that. He got Evelyn back here to spend time with her dad, and he is the one that got her and me together. I feel good about it, so we are going for it."

"What will people think, Dad?"

"I don't know and to quote Clark Gable, 'Frankly my dear, I don't give a damn'."

"Bob and I will be out in a few minutes."

Evelyn and Luther quickly tidied up and placed all of the food in the refrigerator. Evelyn looked at Luther and asked, "Are you going to dress? Luther looked down at his clothes and replied, "I am dressed, and so are you."

Evelyn smiled at him, and went and hugged him. "Well, this is going to be an unorthodox wedding, but hopefully that is the way our marriage will be also. When you take Freddy's advice, you had better get ready to hang on for the ride. He thinks on a different plane."

"I'm learning. It has been interesting. Evelyn, I am a sea of emotions right now. I know I should not be this happy since Mr. Lane is gone, but I love you and I don't want you to be alone tonight. I don't want to be alone either. I think Freddy gave us good advice. He is not encumbered with the thought. '*What will people think?*' When one is free of that, they are free to make rational decisions. This actually makes sense to me. It relieves some of our pain and lets us be together in this time of sorrow. I know he thought all of that through before he made his recommendation. We are not looking back. We are moving forward."

Evelyn quickly packed several items and she and Luther locked the house, and headed to the Overall farm. Luther called Duke and Rosalie and asked them to come over. Velma, Bob and their daughter Nelda arrived shortly after Evelyn and Luther came in. Brother Dan and his wife arrived also.

Brother Dan's first words were, "Luther, this is a little unusual. Have you thought it all through?"

"No, but Fredrick has. This is what he told us to do."

Brother Dan laughed, "Oh, well now, this is beginning to make sense."

On Good Friday evening, Luther and Evelyn stood in the Overall living room and exchanged their vows. It was a touching moment all wrapped in joy and sorrow. Evelyn would be eternally grateful that Fredrick had taken the time to push her to become reconciled with her father before it was too late. Never in her wildest dreams did she think she would fall in love with her former brother in law and become his wife, but at this moment, Evelyn attained true happiness which had eluded her for most of her life.

The memory of Luther and Evelyn's first night together as a couple would remain bittersweet long in their memories. They were so very grateful to have each other to share their sorrow, and thankful to Fredrick for his wisdom and giving them the nudge to exchange their vows. In many ways, the transition to married life at this particular time was easier for Evelyn than she had thought it would be. She was happy for the first time in many, many years.

Fredrick and Eva came in on Saturday morning. They left Austin early and were at the farm by eight to have breakfast with Duke and Rosalie. At eight thirty Luther called to see if they had arrived. Rosalie invited him and Evelyn to join the breakfast gathering, so he and Evelyn came over. Luther and Evelyn each had a deep need to see Fredrick and express their gratitude. That encounter was a touchstone moment. The three wept together briefly and then the expressions of gratitude began. Fredrick was remembering his mother and the many happy years she had told him about when she and Evelyn were growing up together. He reminded Evelyn of things she had long since forgotten, but many of her good memories of childhood began flooding back into her mind from deep within her psyche. The realization of the fact that she had judged her father too harshly hit her full in the face. She finally began to see him in a different light. It was a painful experience and she broke down and wept bitterly. Luther held her close and this helped, but the pain was very intense.

Fredrick took her arm and looked deep into her eyes. "Aunt Evelyn, stop beating yourself up. Granddad also had some regrets that he expressed to me when I got down tight on him. Both of you were as stubborn as a 'humpback mule'. The time for regret is past. You both had your time of reconciliation and you did what you could do. Hind sight is 20/20, but looking into the future, '*we see through a glass darkly*'. He smiled and continued, "That's the King James Version. I know that Mom is smiling down on you for what you did. You gave the old man several good months of joy. He was delighted that you and Dad were going to get married. At least he experienced the joy of that knowledge. What more could you ask?"

Evelyn regained control. She was a pragmatic woman, just like her sister, Mary had been and she set her face toward the task for the day. The time for the visit to the funeral home to make all of the arrangements was fast approaching and she dreaded that. The breakfast together was subdued, but Rosalie was such a good cook that soon all was forgotten briefly until the food was gone. She had fixed biscuits and gravy and that was very high on Fredrick's list of 'food fit for the gods'. It was sausage gravy and sausage didn't 'look like something that had lived' to Fredrick.

After the meal, Luther asked Fredrick to go with he and Evelyn to the Funeral home. Eva had cleared the table and had most of the dishes in the dish washer. Fredrick agreed to go, but Eva was going with him.

Eva spoke up, "You don't need me there, honey."

"I need you wherever I am, Eva."

Eva looked at him and knew immediately that he was hurting. She ran to him and put her arms around him. "Ok, I am going with you."

Evelyn and Luther both smiled. They had gotten a glimpse of what a good marriage looked like. From that point on, Eva had her hand on Fredrick. They were either holding hands or she had her hand on his sleeve. She was not turning him loose until this ordeal was over."

At the funeral home, Luther and Evelyn got the shock of their lives. They discovered that over the Christmas holidays, when Fredrick was at home, he and his granddad had been to the funeral home and made all the arrangements. The old fellow had picked out his casket and paid for it. He had outlined the order of service and even selected what songs were to be used. All Luther and Evelyn had to do was pick the time. All of the dread drained from Evelyn's face. She was aware that she really did not know her father very well and had worried bitterly over this moment.

"How, Fredrick? How did you get this done?"

"Well, Eva and I went to see him one afternoon and he looked terrible. I broached the subject of how I would want my funeral conducted. He picked right up on that and began to tell me how he wanted his.

"I said, Granddad, why don't you go see Mr. Allen and tell him how you want it done. He will pre arrange all of that and you can have it like you want it. He said, 'By dam, that is just what I will do. Will you take me?' I called Mr. Allen and he agreed that if we could come in, he could arrange everything. Eva and I brought him in.

"It was obvious that he had it all thought out ahead of time. He went down the list of things to do just like he had them memorized. He just needed a little push to get the ball rolling."

Luther laughed, "Freddy, you are the best person I know at giving the ball a push. I just wish you had been a quarterback for me. I could have won state again."

"Not with me as quarterback. I get scared when I see a ton of flesh running at me."

There was a tension-breaking laugh around the room.

Mr. Allen brought the matter back in perspective and asked, "Well, what time do you want to have the service? All we need is the time."

Luther and Evelyn put their heads together. Luther looked at Fredrick. "We don't know when James can get here. When do you think we should have it, Freddy?"

Fredrick didn't bat an eye. "Two o'clock tomorrow."

"What if James doesn't make it by then."

Again, Fredrick was ready with an answer. "So be it."

Fredrick and James were not on the best of terms. James didn't care much for his brother. He felt inferior to him in his adult life. He had picked on Fredrick all the time they were at home together when Fredrick was growing up.

Luther sat for a moment sorting things out. "Fredrick, I think James will want to be here."

"You called him last night. It has been sixteen hours already and he still has another 28 hours to get here. All he had to do was get in the car this morning and head out, or get on a plane and fly to Austin. He can make it if he tries. If he doesn't, so be it."

Luther looked at Evelyn. He said two pm tomorrow If Brother Dan is available?"

She nodded her accent.

Mr. Allen had his receptionist call Brother Dan and he was available, so, the funeral was arranged.

*　　*　　*

James came in about ten on Saturday. He brought his fiancé with him. She was an arrogant young lady, obviously very proud of herself and thought the Overall's to be hicks. James had obviously told her that Fredrick was starting a broiler production business. She and James evidently thought this hilarious from their comments.

Luther cornered Fredrick and simply said, "Freddy, please be nice. Don't stare."

Fredrick smiled, "Okay Dad. I promise: I will be nice unless she starts something."

Luther accepted that with some reservations. The "Unless she starts something" worried him.

At noon, the church served a meal for the family. Unfortunately, Marcie, James fiancé sat across the table from Fredrick. She wanted to take a jab at Fredrick for raising chickens. She opened her conversation with, "Well Fredrick, I hear that you are going to raise chickens. Why in the world did you decide to raise chickens?"

Fredrick pushed his glasses back against his face and sat staring at her for an uncomfortable moment.

Luther cringed. He wanted to step in and stop Fredrick, but he knew there was simply no way.

Fredrick cleared his throat and began, "Well, I began with a market survey of the dietary needs of our expanding population and the taste and quirky trends of our elitist. It seems that many are shying away from red meat in favor of poultry, which has increased the demand for poultry products.

"Chickens are very efficient critters with a feed conversion ratio of about 40 percent. In addition, the waste products are high in urea, which is an excellent fertilizer for crop and hay production. This enhances our other farming operations. Why sell our grain to overseas markets when we can run it through chickens right here on the farm? Using our own grain eliminates shipping cost and we put that money in our pockets."

Fredrick went on to pontificate facts relating to environmental impact, mortality rates, problems with disease and how to prevent them, labor force, marketing, space requirement, production facility design and etc. When he finished, he simply said, "So you see Marcie, it is more than simply a few old laying hens that you throw scraps and corn chops to each day and then gather up the eggs."

Color had risen in Marci's face. She had squared off against a superior intellect and she knew it. She stammered, "But, but why did you major in Mechanical Engineering if you were going to raise chickens? Why didn't you major in Agriculture?"

Fredrick again pushed his glasses back against his face and looked squarely at Marcie. "Well, one could just as easily have asked, why did you go to college at all?

"I read pretty well. I can learn about Agriculture by reading. As you may well imagine, Engineering requires learned skills that are more easily learned if taught by a competent instructor. It exercises one's mind in many different disciplines; math, physics, chemistry and just about all of the sciences. Technical writing is also important in the engineering discipline. Project management is also included within the framework of this discipline. These are all skills needed to run and operate a successful business."

Marci couldn't just let it drop. "Well, why didn't you just major in business?"

"Oh, but Eva is getting her degree in business and accounting. She will handle that end of the business. She is also going to become a CPA. You see, I was planning to marry her all along."

Marci's mouth fell open. She was speechless. She had not even looked at Eva as being an intellectual equal, yet she had barely squeaked through college with a liberal arts major.

Her reply was simply "Oh."

That ended the quiz.

*   *   *.

Mr. Lane's service was well done. Although he had some quirks, for the most part, the old fellow was, a good man. He was compassionate at times, but at other times, he was hard as nails. One could never tell which side was going to surface in any given event. Somewhere in the back of his mind was a scale that triggered which personality would surface. Luther and Fredrick were the only two people, after Mary died, who came close to understanding the old man. By the time Evelyn was back in the picture, he had mellowed to the point that he was reasonably docile.

Brother Dan Slade, his pastor, knew many of the good things Mr. Lane had done. He simply overlooked the rest as he delivered his eulogy for a man who had served as a deacon at the little church for over 40 years. Much to everyone's relief, the service was not long.

The Overalls got through the funeral and the Easter weekend without a major confrontation. Luther and Evelyn were delaying a honeymoon until school was out and then they planned a trip. Fredrick and Eva spent much of their time at the Burks avoiding contact with Mark and James. Fredrick and Velma had a reasonably good relationship since Fredrick was matchmaker for her very happy marriage to Bob.

Fredrick did spend time with Gretchen practicing his German. The coaching job at Markel was opening up and Mark had his application in for that job. Luther was doing all he could do to help him secure that position. It was doubtful that James would ever return to the area if he and Marci married. Her dad was in business and it seemed that James was slated to enter that business after the wedding.

*   *   *

Mr. Lane's passing ended an era of farming the old way at the Lane/ Overall farms. He had been an "Old School" type farmer. He held on to his milk cow for years, after most had given that up and gone with pasteurized, 'store bought' milk. He raised hogs fattened on table scraps and for many years he rendered lard and made cracklings. He loved crackling bread, and simply would not give it up. He was a very hard worker, rising at five every morning and working until dark each day except Sunday. Sunday was his day of rest and he held firm with that all of his life. He was frugal, almost to a fault; pushing old equipment way past its practical, useful life. He lived by the old adage, "Use it up—wear it out—make it do—or do without." His fence rows were kept immaculately trimmed and fences were kept in a good state of repair, although patched over and over with old wire. One thing about the old fellow that always irritated Luther was that he would not purchase metal gates or let Luther purchase them. He used homemade wire gaps. His reason given was, "When I open that gap and lay it down, it stays there." Evidently, at some point in his life he had bought a metal gate and put it up. He had opened it and got in his truck to drive through and the wind had blown it closed. He had to get out of his truck and find something to prop against the gate to keep it open. From that, point on he went back to his wire gaps.

Mr. Lane never liked Fredrick. Near the end of his life he respected him. When Fredrick took the old tractor, overhauled it and got it running like new, he began to have a new appreciation for his grandson. He had gone into a tirade when he first learned that Fredrick had the tractor torn down. He tried to fire his farm manager when he learned that he had agreed to assist Fredrick, but Luther stepped in and squished that.

Shortly before the end of his life, he and Fredrick had a heart to heart talk. Mr. Lane admitted to Freddy that he never liked him and apologized for that. Fredrick just as candidly told him that he always thought he was a hard headed, mean spirited old coot and that he didn't like him either.

The two sat looking at one another; Fredrick with his glasses pushed back against his face and Mr. Lane, for one of the first times looking directly into his eyes said, "Son, it's yore eyes. They bug me. 'Em glasses make yore eyes look huge. 'At just bugs the life out of me".

Fredrick didn't cut him any slack. "Well, granddad, I can't help the way I look, but you could help the way you act. When I look at you, I see a mean spirited old man. That bugs me."

"Now just why do you say that?"

"Because it's true. You hurt your daughter terribly and ran her off. Mom was never allowed to enjoy her sister. I am mad as hell at you about that. On top of that, you haven't even apologized to her for that."

"Well, she won't let me. She ain't never come home."

Fredrick was on a roll. "Well, you do know how to write don't you?"

"Naw, I can't write no more, and. I ain't even got her address."

"Well I will write it for you. You can sign it and I'll mail it."

Mr. Lane sat staring at Fredrick for a long moment. "Son, will you write it for me?"

Although the stroke had been somewhat debilitating, Mr. Lane struggled and signed what Freddy had typed. He scribbled at the bottom, "Evie, I'm sorry I dun you wrong. Please forgive me."

Fredrick had included that short note in his letter to Evelyn that had prompted her Thanksgiving visit. It had been enough.

Mr. Lane knew that Fredrick's prompting had brought about the reconciliation. From that point on, he was Fredrick's biggest fan until his death.

Chapter 9

Freddy graduated in three and one half years by going to summer school each semester. Since Eva still lacked a little over two years, he entered graduate school. He set his sights toward a PhD, not that he would need it, but he felt that having the title might be a tool should he ever need to finance a large investment. By the time Eva graduated, Freddy lacked about three semesters finishing course work for his PhD. He had foregone writing a thesis and getting his Masters degree. Eva took a part time job for an accounting firm and began work toward her Certified Public Accountant examination. About the time, Freddy finished his last course; Eva took the CPA board exam and passed it, thus becoming a full fledged CPA. Freddy still lacked a doctoral thesis, but his topic was approved and he was assigned an advisor. It was no surprise that he had selected the design of a new type feed grinding mill for his research project.

Fredrick wrote a grant proposal and received Federal money to work on the project. His grant proposal was a work of art. It was complete with computer-generated drawings, work process descriptions, a time line, and all of the elements of a well run project. Fredrick proposed to supply the location and building, and he in return, could keep the equipment once the project ended. That was a sticky point, but it was accepted. In reality, what Fredrick had done was have the government build a feed processing mill for him that he would have free and clear as well as receive a PhD in the process. It was legal and one would have to say that it was still within the bounds of being ethical, although it stretched the bounds to their limit. It was simply a matter of a good mind using the system to its greatest advantage.

Luther was worried. He questioned, studied, and looked closely at what Freddy was doing. He finally came to the conclusion that what Freddy was doing was ethical and above board. Fredrick gave monthly reports to the Federal Agency that made the grant outlining how each dollar was spent. The Agency did not know what to do with the reports, so they simply filled them. Fredrick and Eva both knew there should be some oversight, but there simply was none.

Fredrick and Eva now had nine broiler houses on their farm. This amounted to 136,000 capacity at this location. They were clearing about $150,000 per year and Freddy was putting all of this money back into the business. The Garcia family was operating the farm and working out great. It was a fantastic opportunity for them, giving meaningful work to a their son and daughter, as well as the rest of the family. Raul, the father saw this as a once in a lifetime opportunity for himself and his family. They had a good home, a good income, and medical and dental benefits. He had found a home and he intended to keep it.

* * *

Evelyn's portion of the Lane farm was fifty percent. Fredrick and Eva worked out a purchase arrangement with her to buy her half of the farm for $562,500.00 They were to pay her $100,000 down and $50,000 per year until the farm was paid off at six percent interest. Evelyn had received the part of the farm with the home. Eva and Fredrick were living there until they were ready to build their own home. Fredrick decided to build a metal building at the farm to house his laboratory. Once his research and thesis were complete, he would convert the Lab to a feed grinding and mixing operation. Fredrick's funds were running lower than he was comfortable with, so he had to slow his rate of growth. He had made some good investments, which were paying well, but he had not made windfall profits the way he did with his penny stock.

He built two broiler houses at the Lane farm and he and Eva operated them for their income to live on. He had his broiler house construction down to a fine art, having designed his own building and having everything prefabricated. Construction on the 40 by 300 building took one week to set the steel frame and one week to install the metal. Plumbing took one day, and installation of the automatic feeding and watering systems required five days. Within one month a house was up and operating. Fredrick had hoped to build at least four more houses at the Lane property, but funds were not available and he refused to borrow money.

Then Eva became pregnant. She and Freddy were overjoyed. Evelyn was beside herself. She was going to be a grandmother; which was an honor she never thought she would experience. Luther was having trouble grasping the concept of becoming a grandfather. Although Velma, James and Mark were old enough to be parents, parenting seemed to be far down on their list of priorities. Fredrick and Eva on the other hand were anxious to start their family.

One evening late, Eva snuggled close to Fredrick. "Freddy, I want to talk to you about something."

"Ok Sweetheart; what is on your mind?"

"I want you to slow down."

"What exactly do you mean by that?"

"Well, if you and I operate these two chicken houses here, We can make about $50,000 per year out of them. With our other income, we can live comfortably. It would be a good life and a good way to raise our children."

Fredrick knew that Eva was a home body and that she was content to simply live on and enjoy the farm. Much like his mother she enjoyed planting, digging in the dirt, romping across the fields and watching the crops grow. She enjoyed raising chickens. Eva was truly a farm girl. She took almost every step Fredrick took on the farm, plus many of her own choosing.

Fredrick considered all of these factors before he answered, "Well sweetheart, I can't really promise you that. I will try, and I will always try to find time for family time together, but you know I have to be involved in some challenge. While I am working on my dissertation, I will slow down on other projects. This is going to take lots of time and energy, but the dynamics of the business that I am trying to build requires a large operation to maximize profitability. I'm sure you understand that."

"I understand it, but I am not sure I like it."

Fredrick pushed his glasses against his face and thought seriously. He was astute enough to realize this was one of those moments that could severely affect his marriage.

He embraced Eva and held her for a long moment and then he quietly explained, "Eva, you and I are a team. Whatever I do will have to be done with your blessings. You are six months pregnant right now and your body is struggling to build another human being. Your job right now is to see that you get ample rest, eat properly, get good exercise and build a healthy baby. For goodness sakes, don't build one that looks like me, and don't run over any opossums."

Eva laughed. The story of Freddy's mother running over the opossum causing its eyes to pop out was rehearsed often in the Overall family. Luther almost believed that was what caused Fredrick to be born nearsighted.

"Freddy, don't put yourself down. If I could make a baby just like you I would be happy."

Eva loved Fredrick. Her main concern now was that Freddy was driven to get even with the town of Pressley. Having grown up feeling the hot winds of prejudice and being reared by a mother who drilled into her the destructive nature of hate, she feared that Freddy's anger at the town would be a destructive force. What Eva and the rest of the family did not understand was that Fredrick loved his hometown and the people in it. He did not like the strangle hold two families held on the economic growth of the town and hoped to change that, but he did not hate people. With his uncanny understanding of human nature, he enjoyed bantering with those who felt they were superior, but this was little more than a game for him. Freddy was a man with a plan, and he intended to stay on that plan. He simply chalked Eva's apprehension up to the fact that she was pregnant, decided to humor her, and go on about his business. He had plenty to do right now getting his research project off the ground. It was well funded and his ideas were already taking shape.

*   *   *

Freddy's design for a new type of feed grinding process was one that used a high speed blower to feed the grinding mill. It fed grain to the chopper from updraft rather than gravity feeding from a hopper. The grinder consisted of a cylindrical worm gear with a fixed clearance which made the product very consistent. The fine gluten from the grinding process was collected and then mixed with a small amount of water and recombined with the ground up grain. The product was then fed through a pelletizer and dryer. Pelletized feed helped reduce waste at feeding time.

Freddy did a search for grinders commercially available, but found none that met his specifications, so he set about designing his own. For the first time in his life, Fredrick Overall met a challenge. He studied metallurgy, machining, metal casting, manufacturing techniques and most of all, politics. Fortunately his laboratory was outside the city limits, so he did not have to deal with all of the required city inspections, but the county inspectors hounded him unmercifully. They constantly sought ways to slow him down. On one occasion the OSHA inspector showed up and he was fined because two workers were inside the construction area without hard hats. It was a token fine of $500 each, but the fact that no construction was being done at the time really angered Fredrick.

After lots of hassle, Fredrick decided that the way around this was to contribute to the right political campaigns. After making four $1,000 contributions, his harassment seemed to fade away. This was enlightening, but also disgusting to Fredrick. It increased his anger with those in power in the town of Pressley. The contributions were not at the local level, but at the state level. No one ever figured out exactly how Fredrick knew just where to put his money, but the $4,000 wound up saving him ten times that amount in harassment and frustration. Freddy did not actively pursue learning the connection between local and state politicians, he just kept his eyes open. He saw more at a glance than most saw with a long look. He decided then and there to subtly work to unseat those he had contributed to.

Folks in Pressley still could not figure out where Fredrick got his money. Jim Turner and Ed Gipson sat in their offices for hours on end trying to figure this out. Both men knew that Fredrick received a $250.000 settlement from his mother's accident, but the level that he was spending did not compute. Neither knew of the windfall profits from the penny stock, and they did not know about his income from computer consulting. He was still on the payroll at two computer companies in Austin. He had saved them big bucks and they were not anxious to lose his services. The bankers did not know about the $200,000 Federal Grant either. Fredrick gave them indigestion.

*   *   *

The telephone wires in Pressley almost went into meltdown when a three by five picture of a smiling Fredrick and Eva Overall appeared in the daily newspaper holding their newborn son, William Luther Overall. Fredrick and Eva honored both of their fathers by naming their firstborn after them. William weighed eight pounds and four ounces. Fredrick was pleased that William's eyes appeared to be normal and Eva was pleased that he had straight hair. He was a beautiful baby and the rumors immediately turned nasty with comments that he couldn't be Freddy Overall's child. This was not believed, it was simply "tacky" gossip.

Fredrick was a doting father and immediately went out and bought the baby a John Deere shirt and Case/International cap. This was a precursor of things to come.

Evelyn and Eva were very close and with the birth of this first child, that relationship grew. One would not have known that Evelyn was not the baby's biological grandmother. In this child she experienced much of the love and affection she had missed by never having a child of her own.

Becoming a grandfather was somewhat traumatic for Luther, but it did not take him long to settle into that role.

*   *   *

One year and sixteen weeks after Fredrick started his research project, he ground his first feed. It was a glorious moment for him because he had poured his heart and soul into the project. Actually, it was an amazing feat for a project of this magnitude to have it completed in this time frame, but to Freddy Overall, a young man on the move, it did not meet his expectations. His next greatest hurdle was obtaining efficiency information from other grain mills. That was a key part of his research since the whole premise of his dissertation was based on comparative efficiency and product quality. Since Federal money was involved, he made several trips to Washington to elicit help from congressional representatives to force cooperation from various mills around the country. It soon became obvious to everyone involved that this young man was not going away until he had what he wanted, so information began to flow in.

For the next several months, Fredrick poured over the information, analyzing and comparing. He wrote an elaborate program which automatically adjusted mill size and output to compare with his mill. Data showed almost immediately that mill efficiency was going to be a wash based on operating cost alone. Unless his cost to maintain proved advantageous, his design had failed in that area, but the premise of his design was broad based. Fredrick considered this as a possibility from the beginning, and he paid careful attention to making the mill reliable and easy to maintain. Whenever possible, he purchased bearings which met NASA specifications to insure long life. He decided that the only way he could salvage his project was to run the mill at least three years and compare the maintenance data He would also look for an improvement in feed conversion from his product.

A positive aspect of the project was the fact that Fredrick was able to process grain from the Overall farm, thus eliminating shipping cost. He worked out an arrangement with the poultry processor to produce his own feed based on their formula for half of his flock and using their feed for the other half. Fredrick ran sixteen batches of broilers making comparisons of the company's standard feed and feed from his mill. He consistently averaged a 2% increase in feed conversion from his mill. The assumption was attributed to the fact that his mill produced a more consistent formula which was more finely ground and more digestible. He knew he would have to prove that to his review committee, so he immediately began to work on that aspect.

Fredrick went to the Biochemistry Departments at both The University of Texas and Texas A&M to engage their services to analyze the two feeds. Both Laboratories concurred that Freddy's feed was more consistent in texture and nutrient value. Freddy's conclusions were that consistency was the key to the increase in feed conversion.

*   *   *

Fredrick's dissertation was six hundred and seventy two pages long. It contained graphs, tables, pie charts (in color), detailed mechanical drawing and parts list for the mill, and materials specifications. It even included design layout of the building that housed the equipment. The attitude of the review committee ranged all the way from being aghast, fascinated, to hero worship. One reviewer commented, "This should be in the biochemistry department"; another, "No, it is clearly Poultry Husbandry", and one reviewer looking at all of the computer technology used in preparation of the document stated flatly, "No it clearly belongs in the Computer Science department."

Sitting stoically and listening to all of the comments, Fredrick just pushed his glasses back against his face and stared down each distracter. He was prepared to defend his dissertation and not one single person in the room was ready to take him on. Fredrick had been in their classes and was well known. There was animosity on the part of some in the room since Fredrick had outfoxed them and wound up with a nice facility, which some felt, should have gone to the University, but he had slipped this by before anyone noticed.

Fredrick fielded each question easily. He would refer to data by page number without even looking at the document. It soon became obvious that he could tell you what was on each page. Four hours and seventeen minutes after the review began; it ended abruptly when no further questions were asked. Fredrick Lane Overall became a full-fledged PhD.

*   *   *

Fredrick's family had not been sitting still while he was working on his doctorate. Eighteen months after William Luther was born, Fredrick Lane II made his entry into the world. He was a carbon copy of his brother. With two in diapers, Fredrick and Eva were busy, but Fredrick was also busily leasing all the land he could find available near Pressley. He now had along with the 2600 acres in the Overall and Lane farms plus his own 400 acres, an additional 4,000 acres with a long term, ten year lease and an option to purchase. This still would not supply his mill and he had to purchase some grain from the local co-op. Since the Turners and Gipsons dominated the co-op this did not set well with Fredrick. He was frequently at odds with the co-op and he was slowly but surely planning his exodus from their grip.

Fredrick worked out a contract with the poultry processor to supply feed from his mill to other producers in the area, and he actually started shipping feed to other locations. The mill became a big business for the Pressley area, and required twenty-five full time employees. Fredrick turned the business management of the mill over to Eva. Eva immediately hired Evelyn to set up the office for the mill and she and Evelyn brought a level of organization to management of this business heretofore not seen in Pressley. The mill became a fantastic moneymaker. Since it was built free and clear with no debt to service, adequate funds for expansion were available, and nothing was static around Fredrick Overall.

*   *   *

In Pressley, the frequent gossip in the beauty and barbershops was that Fredrick Overall was spending the Overalls into bankruptcy. Since the Overalls refused to use the local bank after Karen Boren tried to frame Velma and send her to prison, no one in Pressley knew their financial status. Luther and Velma had turned the management of their investments over to Fredrick and he simply mirrored his portfolio with theirs. They had all done well. Fredrick had written a computer program that automatically bought and sold stocks based on benchmarks. This relieved him of much oversight.

Luther's wealth was now in excess of one million dollars. Velma was close behind. At their rate of earning, Fredrick was doubling their money every five years. Luther finally decided that after 43 years of coaching high school football it was time to give it up. He was now 65 years old and money had not been the reason for his continuing. He loved the game, and he loved making a difference in the lives of the young men he coached.

Mark Overall had been out of the Army for four years and he was coaching at a small school in East Texas. He had done well with his team. He applied for Luther's job and got it. Ben Burks applied for the assistant coach's job and after a bitter fight among the school board members, he was offered that position. Ben clearly had a superior record to all other applicants. Rumors of the bitter debate reached Ben's ears and he started to decline the position, but Luther encouraged him to take the job.

Luther admonished, "Ben, someone has to break the race barrier here in Pressley. It may as well be you. You straightened me out; you may as well educate the school board also."

Mark was a little more personable than Luther, thus he was readily accepted. Luther and Velma were harsh disciplinarians. They were good at their jobs, but with a few rough edges. Mark on the other hand had more finesse. He was boisterous and outgoing and proud of himself, but not abrasive. Luther and Velma were dogmatic and "in your face" when disagreements arose. Many in Pressley were glad to see Luther retire, however, many others, especially the host of young men whose lives Luther had turned around and set on a good path were saddened by his retirement.

*   *   *

Fredrick hosted a banquet at the VFW hall to honor his Dad in his retirement. He sought and attained Evelyn's help in putting together a list of former students who had been on one of Luther's teams. In fact, this became a team effort with the entire family contributing. Each person who had been on a Pressley Athletics team, including those down to the 'water boy' level received a special, engraved invitation. Fredrick spared no expense. Velma and Evelyn both decided they were going to share in the cost and this was one argument with Fredrick they did not intend to lose. He finally acquiesced.

Fredrick even invited the governor, who declined, but sent an emissary in his stead. A state senator and two congressmen attended. Fredrick did not ask any of the dignitaries to speak, although he did recognize their presence and thanked them for coming.

Two weeks before the banquet, Fredrick had Lasik eye surgery. His looks were totally changed. When he stood before the banquet gathering, a new Fredrick Overall had emerged. Opening his welcome address, Fredrick stood and faked an attempt to push his glasses back against his face. He grinned and said, "I started to push by glasses in place the other day and poked my finger in my eye."

The crowd erupted into laughter. The "Fredrick Maneuver" as this action had become known throughout Pressley and Walwick County was legendary. Many in the crowd did not recognize him when he stood before them. Some had not seen him for a long time and the strange looking kid with the horn rim glasses was gone. He was still slender, but at a mature six feet four, he now exhibited an air of authority and dignity, Fredrick Overall was a commanding figure as he spoke.

"With all sincerity," Fredrick began his address, "I wish to thank all of you for your presence here tonight to honor my Dad and to make this a memorable experience for him. After forty-three years of coaching young men and helping start many down a path of success that some might never have found, this is a step of gargantuan proportion. I really don't know what—(Fredrick paused, placed his hand on top of his head and looked at the ceiling as if thinking hard)—Now let's see, is it Aunt Evelyn, Mama Evelyn—oh I know I will just call her Granny Evelyn. I don't know what Granny Evelyn will do with him at home all the time."

Evelyn stood and shook her fist at him. Luther placed his hands over his face thinking, "That name is going to stick. I know it. She is going to kill him."

After the laughter died down Fredrick continued. "No. Seriously, Aunt Evelyn has come back into our lives at a time when most needed and we are overjoyed to have her as an integral part of our family once again".

Everyone in the room knew the devastating effect Mary's death had on all the Overall family, but especially Luther. Most knew of Fredrick's role in bringing Luther and Evelyn together. There was a standing ovation.

After the audience was again seated, Fredrick extended his hand toward Luther and Evelyn and asked, "Mom and Dad, would you stand for a moment?"

Luther and Evelyn stood holding hands. Fredrick continued, "Don't they look good together?"

Another round of applause erupted. Luther and Evelyn beamed. After the applause subsided again, Fredrick continued, "I am not going to stand up here and give a long speech"—Velma clapped.

Fredrick shook his head. "She's one of my greatest admirers."

There was another huge round of laughter. Everyone knew that Fredrick and Velma had been at odds with one another most of his life.

Digressing, Fredrick asked, "You know what she told my mama when I was born. She told her I was one that she didn't need. Isn't that some legacy from your own sister?"

Velma turned six shades of red, and just hung her head. There was another round of laughter and her little brother had again put her in her place. That story was rehearsed often in Pressley and Velma hoped it had finally died down. It was one of those statements thoughtlessly spoken by a young know-it-all fourteen year old teenager, but one that had come back to haunt her many, many times. Now it was in full bloom again.

Continuing, "But I love her in spite of myself." Another burst of laughter.

"I have asked three people, and there could have been hundreds, so, if you are not one of those asked to share your story here tonight, please don't feel slighted. The task of picking was tremendous, but I have picked three of Dad's former students to share briefly some of their remembrances of their time on one of his teams."

The first person to speak was Jim Hodges. Jim had played for Luther when Fredrick was only eight years old. Luther had no idea that Fredrick even remembered him. Jim had received a scholarship to play football for Tyler Junior College. After finishing there, he went to Stephen F. Austin University and received his degree in Physical Education and was now coaching at a school in far West Texas. He had driven eight hours to be present for this banquet.

Jim rose, waved at Luther and went to the podium. "I'm a dumb old coach, not a public speaker, but I would not be a coach today were it not for Luther Overall. I grew up on a poor dirt farm just outside Pressley. My daddy was a hard working man, but he had three faults. He was bad to drink, bad to cuss and bad to beat my butt." There was an explosion of laughter, but then Jim's story turned serious.

"I came to school one day after one of those frequent beating and after I had finished football practice and gotten out of the shower, I was starting to dress when Coach Overall walked through the locker room. He happened to notice my back. He stopped and asked, 'Son, what happened to your back?' I didn't want to tell him but after stammering for a moment, I admitted that my daddy had whipped me. I was afraid I would get daddy in trouble and then I knew I would be in trouble.

"Well, all coach Overall said was. 'I'm taking you home today.' I was petrified. After I dressed, we got in coach's car and he took me home. Coach Overall asked mama where my daddy was and she told him he was in the barn working on a tractor. I knew daddy would already be livid because he and that old tractor did battle all the time.

"We walked to the barn and we could hear daddy cussing that old tractor before we got to the door. I knew he had already been drinking some and I was scared to death. Coach Overall walked up to daddy and didn't flinch.

"Mr. Hodges, Jim has had a severe beating; far outside the bounds of decency. Can you tell me anything about that?"

"Daddy came up off the ground with a wrench in his hand and shook the wrench at Coach and screamed, 'Ain't none of yore damned business!'"

"Coach poked him in the chest with his finger and said, "Well, I'm making it my business. No one beats up one of my students like that and gets away with it".

"Daddy drew back the wrench and tried to hit coach upside the head with it. Coach blocked the blow with his left hand and with his right hand he slapped daddy down.

"My daddy was laying in the barn floor looking up at coach standing over him. Coach said, 'Old man, if you ever beat this boy again, I will find you and give you ten time what you gave him. He is an adult now and you had better wake up to that fact. One other thing, don't try to hide behind your liquor again. That is not going to mean a damn thing to me when I come looking for you. You could and should go to jail for this, but I giving you one last chance to correct your behavior.'

"With that, Coach turned and walked away. Mama had walked out to the barn and she looked at daddy. Coach had given her courage and as she looked at daddy she said, 'If you ever beat any of us again, I'm taking the kids and leaving'."

"She turned and went back in the house. I looked at daddy and I told him, 'Daddy, I ain't taking any more of your beatings and you aren't beating Mama again if I have to take a gun and shoot you.

"I meant what I said. Coach's faith in me—when he told my daddy that I was an adult—Jim had done well up to this point but his emotions got the best of him and he broke down. The audience was patient and sat stoically giving him time to re-compose himself. He brought his emotions in check and continued, "That one statement gave me an inner strength that I didn't know I had. From that day on, I became an adult and I governed myself accordingly. I had thought my daddy invincible, but when I saw him lying in that barn floor, I pitied him. He was just a miserable old man, one who worked hard and then spent most of what he made on liquor.

"Coach had an effect on Dad also. He never beat any of us from that point on. He didn't want to face Coach again.

"Coach helped me get my scholarship to go to college and he, without a doubt, changed my life and is responsible for the little measure of success I have attained. From the bottom of my heart Coach Overall, I thank you for caring."

Jim got a standing ovation. Coach Overall went to him and the two big men embraced. Each had tears in their eyes. Luther marveled that Fredrick had known about this incident and had picked Jim as a keynote speaker. What Luther did not realize was that a young eight-year-old boy, unnoticed, had heard his dad relate this incident to his mother and had never forgotten it. Upon looking for Jim, he discovered he was now a coach himself and figured this was a good person with a success story to tell. Fredrick's hunches generally paid good dividends.

The next speaker's story was better known in Pressley. Benny Hart was a young man whose father was killed in the last days of the Vietnam War before Benny was born. Raised by a single mother, who strived to make a living working at the Dairy Queen, Benny was a latch key kid and had a propensity for picking the wrong crowd. Luther knew his story and encouraged him to try out for the baseball team. He was a reasonable left fielder and could hit pretty well.

Benny approached the podium and his first words were. "Boy, Jim is a hard guy to follow. Thanks Jim for sharing your story with us." There was a round of applause. The audience had been severely touched with Jim's story.

"Coach Overall literally extracted me from jail. As most of you know, I never saw my Dad, and making a living took all of Mom's time and effort just to pay our mortgage and put food on the table. The $10,000 insurance from Dad's death in the service didn't go far in supporting a family. Fortunately, Mom put that into a house, so we had a place to call home.

"There were lots of 'throw away kids' around when I was growing up, and as you know, when there are 'throw away kids' around, that spells trouble. I started down a path of crime by shop lifting, and I got pretty good at it.

"From that, we moved to burglary, and that is when I got caught. We were seen breaking into a garage when the family was not at home, and a neighbor called the police. They were on us before we knew what was happening. The police had been watching for a long time and they were ready to throw the book at us. I knew I was going to reform school.

"Coach Overall came into the Dairy Queen one evening just after I had signed up for baseball. My mom was waiting on him and he told her I was doing well on the team. She broke down and told him about me being arrested.

"Coach simply drank his milkshake, paid his bill and came straight to the jail. He put down bail, extracted me into his custody and brought me home. I am not going to tell you what he told me on the way home, but I can tell you one thing for sure and certain, he put the fear of God in me.

"Fourteen days later, he went with me to my hearing and arranged for us three boys who were involved in the burglary to do community service. I washed Fire Trucks for six hours on four Saturdays. After I finished, I signed up for the volunteer Fire Department.

"Coach Overall called me into his office and laid down the law. He said, 'Son, you have had your chance. Your mother bust her rear end to make a living for you and what kind of appreciation have you shown her. If you pull a stunt like this again, I am going to personally kick your butt all the way to Gatesville and let you get a taste of what reform school is like."

"There was no doubt in my mind that Coach meant what he said, but more than that, I did not want to disappoint a man that believed in me.

"When I got out of High School, Coach encouraged me to go on to college. Since my Daddy was killed in service, I did not have to pay tuition. I started to college and discovered that I liked it. In fact I liked it so well that I stayed in school until I finished Law School. I'm a corporate lawyer in Houston, Texas, married and have two wonderful children.

"Thanks Coach. You probably saved my life. I shall always remember looking down the barrel of that .38 police special when the cops came to arrest us in that garage. I could see that cop's finger just itching and hoping that one of us would run. Thanks for caring enough to make a change in a young boy's life."

Again there was a standing ovation. Luther and Benny embraced, each weeping. After Fredrick had given the audience time to become quiet, he again went to the podium. He placed his finger on the bridge of his nose like he was pushing his glasses back against his face. Everyone began to understand that this was a maneuver, which helped Fredrick place all his thoughts in order.

"I face this next addressee with fear and trembling. I felt that someone from our family should give some insight into my Dad, so, I have asked my sister Velma to give that insight. Now I know she is going to bawl, but that's okay, Velma. This is an emotionally charged evening for the Overall family."

Velma arose and went to the podium. She was very well groomed and did not look like Coach Velma Overall. She was an attractive woman when she made any effort at grooming.

Velma began, "My Daddy is a saint. I have proof of that. He has lived with Fredrick for twenty six years and has not killed him—yet."

This drew a tremendous laugh. Fredrick simply sat stoically and stared at Velma. His look simply added fuel to the laughter.

"Growing up in the Overall home I saw my Dad struggle with many of his students and players problems. He loves each of you. I have seen him fret over those who were not doing well academically. I have also seen him hurt for those who were hurting due to family problems at home. He knew your problems. Don't ask me how he knew, he simply knew. He knew of your failed romances. All the little details that seemingly go unnoticed by others. I guess it is an Overall curse since in many instances I find myself following in my dad's footsteps, but his steps are simply too big for me to follow. He did not make many of the mistakes that I have made. He has been an inspiration for me to strive to do a good job and always give my best effort. Dad simply doesn't settle for second best. He expects everyone to carry their own load to the best of their ability, but he seemed to have an uncanny ability to recognize when that best was not quite good enough and could accept a defeat gracefully.

"I haven't learned that yet. When I lose, I want to hurt somebody."

There was a loud "Amen" from Fredrick, which drew a round of laughter from the crowd.

"Dad has been a great example for all of us to follow. We are grateful for his stability, his love, and most of all for being a good daddy. Thanks Dad for your example."

Velma also drew a standing ovation from the crowd. She made it through her speech, but then just as Fredrick had predicted, she bawled.

Fredrick went back to the podium. "We have deliberately kept the speeches short this evening in order to give many of you opportunities to visit with Dad.

I am going to give Dad and opportunity to share a few memories and plans, but before I turn the mike over to him, I wish to charge my brother Mark to continue on in the Overall tradition as he follows Dad as the new heard coach of the fighting Pressley Blue Devils.

"Mark, you have a hard act to follow, but you have had a great teacher and I am sure you will carry on in the tradition of excellence."

Mark nodded and acknowledged Fredrick's charge. He received an ovation.

After all of the clapping again died down, Fredrick turned to his dad, "Dad, we would like to hear a word from you."

Luther went to the podium. He was visibly overcome with emotion. "Thank all of you for coming and Fredrick, thank you for arranging this celebration.

"I face retirement with fear and trembling. I have loved my years of coaching. Many have so beautifully expressed how I have touched their lives, but I can tell you right up front that it is a two-edge sword. Each student has touched my life in some way. I have so many grand and glorious memories of students I have coached and taught over the past 43 years. Fortunately I have enough memories to carry me through a few years of retirement, and I am so very grateful to have Evelyn to share those memories with me."

The audience erupted with applause. "Fredrick arranged that. He is a pretty good arranger. As I look out over this gathering I see several that can attest to that. There is Velma and Bob, and Miss Emily and Dr. Hill are also here tonight. There are at least three couples here tonight who will be eternally grateful to him for his match making.

"Evelyn and I have a few plans. We plan to travel some, play on the farm, visit old friends, and play with grandkids. Looks like Fredrick is going to keep us supplied in that area. I heard someone ask Fredrick the other day how many kids he had and he said, Two and another one on the way."

Eva looked hard at Fredrick and frowned. Luther continued, The fellow asked, 'Oh really, when is the other one due?' Fredrick answered, 'Oh, ten or eleven months'."

Eva slapped Fredrick on the arm and he just put his finger on the bridge of his nose and smiled at her. The crowd roared.

Luther continued, "I think we will find enough to keep us busy for a while, and then when my mind goes, I'll just go home and watch Television."

After another round of laughter died down, Luther ended his speech. "Thanks to all of you for being here tonight. What a grand tribute this has been. I was sure Fredrick would roast me, but this has been a delightful surprise. My son is full of surprises." Another round of laughter.

"Thank you and may God bless you each and every one."

Luther also received a standing ovation.

Fredrick went back the podium. "Thanks Dad. I may never get back in my bed now."

This was a rare moments. Luther finally came out on the plus side with Fredrick. It was generally the other way around.

"May I add my thanks to all of you for being here tonight, and Dad, Thank you. You have taught us compassion, stability, integrity and perseverance. What a grand legacy to leave your students and family.

"And my thanks to all who made this event possible with a special thanks to Aunt Evelyn, Eva and Velma for all of their hard work in making this a grand event."

There was one final standing ovation and then Fredrick said, "In order for everyone to have a chance to speak with Dad, I think I will ask he and Aunt Evelyn to go to the East wall of this building and form an informal receiving line. Just sort of drift over that way as the crowd allows and each of you visit with Dad.

"Velma, Mark and James, You may wish to join Dad and Aunt Evelyn in greeting folks."

That ended the formal presentation and Luther and Evelyn had a chance to visit with each person. Fredrick and Eva just circulated the crowd to see that everyone felt at ease. Fredrick met each person and called them by name, which endeared him to many. He never forgot a name or a face. Surprisingly he came face to face with Karen Boren Williams.

"Why hello, Karen, Nice to see you."

"Don't lie Freddy. You know you hate my guts. Jim wanted to come so he drug me along. I'm so embarrassed to be here."

Fredrick placed his arm around her shoulder and said, "Aw Karen, I don't hate people. I like everybody if they give me half a chance."

"But I tried to send your sister to prison. How could you not hate me?"

Fredrick looked deep into her eyes. It was the first time she had ever seen Fredrick Overall. He smiled a guileless smile and answered, "Well I don't hate you, Karen. I didn't like what you did, but I didn't hate you. I sort of figured I evened up the score. I went for a knockout punch to protect Velma."

Karen smiled, "Well, you burned my butt good Freddy and I deserved it. I was so stupid."

"Well, it turned out alright. You are here and all is forgiven on our side. I hope it is the same with you."

"I have hated you Freddy for what you did to me, but I just got what I deserved. I have never apologized to your dad for what I did and that has eaten my guts out."

Fredrick took her arm and said, "Well, let's just take care of that." He ushered her to Luther who was visiting with a former student. After waiting for two ex-students to greet Luther, Karen and Luther were face to face.

Luther was stunned to see Karen, but he recovered and extended his hand. Karen, (although feeling faint), approached Luther and in a very meek voice finally expressed what she had wanted to say for ten years. "Coach Overall, I am sorry for what I tried to do to your family. I was young and stupid."

"Karen, that means so very much to me. Thank you so much for that. I can assure you that all is forgiven."

Karen felt forgiven and she felt a load removed from her shoulders. Fredrick still held her arm. He was afraid that she would collapse if he turned her loose. Karen was aware that he was holding her arm. Fredrick Overall, now that he had his eyes 'fixed' as Presslians liked to refer to his surgery, was now an imposing figure. Karen had already decided that he was handsome. Tingles were running up and down her spine and her eyes were dilated. Eva had been watching Fredrick and she did not like what she was seeing at all.

The moment Fredrick turned Karen loose and moved on, she faced him and in her black accent admonished, "You keep yo hands off dem gals." Now Eva spoke English as well or better than most, but when she reverted to her black accent, Fredrick knew it was time to listen up.

"What on earth are you talking about Eva?"

"I saw that look that woman gave you. Don't you try to lie to me boy."

"Why Eva, I believe you are jealous."

"Well, I can tell you one thing, If women keep looking at you like that, I gonna put them glasses back on you."

Fredrick knew that Eva was kidding: almost at least. He hugged her and remonstrated, "Aw Eva, it's just because you are almost pregnant that you are acting this way."

Eva slapped his arm, "I'm gonna knock you in the head."

They both laughed and Fredrick reached out and hugged Eva. Just at that moment, they heard, "Hold it," and the photographer for the Pressley Daily News snapped their picture. That picture along with a picture of Luther and Evelyn made the paper with almost a full page write up of the Banquet. Eva was a beautiful girl and since Fredrick's thick horn rim glasses were missing, they were a very handsome couple. Fredrick and Eva's successes were very well known throughout Walrick County, this write up just added fuel to the fires of jealously.

Dr. Hill and Miss Emily (she simply could not shake that handle), had driven up from Austin for Luther's Banquet. They were staying with Fredrick and Eva. They were all just sitting down to lunch when Luther and Evelyn came in with a copy of the newspaper.

Evelyn opened the paper and showed the picture, commenting, "You two make such a beautiful couple."

The picture was done in color. Eva and Fredrick were both smiling and beautiful. Eva was tremendously attractive in the picture. To many in Pressley, before this picture came out, she was simply that "little nigger gal" that Fredrick Overall married. This picture single handedly changed most all of their minds, by that tacky comment, which was fed by the Turners and Gipsons.

Eva said, "Let me see that." She scanned the related article quickly. "I was afraid they might have heard what Freddy had just said to me before they snapped that picture."

Luther asked, "What had he just said, Eva?"

Eva looked a little embarrassed. "Well, he had just told me I was almost pregnant."

After a round of laughter. Miss Emily's humor came through, "Well honey, maybe that's better than being a little bit pregnant."

There was another round of laughter.

Mortimer, Miss "Emily's old cat, who had really become Fredrick's cat was sitting beside Fredrick. Fredrick looked down at Mortimer and pretended to be in conversation."

"Umm,—Oh really,—Well, Why?—Oh, I see." Mortimer got up and ambled out of the room.

Miss Emily, as always, asked, "Well, what did he say?"

"He said, we don't need any more younguns around here. He said he has all he can take care of."

Mortimer watched the kids like a hawk. If one cried, he would not rest until it got attention. He would sit and watch each child as they were bathed and take each step until they were in bed. It was just as in his old age he finally had a child of his own. Eva got up, went and found him. Picking him up, lovingly she petted him. She coaxed, "You have a heavy load don't you Mortimer, but you are such a good grandpapa."

Fredrick related to everyone how Mortimer watched the kids and alarmed them when one was crying. With one at twenty-eight months and one six months old, Fredrick and Eva had their hands full. They were amazed that the old cat, now twenty-two years old showed so much affection for the babies.

Eva set two more plates and Luther and Evelyn joined them for lunch. Luther was on cloud nine and still hyped-up from the banquet. Repeatedly he thanked Fredrick for pulling it all together. This had been one of those touchstone moments for this family.

* * *

Mark and Gretchen had bought a house in town. James and Marci were staying with them. They decided to go out for lunch and had called Velma and Bob to join them. The meal quickly turned into a bash Fredrick fest by Mark and James. Finally, Velma could stand it no longer.

"You two are just jealous. He is bright, vivacious, smooth as silk and just glides through life. He is already a millionaire and climbing. He has more irons in the fire than you can ever imagine."

James replied, "Well, he is going to go bankrupt one of these days. I just hope he doesn't take Dad down with him."

"Dad down with him? He isn't using any of Dad's money. He has made a mint for Dad and I both."

"Well, what about Aunt Evelyn?" Mark asked? "How did he get the farm away from her?"

"He bought it. She would have given it to him, but he bought it. Paid top dollar."

"Well, I just don't see where his money is coming from. He must be head over heels in debt." James said.

"Nope, The only debt he has is with Aunt Evelyn. He paid her $100,000 down and is paying the rest out at $50,000 per year with six percent interest."

"Well, where is he getting that kind of money," asked James?"

"He is earning it. He has his farm, Aunt Evelyn's farm, his part of our farm, and the feed mill. You have no idea how much he is making off all of this. That feed mill is going to be a money maker for the farms. He has a long term lease on 4,000 additional acres. He is processing his own grain and feeding it, plus he is selling the excess. His intention is to build enough broiler houses to sell all of our grain through them. Your little idiot baby brother as you like to refer to him has an eye for business and he is using it to the hilt, and Eva is just about as sharp. She handles all of the finances from an accounting standpoint. They planned all of this before either of them started college. Now you tell me how dumb they are."

Velma had summed things up well. Over the past ten years she had watched Fredrick and Eva. They were a well oiled machine. Fredrick was not driven to making money, it was just one of those necessary evils that went along with meeting challenges. Mark and James were aghast at Velma's revelation. How could frail Freddy be outstripping them? They were the athletes. They were the ones with the charisma, the ones who had followed in their father's footsteps. Everything either one had done was tied in some way to sports. Marci's dad was a distributor for a major sports equipment supplier and James' interest in sports had cemented their relationship. How could anyone who did not play sports be successful?

James was the first to speak. "Well, I just don't understand it. How was he able to do this?"

Velma had learned her lesson well. "For one thing, he keeps his mouth shut at the right time and listens. He misses nothing. He assimilates information, categorizes it, understands every detail before he makes his move and then barrels ahead. You best get out of his way when he starts to move or get run over, and don't overlook that little mild mannered Eva. She can be a tiger. Fredrick has assembled a fantastic work force of people that everyone else would have discarded. He has given them opportunities and they have jumped at them. No one ever thought that Tommy DeVaney would amount to a 'hill of beans', but Freddy has taken him and made him his construction manager. He is doing a fantastic job. He has brought in two Latin American families and given them an opportunity for a better life. The whole family pitches in and they do a tremendous job raising chickens. It is amazing to watch."

Bob had been listening to Velma and marveling that she had expressed herself so well. She was somewhat self conscious and seldom put two sentences together. He reached under the table and took her hand. She grabbed his hand and squeezed it tight.

Marci was never at a loss of words. "Well, I just don't understand how chickens can amount to anything. Who in the world would want to mess with those things?"

Velma jumped back in. "Well, Eva for one. She gets right in the middle of raising chickens. You should go to one of the houses when baby chicks arrive. After they get their tummies full and settle down around a brooder, it is a sight to behold and there has never been a more peaceful sound that 15,000 contented chickens."

"Eva would be content to simply stop where they are and raise chickens, but Fredrick is already talking about raising laying hens and putting in a hatchery. I have no idea where he will stop. I imagine a processing plant is in the works somewhere down the road."

Bob spoke up. "Oh, knowing Freddy, I doubt that. He can't stand the sight of blood."

Velma smiled, "Yes, you are right. I had forgotten about that. That won't happen. Not by Freddy anyhow. He may con the town into that."

The meal ended with lots of food for thought by James, Marci, Mark, and Gretchen. Marci was appalled, but Gretchen was fascinated. The two sisters-in-law's opinion of Fredrick were diametrically opposed.

Fredrick not only gave the town of Pressley heartburn, but it spread over to his brothers. Velma on the other hand, since Fredrick had saved her from going to prison and found her husband and stepdaughter that she truly loved, was now his biggest fan. No one was going to "trash mouth" Fredrick in her presence.

Chapter 10

Fredrick slowly but surely built his business. He bought more land, he leased more land, he built more chicken houses and five years down the road, he had one million chickens on feed with six families profit sharing and caring for the broilers. He had to expand the feed mill to handle his grain production. The Pressley Co-op which had a strangle hold on farmers for years was almost defunct. The Turners and Gipsons tried to hold it together, but could not compete with Fredrick. Walmart built a big new store just outside the city limits. Fredrick just happened to own the property that Walmart bought and they paid him enough for a small 10 acre plot to cover what he had paid for the property originally. He then built a strip center next door to Walmart, which in reality spelled disaster for the downtown area of Pressley. It was not a vindictive move on Fredrick's part It was simply progress that was going to happen and Fredrick decided he may as well profit from it to feed his other businesses.

Fredrick Overall's name was MUD with most of the old time power broker Pressleyites, but he was a breath of fresh air to others who had been held in an almost subservient status. There were several individuals working in the Turner's and Gipson's businesses who had been working for twenty years for minimum wage. The crowning blow came when Fredrick decided it was time for Pressley to have a McDonalds. Since Luther and Evelyn had done about all of the traveling they wanted to do, he talked his dad into taking on that responsibility. He, Luther and Velma pooled their funds and plunked down the money for the McDonalds franchise. Since Mark had spent just about all of the funds he received from the insurance settlement from his mother's death, he was left out of the deal.

Tommy DeVaney took charge of the construction project and six months after construction began, the Pressley McDonalds opened. It was an instant success. Luther loved running the place. It immediately became the gathering place for seniors and Luther could hardly wait to get there in the morning to visit old friends.

The Dairy Queen business, owned by the Turners and Gipsons dropped by 75 percent when the new McDonalds opened. With their senior coffee for thirty-five cents and their sausage and biscuit for one dollar, McDonalds became a very popular place with seniors. Dairy Queen's building had not been maintained and on two occasions, the Turners and Gipsons almost lost their franchise. After the McDonalds opened, Dairy Queen Cooperate ordered a refurbishing of the facility or give up their franchise. Refusing to use Fredrick's construction company, which was equipped to do the job in a timely manner, they opted to go with local, individual refurbishers. None was equipped to handle a commercial project of this nature. It was a disaster and the job took three times longer than it should have, and was more costly and unsatisfactory. Dairy Queen Corporate would not accept the work and it had to be redone. Loss of revenue plus the bungled construction stressed the budget to its limits. Fredrick was called every name in the book in the Turner and Gipson camp.

Unfortunately for the downtown area, the strip center next door to the Wal-Mart almost gutted the old downtown area. The Turners and Gipsons owned seventy five percent of the buildings and now they were fifty percent vacant.

Pressley Hardware was one of the few building not owned by the Turners and Gipsons. The hardware store had been there for fifty years. Since no one else could find anything in the store except the owner, Mr. Howard, his family decided to close out the business. Mr. Howard died behind the counter at 89. Fredrick bought it "lock, stock and barrel," He moved all of the hardware stock to the farm and refurbished the building to become his corporate office.

Fredrick and Eva spared no expense in refurbishing the building. Fredrick needed something to keep Tommy DeVaney busy when he did not have other work for him, and the building was excellent for that. The building inspector was waiting to give Fredrick a hard time about the old building. He was all set to condemn the plumbing, wiring and structural integrity of the building floor. In fact, he had sat in Jim Turner's office and laughed about how Fredrick Overall had finally gotten taken and that he would never be able to use the building. Much to their dismay and surprise, the first thing Fredrick had Tommy do was completely gut the building. Before they started, Fredrick had metal trusses fabricated and ready to set in place, and then he had the old roof and ceiling completely removed. The Metal trusses were set and a new metal roof was installed.

The inspector complained about the metal roof and tried to convince Fredrick that it violated city building codes. The metal chosen was a good heavy duty commercial metal. Fredrick simply said, "Show me the code violation Tony and we will take it off."

Tony could not show him the violation, since there were no city specifications for the roof material.

After the roof was on, the inside of the building was taken down to the ground. Tommy shored up the old brick walls and left them, but everything else was removed. With proper permits, new sewer piping was installed,. New water and gas piping, and new electrical was wiring installed according to code. The building was built peer and beam construction, and Fredrick had the old faulty peers and beams removed and new ones installed. Architectural drawings and specifications were made available to the code inspector He tried hard, but could find no fault. They faced the building with marble and used lots of bronze and wrought iron trim. The building made everything else on the square look drab and dingy. In six inch bronze letters over the door of the building, Fredrick had Overall Enterprises installed.

Fredrick and Eva had just moved their office into the building and settled in when the buildings on each side of their building caught fire about two AM. They were raging infernos before the fire trucks arrived. Both buildings were vacant and only housed junk which had been stored in them. One housed a lot of old bank records from Pressley National Bank, and the other had lots of used office furniture and some new furniture from Pressley Furniture, which incidentally, was owned by Karen Boren's father.

When the fire department arrived, they squirted a little water on the buildings next door and then they seemed to delight in the opportunity to break in the windows of Fredrick's building and then flood the place with water. A new computer system complete with backup was destroyed. They did not even bother to cut the main breaker before they started squirting water into the place. The fire department demolished everything with their high pressure water.

Fredrick got a call at 3 Am informing him of the fire. When he drove in and looked at his building, it was obvious that this was a deliberate act of violence toward him. Fredrick just quietly walked around and surveyed the damage. The fire marshal walked up to offer Fredrick his condolences.

Fredrick asked, "How did it start?"

"Probably lightening. We will be looking at it a little later."

"Fredrick just smiled. "Must be the phenomenon of the century."

"What's that Mr. Overall?"

Building on each side of me hit by lightening. Looks like 'Lightening' was a busy little man last night. The fire chief walked up about the time Fredrick made his comment. Fredrick turned to him. "Why did you guys flood my place. I had a mist system. It would have protected my place. You have destroyed everything."

The chief did not have an answer. Fredrick just got in his car and drove away. A chill fell over the fire chief as well as the fire marshal. Lee Boren walked up to the two men and asked, "Where's Overall? I thought I saw him here."

Bill Hill the fire marshal answered. "He just got in his car and left."

"Well, what did he say?"

He didn't say much. He wasn't happy that his building was flooded. Said he had a mist system that would have protected his building. Said it must be the phenomenon of the century, building on each side of him struck by lightening."

Lee Boren turned white. If Fredrick had ranted and raved he would have felt better, but the fact that Fredrick was quiet made him nervous.

For two weeks, no one saw Fredrick. He didn't even come in to secure the building. He just let it sit with the wet paper, wet carpet, wet sheetrock. In a few days, it began to stink. After the insurance adjuster had accessed damages, Fredrick had a cleanup crew come in and clean up the building, tearing out walls, floor, sheetrock and everything. It wound up completely gutted. Fredrick then had a brick mason come in and brick up the front of the building and the back door, making it totally un-accessible Then he walked away from it.

The Fire Marshall completed his investigation and issued a report that the fire was started by lightening striking the buildings. The result of his so-called investigation was published in the Daily News. A reporter went to Fredrick and asked him to comment on the report.

Fredrick was candid. "I simply know one thing. Lightening did not strike the buildings. I have a radio antenna on the top of my building and it was properly grounded. The adjacent buildings are within the cone of protection of that antenna. There is no way lightening could have hit those buildings."

"Mr. Overall, how do you think the fire started?"

"I have no comment on that at this time."

"Mr. Overall, are you going to rebuild?"

"No way. It has been made perfectly clear to me that I am not wanted in the town of Pressley. It is a shame though. There were several jobs opening up in our office."

"Where do you plan to build your office?"

"Right here on the farm, so Pressley won't be able to tax it. The town is the loser not me. I was adequately insured and I keep two sets of records isolated from one another, so, that is not a problem.

"Looks like the only thing that is going to be left downtown pretty soon is Pressley National Bank. Sure is gonna be lonesome downtown."

When Fredrick's comments made the paper, the Turners and Gipsons were livid, but scared. There had been a huge lightening storm the night of the fire and they thought the lightening explanation would be a grand cover up. They didn't understand Fredrick's comment about the buildings being under the cone of protection of the antenna and that worried them. They couldn't stand an in-depth investigation of the cause of the fire and they were terrified. They were insured to the hilt on the two old buildings and already afraid that the insurance company would do an investigation. They were right. The insurance companies talked to Fredrick. His comments sparked an investigation and they immediately determined that the cause of the fire was arson, started by the use of flammable liquids, probably kerosene or diesel fuel. Local law enforcement did not cooperate very well and the Texas Rangers were called in. Nothing was ever proven, but suspicion had been laid squarely at the feet of the Turners and Gipsons and their reputation plummeted. A branch bank opened in Wal-mart and Pressley National Bank immediately began to lose customer base.

Fredrick went about his business as though nothing had happened. He was adequately insured to fund the construction of a nice office at the farm. In some ways, he was glad that he and Eva did not have to drive into town each day. His reasoning that caused him to build his office in town was to help revitalize the downtown area. He let that be known around Pressley; always ending his statement with "Too bad it got burned out." He never accused anyone of anything. He appeared to hold no hard feelings toward those he knew were responsible. He simply asked hard questions like the one he asked the tax appraisers, "Why are the taxes on my burned out building ten times that of the adjacent property?"

Since there was no legitimate answer, his taxes were immediately lowered.

*   *   *

Fredrick and Eva had another son born just after the fire that destroyed their office. Benjamin Marcus was another carbon copy of his two brothers. Then two years down the road, Mary Evelyn was born. The first thing Eva said to Fredrick when she discovered she had a girl was, "I ain't havin no more younguns."

Fredrick countered, "But I wanted ten."

"Then you better get you a concubine."

Fredrick smiled at his wife and countered, "But then they wouldn't look like you and I wouldn't want them."

"Eva countered, "You are pretty cool. You always know what to say."

Fredrick did a soliloquist, took her hand and in his Shakespearian voice, "Only from yon fair maiden woudest I have kids."

Fredrick took his tiny daughter from Eva and continued, "Sweetheart, she is beautiful. We are very blessed."

Eva and Fredrick were two people who truly loved each other. The "nay sayers" had predicted nothing but doom and gloom for their marriage. They had never dated anyone else. From the beginning of their lives they were together, raised almost like sister and brother. As a baby, Rosalie brought Eva with her when she came to keep house for Mary and as babies they generally wound up on a pallet on the floor or in the same crib. Even Freddy's family predicted that he would tire of Eva after a while, especially when the money came rolling in.

His brother James frequently predicted, "Just wait until some little old secretary figures out that her boss is rich. She will shake that fanny at him and he will fall right into her trap."

What James did not seem to realize was that Fredrick Vines Overall was a man with a strict code of ethic, and strong moral fiber based deeply in his Christian faith. Fredrick was not a "Bible thumper" and did not often quote passages of scripture to make his point and look religious, but he had an enduring faith. It was a faith that had come out of struggles with doubt. By many, more fundamental in their belief, Fredrick was seen as an unbeliever because some of his beliefs pushed the envelope of orthodoxy. But Fredrick was a good man and never tried to push his belief off on someone else. He quietly and behind the scene lived out his Christian faith.

Fredrick went to his pastor and told him, "Don't let any child be left out because of lack of funds."

Quietly and behind the scene without anyone's knowledge, he sent kids to camp, on mission trips, trips to amusement parks and any other activity the church young people participated in. He set up a $5,000 slush fund for the pastor to use for this purpose and he kept it stocked. No one except Fredrick, Eva, and Brother Dan knew this.

The same thing was true at school. Fredrick instructed the Elementary, Middle and High school principles to let him know when a child was being left out of something that was important. and Fredrick also told them to insure that no child in Pressley went hungry.

After the McDonalds had been opened a couple of months, the Youth minister at Fredrick's church decided that he would try a Thursday morning "Meet me at McDonalds Bible Study."

Kids were invited to meet early at McDonalds for a brief devotional and prayer. Luther reserved the kids section for that purpose every Thursday morning. Eight kids were fairly regular and Fredrick told his Dad to simply give them a drink cup and place a stack of sausage and biscuits on a table in the kids section for free. The next Thursday morning after the first free food, thirty-five kids showed up. The crowd leveled off at about thirty-seven regulars.

Fredrick took all kinds of verbal abuse over the free food for the 'Thursday Morning Club'. There were complaints that Fredrick Overall was ruining the health of Pressley youth with sausage and biscuits. Others complained that he was trying to proselyte the young people from other churches. Others complained that he was just trying to get free advertizing for McDonalds and that he was writing the food off on income tax as advertizing.

Fredrick invoked the wrath of the whole town with a comment he made to a very conservative, fundamentalist pastor of a small independent Church.

The Pastor had learned that two of the young people from his church had attended the Thursday Morning Club. He met Fredrick in the post offic and really dressed him down about the free food. The Pastor told Fredrick, "I am appalled that you would use the Lord's work to grab free advertizing for your establishment."

Fredrick placed his finger on the bridge of his nose and stared at the old fellow for a few moments before remarking, "Suffer the little children to come unto me and I will give them Sausage and Biscuits."

He was so disgusted with the whole affair that he simply turned and walked out leaving the poor old fellow speechless for a few moments. When the old preacher finally got his wits back, he preached a sermon right there in the Post Office. The whole town was inflamed and threatening to ride Fredrick out of town on a rail.

Fredrick's pastor decided that things had gone too far. He shut down the 'Meet at McDonalds Club' and tried to move the meeting to the church parlor. That move failed miserably and the 'Thursday Morning Meet at McDonalds Club' died, or was murdered by hate and jealously.

*   *   *

Almost immediately after the demise of the "Meet at McDonalds Club' fiasco, graffiti appeared on Fredrick's burned out building. A huge picture of a red devil appeared. Fredrick simply left it. The city counsel voted unanimously to require Fredrick to remove the graffiti. Fredrick sent a painter and told him to paint over the front of the building with the ugliest brown paint he could find. The painter mixed several buckets of old paint and came up with a sickening dirty purple/brown. Two days later, graffiti again appeared indicating that Fredrick was gay. This time Fredrick told the painter to use iridescent pink paint.

Several days later graffiti appeared again. Fredrick left it until the city council again required that it be removed. This time he had it painted a pale iridescent lime green. The president of the city council called him and told him he would have to have the building painted again. Fredrick had been pushed far enough and his 'buck was up.'

"Mr. Smith, you will have to get a court order and I can assure you I will fight it. I like that color. I think it is pretty. If the Pressley Police Department does not stop the abuse of my property, I am going to file a complaint with the Texas Rangers as to why I am being harassed. I have everything documented. Someone has to be turning their face away for kids to spend the amount of time it takes to paint that graffiti on my building. This should have been stopped long ago. I have had enough."

The president of the City Council took Fredrick's message back to the other members. Jim Turner, who was on the counsel, spoke up, "We better back off. There is no telling what that fool will do."

This view was shared by all members of council. So, Fredrick's lime green wall remained a sore spot for all of Pressley for about six months and then Fredrick decided he could use the metal trusses out of the building. He had a construction crew move in and tear down the false brick wall covering the front of the old store, take the trusses down and demolish the building. He had the bricks from the old building moved to the farm.

Just off the sidewalk Fredrick had a plaque set in concrete. It read, Pressley Historical Site. Former location of Pressley Hardware. Building maliciously destroyed by arson.

Chapter 11

William Luther did not attend kindergarten. Eva followed Mary's footsteps and taught him at home. She and the kids roamed the farm almost daily and on rainy and cold days, they played school. Grandmother Evelyn was right in the middle of their activities. She and Eva became inseparable. Evelyn was not accepted back in Pressley and this pushed her and Eva together for companionship. All of the kids were smart, approaching their daddy's intellect and having his humor and temperament. Normally all kids in a family are different. In Fredrick's case, this was not true. Everyone who knew them accused Eva and Fredrick of using a cookie cutter. The boys all looked alike; Mary Ellen looked like her mother. When they were born, they were all within four ounces of eight pounds. Dr. Elliot accused Eva of being a baby machine. She was not impressed with this and told him as much.

Bill Griffin, long-term principal of the elementary school, decided to retire when he learned that Fredrick had a child starting school. He told his wife, "I don't believe I can take another Fredrick at my age."

Mrs. Griffin let this slip and Bill had to face Fredrick one day coming out of the post office.

Fredrick placed his finger on the bridge of his nose and made eye contact with his ex principle. "Mr. Griffin, what's this I hear about you not wanting to teach my child?"

"Oh Fredrick, I am and old dog now. I am afraid I am not up to your son."

"Well, he doesn't bite and he seldom barks."

Bill laughed and was almost sorry he had elected to retire. Even as a small boy, Fredrick exhibited the same good natured sense of humor.

"Fredrick, I am just getting old. Your son will be on the cutting edge of everything. I did not think I would be up to challenging him. I'm told he is very bright."

Fredrick was quiet for a moment with his finger on the bridge of his nose before he answered. "Just what does that mean Mr. Griffin? I have wondered about that for years. People have said that about me from time to time, but I don't feel bright. I feel normal. You know, God gave us all a brain. Some just don't do much with it. I really doubt there is a lot of difference in the intelligence level of most of us. If you watch a man who has dug ditches all his life you will probably learn the easiest way to dig ditches. If you watch a professional truck driver or bulldozer operator, you will see a work of art. You can pick almost any endeavor and you will find uncanny wisdom and knowledge. So, what is this business of being bright? Eva and I have tried to follow Mom's example and teach our kids, expand their boundaries and stretch their minds, but I don't know that they are any brighter than anyone else's kids."

Now it was time for Bill Griffin to think before he answered. "Well Fredrick, I don't think I agree with you. I can see your point about folks learning skills and better ways of doing things, but some are just smarter than others."

"Oh, but Mr. Griffin, I think that is because of the way we judge intelligence, not raw intelligence per se'. According to the Bible, God gave different gifts to everyone. Wouldn't we be a boring bunch of folks if we all had the same gifts. I think one of the reasons some individuals don't do as well as they should is because they are too busy coveting someone else's gifts."

The two men stood looking at one another for a brief moment and then Bill Griffin commented, "Well Fredrick, as usual, you have given me something to study about. You seem to have a gift for that."

"Oh, you mean being a pest?"

Bill Griffin laughed a huge belly laugh, waved and turned to walk away. "Yeah and that too. I'll see you Freddy, and I hope your son has a great school year."

"Thanks, Mr. Griffin. I am sorry you won't be there to enjoy him."

"Me Too."

After his confrontation with Fredrick, Bill was already missing the start of the school year. He was a very good principal. After he had gotten to know Fredrick, he enjoyed every minute of his association with him.

Fredrick always had a question for him each time he met him in the hall throughout his elementary school days. He stretched the boundaries of imagination on all fronts. Bill remembered Fredrick as a delightful child and now after seeing him six inches taller that himself, he felt very small and very old. "Why do I always feel inferior to Fredrick?" he asked himself. "He just tried to give me a crutch to alleviate that. Why don't I feel any better?"

He concluded, "Oh well, I suppose it is because it is true. I had always thought he was one of a kind, but now they tell me there are four more waiting in the wings. Poor teachers. I think I made the right decision."

The new elementary principal was a young lady that the new Pressley Superintendent brought with him from out of district. She was a cocky smart aleck who looked at Pressleites as just a bunch of hicks. During one of the staff meetings before start of school, she heard teachers discussing, "I wonder who is going to have William Overall."

She asked, "Who is William Overall?"

Several teachers answered in unison," Oh, he is Fredrick's son."

"And who is Fredrick?"

The teachers all looked at one another. One asked, "Just how does one describe Fredrick?" They all looked blank, and finally one answered, "Different."

"Different, That's all? Different."

They all nodded in agreement and answered, "Different."

"Well, what makes him different?"

One teacher answered, "Well, he is just different. He calls himself 'The Twerp'."

"The Twerp! What does that mean?"

One teacher was in the third grade class the day Fredrick entered. She still remembered the definition Fredrick read to the class. "A contemptible or insignificant person," she answered.

Continuing, she asked, "May I have William in my class? I was in third grade with Fredrick. I imagine William will wind up in third grade also."

"What do you mean wind up in third grade. What grade is he supposed to be in?"

"Well he is starting school, but I can assure you he will be beyond first grade level. They aren't normal."

The young principal was adamant. "Well if he is supposed to be in first grade, he will start in first grade and that is final."

Two teachers looked at one another and smiled. They did not speak; they simply looked. The look was a bit unsettling to the principal. She had only been in Pressley for two weeks before the start of school. She knew that Luther had been a coach, and she had met Velma. She had not met Fredrick and she had him pegged as just another sports nut like the rest of his family. In Pressley she had heard that Velma's brother was married to a half black girl and that "colored" her opinion of him, since she was very prejudiced herself.

*   *   *

School started and William showed up, a happy precocious little boy. Quite unlike his father's first day, William looked like a normal first grader except he had his book bag stuffed with books. Eva has quietly been coaching him that books would be his salvation at school since he would probably be bored. Fredrick and Eva had decided not to push to have him elevated to a higher grade. Fredrick could not decide if that was good or bad. He had taken all kinds of abuse from older kids. William was a little more sensitive than Fredrick had been. Since Fredrick's looks were so very different, Mary had coached him to the point that he had a very thick skin which outwardly seemed impervious. William on the other hand was a sensitive child. Eva and Fredrick both worked on this because they knew he would take abuse because of his intellect.

William's teacher was a kindly lady in her forties. She had taught first grade for fifteen years and had three sons of her own. Two were in middle school and one in high school. She paid special attention to William and after about one week she went to the principal and told her, "There is no way I can teach that child along with the rest of this class. He reads, he writes cursive, he can do third or fourth grade math, his science knowledge is middle school level. He has already taught me things about nature that I did not know. It is a travesty to try to keep him in first grade."

The principal was unbending. "If he is supposed to be in first grade he will stay in first grade. That is final."

Mrs. Simmons was a meek and mild person. She did not like any kind of confrontation, so she backed off. Before she left the office though, she left a parting shot. "Mrs. Hensley, sooner or later you will have to face Fredrick Overall. I pity you when that happens. Fredrick is normally a kind and gentle man but he can take you down and never fire a shot. He generally lets his enemies self-destruct. He is masterful at that."

Mrs. Hensley sat in her office for the next few minutes thinking about Mrs. Simmons warning. She could not imagine what she was talking about and decided to document every incident involving William Overall. Already she hated that kid. She had not even talked to him personally, but she hated him and looked forward to the time she would see him in her office.

It did not take long for that to occur. Other first graders sensed right away that William was different. They disliked him because of that. During the second week of school, several of the first grade students were in the rest room and they began to wad up toilet paper, wet it and throw it against the ceiling to see if they could make it stick. Teachers began to receive reports that the rest room was in a mess. The first grade pupils told Mrs. Simmons that William Overall did it.

Word soon spread to the principal that William Overall had messed up the restroom by throwing paper on the ceiling. Mrs. Hensley did not even consult with Mrs. Simmons, she sent a secretary to bring William to the office. She let him sit outside waiting for about 30 minutes thinking that would cause intense anguish and soften him up, but William was made of the same metal from which his dad was formed.

When she finally told the secretary to bring him in, much to her surprise he was calm and poised.

Mrs. Hensley looked sternly at him and asked, "Young man, what do you have to say for yourself?"

William sat for a moment without answering. He had his hand on his chin, much like he had often seen his father do when he was thinking and then he looked the principal squarely in the eyes with that Fredrick Overall stare and answered, "I'm William Luther Overall, age six, and I am in Mrs. Simmons first grade class at Pressley Elementary School."

"I don't mean that, I mean about the restroom."

Again, William was slow to answer. "It is convenient to the classroom, well kept and well lighted. I like it."

Mrs. Hensley became livid. She screamed loud enough that the secretary heard her outside the office, "Young man, you know what I mean. I mean about the mess in that boys' restroom."

William ducked his head, put his hands over his ears and closed his eyes. Mrs. Hensley jumped up out of her chair, came around the desk and grabbed his arm and tried to pull his hands away from his ears. He just held on tight and she jerked him up out of his chair. She was so surprised that she turned his arm loose. He went crashing to the floor and rolled into a stand, which held a self-wind perpetual clock causing it to come crashing to the floor. The secretary heard the crash and came running into the office.

William was lying on the floor in a fetal position saying, "Don't hit me; please don't hit me again."

The secretary with mouth open and wide eyed, along with two teachers and a parent who had been in the outer office stood looking at the principal.

She stammered, "I didn't strike him. Honestly, I didn't strike him." The secretary got down on her knees beside William and asked, "William are you okay ? Are you hurt?"

He just lay there trembling, or at least that was the way it appeared. The secretary looked up and said, "Someone call 911 and we had better call the parents." Mrs. Hensley was terrified. It took Eva five minutes to arrive at school. The police, fire truck, and ambulance were all there and Eva was beside herself.

She went running into the office and William was still lying on the floor, with a cushion under his head, but he still had his eyes closed and his hands were still covering his ears. She got down on her knees beside him and he appeared to want to tell her something, but she couldn't hear what he was saying. She put her ear close to his lips and he whispered, "Mama, I'm faking."

Eva stood up and said, "Get him to the hospital. The paramedic transferred him from the floor to a stretcher and headed to the ambulance."

Eva stood, looked at Mrs. Hensley and said, "I don't know what went on here, and we will sort it out later, but I don't think I like what I see."

Eva was almost six feet tall, slender and in excellent physical condition. Mrs. Hensley wilted. She had never seen a more attractive woman. She had no desire to tangle with this lady, and from all she had heard, she was the calm one of the family.

Mrs. Hensley started to answer, but all she could get out before Eva walked away to go to her car to follow the ambulance was, "I—I—"

After Eva left, she tried to explain that she really did not strike the child, but her words fell on deaf ears.

Mrs. Hensley went to the hospital. In the emergency room, Dr. Elliot came in and began to examine William. His blood pressure was 110 over seventy. He had no physical marks of abuse except on his forearm where there were red marks, the results of the principal grabbing his arm. Dr. Elliot asked, "William, do you want to tell me what happened?"

William looked at the nurse who was assisting the doctor. Dr. Elliot sensed immediately that he wanted this to be a private conversation. He asked his nurse to leave the room for a few moments. After the nurse was out of the room, William began, "Kids in my class do not like me. They pick on me all the time. Several of the boys trashed the restroom and blamed it on me. I knew there was no way anyone would believe that I didn't make the mess. Mrs. Hensley called me into the office and made me sit outside and wait for about 30 minutes before she had me come into her office. That gave me lots of time to think and plan how to handle the situation I found myself in.

William repeated his conversation with the principal word for word "I made her mad, which is what I intended to do. I figured that if I got her mad enough she would do something foolish." He looked at Dr. Elliot, "You know, daddy says you do foolish things when you let your anger control you."

Dr. Elliot burst into laughter. "Yes, I know your daddy well."

"Well, she started screaming, so I put my hands over my ears and closed my eyes. I have real sensitive ears. This just made her angrier and she grabbed my arm to pull my hands away from my ears. I held on tight and she jerked me up out of my seat. That startled her so she turned me loose and I just fell down and rolled into her clock stand. I am sorry I broke her clock."

Dr. Elliot looked at Eva. "Like father, like son."

Fredrick came rushing in about this time. Mrs. Hensley, who was waiting outside the emergency room finally got a look at him. He took in everything in the room with one look. She did not miss that. The emergency room nurse showed him to William's room.

Fredrick burst into the room and William smiled at him. Fredrick grabbed his hand and asked, "What's up little buddy?"

"A little situation, Dad. No big deal."

"You got it covered?"

William gave him a thumbs up sign. "Got it covered."

Dr. Elliot threw back his head and laughed. Eva smiled at Fredrick, and hugged him. "We will talk about it later."

"I am going to keep him in the hospital for a few hours for observation and then we will release him."

Mrs. Hensley went running to Fredrick and Eva as they came out with William being wheeled off to a room. She attempted to touch William and he flinched like she was going to strike him. Eva put her hand out and took her arm firmly. The poor lady wilted. "Honestly, I didn't strike him."

Fredrick looked at her and remarked, "We will sort this out later. Right now we are taking him to a room for observation."

Mrs. Hensley did not know the relationship between Fredrick and Dr. Elliot. She was a basket case.

* * *

Fredrick and Eva kept William home for two days and then he went back to school, but Fredrick was not finished playing. He hired a bodyguard for William that went everywhere he went. He sat in class with him, went to the restroom with him and to the cafeteria. At the end of two weeks, Pressley was up in arms, calling for Mrs. Hensley's resignation.

At the first school board meeting after the incident, a petition was presented to the board calling for termination of her contract.

Fredrick was at the meeting and asked to address the board. Fredrick took a seat on the platform and placed his finger against the bridge of his nose before he began. He sat for a pregnant moment and then began, "Gentlemen, I think that one month is entirely too short a time to decide if Mrs. Hensley is qualified to serve as principal of the Elementary School. She may be quite good at her job. Her former boss evidently thinks so. All my family desires is the assurance that our son will be in a safe environment at school and we will remove the bodyguard. This includes not only the principal's office, but in the class and restrooms.

"The problems began when my son was falsely accused of making a mess in the restroom. People like William and I are 'picked on' from time to time, because everyone thinks we are different. We are not different. We love, we hate, we hurt just like everyone else. No one likes to be considered weird. Now William has a good mind and it is incumbent on parents in this town to realize that he is not some freak who belongs in a sideshow simply because he can think. Children need to be taught to be just a little bit understanding of those who do not fit into their mold. They need to understand those whose skin is slightly different, who speak with an accent, who think differently are God's children also. No amount of principal firing is going to correct matters of the heart and mind in our schools.

"Let me go on record that the Overalls are not calling for this principal's resignation. We will support her in any way we can to help Pressley Elementary School become an exemplary educational establishment. Thank you for your time and your indulgence."

The motion was made that Mrs. Hensley be placed on six months probation. This was the best she could hope for. At the end of her probation she would still have time to redeem herself and have her contract renewed at the end of its term. She was extremely grateful to Fredrick for his vote of confidence. She wished to thank him, but after he finished he did not even wait around for the outcome. He simply walked out and left. After the meeting was over, She went home and called him to thank him. He was gracious and assured her that he meant what he said.

Before their conversation ended, Mrs Hensley asked, "Mr. Overall, what grade do you think would best suit William.?"

"Well, Mrs. Hensley, I started in the third grade. My mother thought that was probably about as high as I should go and still develop some social skills. William is more social than I was. Third or fourth is probably fine. Why don't you test him and decide. We will accept either one."

William tested beyond fourth grade, so he was placed in fourth. He hit the ground running, quickly caught up in all areas and continued on. Socially he was a nightmare, pestering the life out of the older kids, but with his sense of humor, he got along okay. He never looked back. Fredrick's idea of the bodyguard worked wonders. The person he had hired was big and mean looking. He terrified the kids and no one, kids, parents or staff wanted him back on campus, thus they left William alone after the bodyguard's presence for two weeks.

Chapter 12

Fredrick got the wild idea that his chicken houses should all have concrete floors to make them more disease retarding and for ease of cleaning. He had been toying with a mechanical design that worked somewhat like a snow blower, but it also had a chopper/grinder element that made breakdown of the litter faster when spread on fields and pastures. Fredrick's idea was that with the blower, one could clean a house in record time.

He went to Pressley concrete and tried to work out a deal on concrete in large volume lots. For a five sack mixture he was quoted $67.50. When asked if he got a volume discount, he was told, "It is $67.50—take it or leave it."

Fredrick replied, "I think I will leave it. Maybe I'll just build my own plant." With that, he left.

Checking around, Fredrick discovered that the concrete plant was not locally owned, but owned by a company in Waco and operated by Jim Turner's brother in law, Lew Tucker. Fredrick called the company who owned the business and asked if they would be interested in selling the plant. He wound up talking to the CEO on the phone.

Fredrick did not beat around the bush. "Mr. Holmes, I am Fredrick Overall from Pressley. I have been trying to buy concrete from your plant here in Pressley and can't seem to do business with them. I was wondering if you would be interested in selling the plant here?"

"Well, Mr. Overall, we try to keep our prices competitive. I am surprised that you can't do business with us. How much concrete are you looking for?"

"I am planning to concrete 50 broiler houses that are 40 feet by 300 feet each. That is an excess of 7000 yards of concrete over the next few years. That is probably enough for me to build my own concrete plant, but the town is not big enough for two concrete suppliers."

"Well, Mr. Overall, are you using five sack mixture?"

"Yes."

"You know, $60 per yard is not a bad price. We purchase in large quantities and you will have a little trouble beating that by mixing it yourself."

"Well, $60 might be acceptable, but I haven't purchased any concrete from you for less than $67.50 in two years, and my company has poured some good size jobs."

"Oh no, Mr. Overall, you must be mistaken. I have looked at the invoices myself."

"Mr. Holmes, would you like to see my receipts. I know what I pay for concrete, and I know what I was quoted."

There was a long pause on the phone and then, "Mr. Overall, if I came to Pressley this afternoon, would you have time to meet with me for a few moments and let me look at your receipts?"

"I would be happy to do that."

"Perhaps we should keep this conversation confidential until after our meeting, Mr. Overall."

Fredrick asked Eva if she could extract all of their concrete receipts for the past five years. She was able to do that in short order since they were filed by company name.

Two hours later Mr. Holmes and a clerk drove into the parking lot at Fredrick's office. After pleasantries, the two men got down to business. Mr. Holmes had copies of all the receipts supposedly signed by Tommy DeVaney. Fredrick's invoice showed the price at $67.50. The invoice received in Waco showed the price at $60. It was obvious that the locals had been adding an extra $7.50 to each yard of concrete, and sending the parent company a phony invoice.

Mr. Holmes was stunned. He was an honest business man. One who believed in integrity in business and maintained high standards of business ethic. He simply sat overwhelmed for a few moments.

Fredrick had his finger on the bridge of his nose in thinking position. Finally, Fredrick spoke up. "Mr. Holmes, how much concrete do you see that we purchased for the McDonalds job?"

Looking at the invoices, "We show 700 yards."

"I show that we purchased 840 yards."

"Oh, but that can't be we monitor the amount of Portland used."

Fredrick thought for a moment. "I paid for six sacks of concrete. That probably means I got five sacks."

Mr. Holmes turned white. The implications of that chilled him to the bone. "Oh my! Oh my! Mr. Overall that could ruin us. Oh My!"

Both men sat thinking for a long time. Neither spoke. Fredrick broke the ice. "I wonder just how many jobs I have poured like that."

For the next hour, the two men went over the invoices. The McDonalds and the office building were the only two where there was suspicion that the formula may have been altered.

"Both of those were my buildings Mr. Holmes. Looks like they were mainly taking a shot at me."

"Mr. Overall, I don't know what to say. These were supposed to be upstanding people that we hired. The manager is a deacon in the church and talks a good religious line."

"Mr. Holmes, when a man has to tell you how religious he is, you had better grab you billfold, because he is fixin' to try to get in it."

Joe Holmes laughed, although he was not feeling very happy at the moment.

"Mr. Overall, would you still be interested in buying this plant?"

"No sir. Nada, no, no! Too much liability!"

"The only way I would purchase the plant now is for you to shut it down. Let me purchase the equipment and open as a totally new business. Then, I might be interested."

"I suppose the next move for us is to subpoena their records and go from there."

"Well, my suggestion for you is to get the FBI involved. There has to be tax fraud involved here. You might go from that angle. If the locals are involved, they will somehow cover everything up."

Joe sat thinking for a moment, but then responded, "Since we are the parent company, the responsibility falls on our shoulders, but I guess there is no way around that."

"Well, if you don't report the fraud, and it does surface with the IRS, you will be in even bigger trouble."

"Yes, you are so right."

"Thank you for your help Mr. Overall. I do not know what to do about your buildings."

"Well, they have already burned one of them down, so you don't have to worry about it. Hopefully the McDonalds will stay together. You have enough on your mind right now. We will worry about that later. The parking lot is mainly what I am worried about. It takes some heavy traffic. If I can help you further to stop these crooks, just let me know. I never thought they would stoop this low."

With heavy heart, Joe Holmes and his clerk began their trek back to Waco. The next evening, there was a knock on Fredrick's door and two FBI agents showed badges. Mr. Overall, we are going to put security tape on the door of your office building. You are not to enter until we are able to look at your records. If the tape is broken, You are committing a felony."

"Sirs, that is unacceptable to me. I will not be subjected to that kind of risk without you providing around the clock surveillance. I don't know who might come up and break that tape. I will not have my reputation subjected to that kind of risk."

The two agents were stunned. They had never had their authority questioned before. "Well, you don't have a choice Mr. Overall. You will have to provide your own surveillance."

"This is not fair. I have agreed to co-operate with this investigation. I do not think you are within the bounds of civility to require this of me. I have committed no crime, and as far as I know, I am suspected of no crime other than as the victim. Now if you wish to go inside the building and place security tape on the file cabinets which are inside my protective alarm system, I will be happy to comply with that request."

The two agents put their heads together and decided that was a reasonable request. Fredrick got in his truck and drove the short quarter mile down the road to his office with the two FBI agents following. At the office he disarmed the alarm system and invited the two men into the office. Looking around, they decided that the place was secure enough so they simply excused themselves and left.

Fredrick studied on this turn of events some, but could not figure out what that was all about. There was a nagging suspicion in the back of his mind that it might be more than simple government red tape.

Back at home, he told Eva, "Boy, I hope we have all our ducks in order. They are going to be looking us over while they are digging around."

She grinned at Fredrick, "I be ready, hon. We have nothing to hide."

*   *   *

Freddy had read the situation correctly. The agents along with an auditor poured over Fredrick's books. Eva was correct. Evelyn kept the kids for her and she was available to answer any question. She gave them spread sheets of accounts payable and receivable from all businesses.

The Auditor commented, "This is a work of art. Who is your CPA?"

"I am," Eva answered.

"Oh!"

Fredrick had sandwiches catered from the HEB store in town. He went in and picked them up. While at the store, he was informed that the FBI was in the bank and at the concrete plant going over records. His answer to his informant was a surprised, "Is that so? I wonder what that is all about?"

No one was speculating. But then, the phony records were found in a safety deposit box in Lew Tucker's name. That is when the lid blew off. Jim Turner was scrambling, trying to distance himself from his brother in law, but having a hard time doing that. Everyone in Pressley knew that Lew was not the "brightest star in the constellation" and there had to be someone else involved. A poor little clerk who thought she was going to prison spilled the beans. She implicated Jim Turner as the mastermind.

Jim thought that by burning Fredrick's office building that all records would be destroyed. What he did not know was that only computer records and very recent transaction records were in the new office building, and that

Fredrick kept records on separate computers in two different locations. The receipts on the McDonalds and the refurbishing of the old hardware store were enough to convict. Both men were headed to Federal Prison for tax evasion. Fredrick Overall's name was again MUD in Pressley.

Pressley National Bank folded and was purchased by Wells Fargo as a Branch Bank. The Turner and Gipson dynasty was ended.

Fredrick went on his way as though nothing had happened. He was friendly and pleasant to everyone. As someone described him, "He just lets the warm glow of sunshine shine on everyone he meets." He wound up with the concrete plant and three trucks. Whenever the plant was not busy with commercial jobs, Fredrick was pouring concrete in chicken houses. His new litter extraction process worked wonderfully well cleaning out houses with concrete floors. He then started work on a device to mechanically install the litter for new batches of chickens. Fredrick was big on the use of blowers and that entered into the design. The two mechanical masterpieces cut turnaround time by 70 percent. Fredrick continued to make money. Everything he touched flourished. His stock market investments were showing outrageous earnings. He could not expand businesses fast enough to stay in a reasonable tax bracket.

The entire west side of the Pressley square came up for sale after Jim Turner went to prison. The buildings were in such a sad state of repair that Fredrick immediately started having them demolished. He purchased an old service station and Garage immediately behind the buildings and had them demolished as well. No one knew what he had in mind for the property. Some speculated that he was going to build a huge new corporate office, One rumor was that he was going to build a large multi story chicken house right in the middle of town. This rumor was repeated so often that the town council finally went to him and asked if this was true.

Fredrick placed his finger on the bridge of his nose and just stood for a long moment, and then asked, "Do I really look that stupid?"

"How in the world do you think I could clean out a two story chicken house? It is only going to be one story and I'm going to raise guineas. I'm going to try to start a new fad guinea egg diet."

Fredrick went into a long dissertation on the merits of guinea eggs over chicken eggs. He threw out all kinds of facts and figures relating to longevity, production expectancy, feed conversion (all made up of course).

One poor lady on the council became all worked up and blurted out, "But, Mr. Overall, you couldn't stay in town with that many guineas. They are so noisy."

"Oh, but I am going to play classical music for them. They love classical music. That will keep them quiet. You should see them march to Tchaikovsky 1812 Overture." He hummed a few bars while he marched in place and then, he placed his hand over his heart and swooned, "Oh it's a sight to behold. People will come from miles around just to get a glimpse."

Most on the council realized that Fredrick was toying with them and had gone along with his ruse. They were tremendously embarrassed that one of their members had swallowed Fredrick's tale, hook line and sinker. Bo Wade asked, "Fredrick, what are you really going to do with that property?"

Fredrick looked at Bo and could see his sincerity. "Bo, I am not quite ready to make the announcement just yet, but let me assure you of one fact. It will make Pressley proud. Will you trust me on that. I give you my promise that when I make the announcement, if this council objects, I will stop the project. Is that fair enough."

"That is fair enough Fredrick. We will accept that."

Mrs. Hill looked at him. She was angry. "You made a fool of me, Fredrick. I don't like that. I don't like it one bit."

"Oh Mrs. Hill, I imagine you will get over it. You should know me by now. I used to have a crush on your daughter. Did you know that?"

"Really?"

"Oh yes. She was so pretty. Too pretty for Fredrick Overall."

Mrs. Hill was startled by this revelation and tremendously flattered.

Fredrick had forgotten that Eva was in the room. When the council left she looked at Fredrick. "You gonna go to hell."

"What for?"

"Lying."

"Well, it was just a little one. She was pretty shapely you know."

"Yea, round is a shape."

He and Eva both laughed. Eva was not ready to let him off the hook. "You told me I was the only girl you ever noticed."

He attempted to push his glasses back against his face, an old habit that he could not seem to break, and stared at Eva for a long moment. "Eva, I love you more than life. My life would be totally empty without you."

Eva looked at Fredrick with dilated eyes. She had loved Fredrick Overall since the day she was born. She knew his heart and soul. She rushed to him and fell into his arms for a long and passionate kiss.

When Eva came up for air she asked, "Fredrick, do you think those stupid people actually thought you would build a chicken house downtown?"

"Of course they believed it. Eva, folks in this town think I am crazy. They will believe anything in the world about me. I should have told them I was going to build a 47 room cat house. That would have gotten their attention."

Eva laughed a deep belly laugh. "Oh no, Freddy. Don't do that. I would have to handle the job applications and I don't have time for that."

Now it was Freddy's turn to laugh. Eva did not have a very high opinion of the town of Pressley. She had felt the hot winds of prejudice all her life and she could have dealt with that, but Pressley gossip was ruthless against the man she loved and that forgiveness hill was simply too high to climb. Their children were beginning to feel the barbs because of their mixed race as well and Eva was struggling with that.

Seemingly, nothing seemed to bother Fredrick though, except one day Fredrick and Eva were exiting the grocery store and they found themselves face to face with Karen Boren Williams. Karen looked at Fredrick and in a very angry voice she exploded, "Well I guess you are happy now that you have sent my Grandfather to prison."

Fredrick was stunned. His eyes met Karen's and they held for a moment. Quietly he answered, "Karen, I am heartbroken that your grandfather is in prison. I did not cause that. My records were used in the trial, but I did not deliberately expose your grandfather. This all came about simply because I was trying to purchase concrete at a decent price. I am truly sorry that your family has to go through this. I did not know your family was involved except that your uncle ran the plant. I take no pleasure in what has happened."

Tears were streaming down Karen's face. She believed Fredrick and wailed, "I am sorry Fredrick. I so very much wanted to blame you. I just wish there was someone to blame. It would make things so much easier."

"Oh I doubt that Karen. We all have to stand in front of the mirror each day. Sooner or later we all have to face our imperfections and we all have them. None of us have perfect families. I was blessed to have parents who taught me integrity. If I can pass that on to my children, I will feel that I have been successful. I hope the same for you."

Fredrick's words stung Karen deeply. She had two sons who were 13 and 15. They were feeling the effects of the family's disgrace in the town. She knew that Fredrick had zeroed in on her problem. Karen's husband was on the fringe of the concrete scandal. He had driven one of the concrete trucks. He had been out of work since the plant closed and he was too ashamed to approach Fredrick for a job when it reopened. He was drinking heavily and in situational depression. Karen was having a terrible time.

Standing and looking at this broken woman, Fredrick's heart melted. "Karen, is Tom working?"

"No."

"Is he able to work?"

Karen broke down. "I don't know Fredrick. He is drinking heavily. I don't know what to do."

"Will you ask him to come see me?"

"I'll ask him. I don't know if he will come or not. He is very angry at you, Fredrick."

Eva had placed her arm around Karen's shoulder as she sobbed. She said, Karen, why don't you come home with us for a little while and let us talk in private."

"But I have hamburger meat that needs to go in the refrigerator."

"We will put it in mine for now."

Karen agreed to go with Eva and Fredrick. Eva decided to ride with Karen. On the way to the farm, Eva counseled, "Karen, Freddy has been worried about you and Tom. He has mentioned this over and over. He has wanted to come talk to you for some time now, but did not know how you would receive him."

"Why Eva? Why would he care about us?"

"Because he is Fredrick Overall. Karen you do not know the heart of this man. He has a heart as big as all of outdoors. He cried when Mr. Jim was sentenced to two years in prison."

"Eva, I just can't believe that."

"Its true. I caught him. He has a crying place. I couldn't find him and I went to his crying place. That is where I found him when his mother was killed. He had the newspaper with him and I could tell that he had been crying. Don't you ever tell this, but I thought you needed to know."

This revelation stunned Karen more than anything she had ever heard. "Pressley doesn't know Fredrick Overall does it? Everyone simply thinks he is a money hungry tyrant grabbing all the land and business he can grab."

"Oh, that is just nervous energy. He has to have some challenge going all the time. He has a knack for making money, Karen. I tried to get him to stop when we had eight chicken houses. I thought the two on the farm would be a good way to teach the children responsibility. I wanted to stop right there, but now we have 50. Fredrick just picks good people, shares the profit and turns them loose."

They were now at the farm. Karen dug her hamburger meat out of her bag and carried it inside with her. Karen had often wondered what Fredrick and Eva's house looked like inside. It was comfortable, serviceable, and not extravagant at all. It was decorated with bright cheerful colors.

Eva started a pot of coffee, and invited Karen to sit down at the dining table. Rosa, Miss Emily's old housekeeper, came to Pressley when Fredrick and Eva graduated from college to live with them. Fredrick built her nice little quarters on the back of the old Lane house. It was somewhat detached from the main house, but connected by an enclosed walkway. She kept the children occupied while Fredrick and Eva were grocery shopping. She was also in the kitchen preparing lunch.

When Fredrick came in, the two youngest boys ran to him and he picked them up. It was obvious that they adored their daddy. Karen missed none of this. Fredrick introduced each child to Karen. Mary Evelyn crawled to her and Karen picked her up. Karen wanted a little girl but she could have no other children after her two boys were born. The little girl melted her heart.

Eva moved about the kitchen retrieving cups and such preparing to serve the coffee. For the first time ever, Karen suddenly realized how beautiful, poised and graceful she was. To Karen Eva had simply been that 'nigger gal' that Fredrick Overall married. She studied her as she moved about the kitchen interacting with Rosa like she was her own grandmother. Her attitude changed immediately. Here was a grand lady of the manor. Educated, successful, wealthy enough to have a live in servant, and married to Fredrick Overall.

After a bit of small talk, Fredrick got down to business. "Karen, I've been told that you and Tom are struggling. I know that you work in the tax office, but Tom is not working?"

"No, since he lost his job at the concrete plant he has not found a steady job. You know we married when we were freshmen in college. Frankly, Fredrick, I got pregnant and we had to marry. I'm not proud of that, but that is just the way it is. Tom does not have many skills. My uncle gave him a job driving a concrete truck when we got married. That is all he has ever done. He has a promise of a job with a gas company hauling propane, but that hasn't come through."

"Karen, I am going to be very frank and up front with you. The word on the street is that Tom is an alcoholic. From what I hear by just keeping my mouth shut and listening, that is the reason he has not found a job."

Karen hung her head. Things had not gone well for the Turners and their extended families. They had built a house of cards and it had come tumbling down. With tear filled eyes, Karen gushed, "I do not know what to do, Fredrick. I wish he would leave and not come back. I sometimes think I hate him."

Eva had not said much since Freddy came in, but now she jumped into the conversation,

"Oh honey, you don't hate him. You just don't like the way thing have turned out. Your world has fallen apart, but just remember, Tom's has too. You need each other, but he needs to give up alcohol. He probably can't do that alone. You lay down the law to him."

"How in the world do I do that, Eva?"

"Has he ever struck you when he is drunk?" Karen hung her head but did not answer. That was too painful for her to admit, although by her silence, Eva had her answer.

"Does he ever pass out when he is drunk?"

"Sometimes."

"Well let me tell you what you do. The very next time he gets violent with you, when he passes out, you get yourself a good strong sheet and roll him up in it. Take you a carpet needle and some good strong thread. You sew him up in that sheet as tight as you can. Wait until he sobers up and is conscious. Then you take a good bar of new soap and slip it into a sock. You climb right up on top of him and beat the hell out of him with that sock and bar of soap. When you get through, you tell him if it ever happens again you will cut his throat. You won't have any more trouble with that young man."

Fredrick exploded, "Good lands. Eva. I sure hope you don't get mad at me."

"Well that works. My Mama has told me about two different women who have used this technique and they haven't had any more trouble."

Eva was one of those people who looked around seemingly not seeing anything, but taking in everything down to the minutest detail. She noticed what appeared to be a welt on Karen's face, covered up with makeup. She knew exactly what had happened.

Karen sat thinking for a few moments. One could see the resolve forming in her face. She was an athletic woman and she had always been very competitive.

Fredrick stepped back into the conversation. "Karen, if Tom will go to AA and make an attempt to give up alcohol, I will find a job for him. Now he may not like what I find, because I cannot turn him loose in a company truck until he proves himself, but I will find a job for him. Tommy DeVaney always has work. It is good honest work and pays construction labor wages."

"Freddy, Tom doesn't know how to do anything but drive a truck."

"Well, if he can drive a truck, he can probably drive a tractor. He probably can't tear up too much out in the fields that we can't fix. You tell him to come see me when he dries out."

Mary Evelyn was still sitting in Karen's lap. As tears streamed down her cheek, the little girl wiped them away with a napkin. This pushed Karen further over the edge emotionally. She hugged the child and Mary Evelyn responded by hugging her back.

Karen regained control of her emotions and thanked Fredrick and Eva over and over again. She retrieved her hamburger meat from the refrigerator and made her exit with lots to think about. When she arrived home, Tom was passed out in the den. She went to work immediately. When Tom started to sober up he found that he could not move. He screamed for Karen to come set him free. She told him no. He screamed and hollered and cussed. Finally he pleadingly said, "Karen I have to go to the bathroom. I'm about to pop."

Karen had experienced all the violence from her husband she intended to take, and she had her plans already worked out. She informed him that nothing was stopping him from relieving himself. That he could clean it up later. He bawled, pleaded and screamed. Just as Eva had instructed, Karen got her soap and sock and went to work. She, not too hard, but hard enough to be extremely uncomfortable, beat the tar out of him. The neighbors heard him screaming and called the police.

When the police came, they found Tom in his homemade straight jacket. It was all they could do to keep from laughing. They cut him loose. Karen stood her ground. She informed the police that he had just gotten a taste of what would happen if he ever struck her again. The incident was observed by all the neighbors and spread like wildfire throughout the town of Pressley.

Karen's mother had to go to bed when she heard the word at her bridge club, but Karen made no apologies to anyone. Tom knew she meant what she said about "Next time." He immediately signed up for AA. Tom boasted that one day he was going to beat up Fredrick Overall for destroying his family. Fredrick had heard of the threats, but as usual, paid little attention to them.

Fredrick was no small man now that he was grown. He was not athletic, but he was always busy. He enjoyed physical labor as long as it profited something, and in reality, he was 'strong as an oxen'. Tom on the other hand had really become quite lazy and somewhat overweight. He had a beer belly, double chin and looked sloppy He was a far cry from his high school days when he was a running back.

Two weeks after his first AA meeting, he went to Fredrick's office to ask for a job. Fredrick's office was not fancy, but well apportioned. It had a double steelcase desk with the attendant file cabinets and a credenza. It was loaded with computers. The office was neat as a pin.

With hat in hand, Tom approached Fredrick. Fredrick came around the desk and faced Tom, face to face extending his hand. The first words out of Tom's mouth were. "Fredrick, Karen told me to see you about a job.'

Fredrick smiled and commented, "Well, I see you finally figured out who's boss."

This flashed Tom. He figured that Fredrick was referring to the beating Karen had given him, but Fredrick continued, "The sooner us guys realize that, the better off we are."

Since Fredrick included himself in his generalization, it eased the tension somewhat. Tom faintly smiled.

"Have a seat, Tom, and let's talk about this."

Fredrick did not go back around the desk, but pulled up a chair close to Tom in a more casual setting. He didn't beat around the bush.

"Tom, I will find a place for you, but I will tell you up front, your alcohol problem is going to limit your options. Now I have several responsible jobs that I am looking to fill, but quite frankly I don't think you are ready for any of them. I can't put you in a truck because of the liability. I can't put you in a position where you handle receipts because I don't know your involvement with the concrete scam. I can't put you over people because you haven't proven yourself. You will have to start at the bottom and work your way up. That is going to be a bitter pill to swallow. Do you think you can handle it?"

Tom sat thinking for a moment. He had always been a big man in his own mind. He had married into the Turner family. That set him apart from the peons. Fredrick had not left him any wiggle room and Karen was right there to back him up.

After setting reflectively for a moment, he answered. "I don't have a choice do I, Freddy?"

"As I see it Tom, unless you want to start robbing banks, you don't have a choice."

"Well, I ain't got no hankering to rob banks and go to prison. I thought shore I was going a while back. Scared the hell out of me."

"Tom, you have one more hill to climb."

"What's that?"

"You have to go see Tommy DeVaney and tell him that I said to put you to work."

"Tom groaned, "Oh!!!"

"Now Tommy is going to put you on the worst jobs he can find. You picked on him pretty hard when we were in High School, but you prove yourself and he will move you up. You are not dumb, Tom. You can learn and if you try, you can amount to something with us."

Sensing the interview was over, Tom and Fredrick arose and shook hands. Tom went to see Tommy and just as Fredrick predicted, Tommy assigned him to a concrete crew. It was hard back breaking work until you learned the tricks of the trade. Pretty soon, Tom's muscles began to develop in the right places and he started to enjoy the work.

Tom was in a crew of concrete laborers consisting of Bo Walsh and Willie Hudson. Both were huge black men, quiet, and outwardly appeared to be lazy, dim witted individuals until one began to observe closely. Tom quickly began to realize there was no wasted motion about either man. Each knew his job and did it well. If they had a large job, they sometimes brought their kids along to help and they were a delight. When their sons were present, there was a constant stream of chatter that kept everyone in stitches. Tom began to look forward to the time the boys would be with their dads. At other times they simply hired day laborers who in most cases took no ownership for their work and those were hard days. Tom quickly learned there was an undercurrent of depth and stability about these two men. He mentioned that to Fredrick one day when Fredrick came to check on a job.

Fredrick placed his finger against the bridge of his nose, (old habits are hard to break) and simply commented, "Yep, Bo and Willie each have lots of 'walking around sense'."

After he and Fredrick parted, Tom thought about this for a long time. He finally uttered a little prayer, "Lord, please grant me lots of walking around sense." He had to smile to himself as he thought, After all these years, here I am praying to be like the two black men in a position of authority over me. He almost laughed out loud when this thought came to mind.

Karen began to notice that Tom constantly talked about Bo and Willie every evening at dinner. One night after the boys left the table and only she and

Tom were left there alone, Karen turned to Tom and asked, "Honey, you really like Bo and Willie don't you?"

"Karen, they are the best thing that has ever happened to me except you. They are kind, compassionate and not an evil bone in their body. I have never heard one of them use bad language and they chastise me if I do. Yes, I like them. I like them a lot. Fredrick Overall handpicked that crew to teach me. He knew exactly what he was doing."

Karen smiled a faint smile. "I didn't like Fredrick very much for making you work for blacks. I thought he was just making you eat crow."

"He knew exactly what he was doing. I hated him for that at first and started to quit the first day out, but there was just a quiet dignity about these two men that wouldn't turn me loose. They are both good men."

*   *   *

Tom learned quickly and before very long, much to his chagrin, he was made foreman over his own crew. He complained to Bo and Willie that he didn't like this, that he wanted to continue to work with them. Bo simply said, "Mr. Tom, Mr. Fredrick know what he doing. You smart. You been to school. Me and Willie never had much of a chance to go to school. We doing 'bout all we can do, but you can do more. Mr. Fredrick know that. Don't you worry 'bout it. Me and Willie doing better than we ever done before and we happy."

Tom's eyes misted as he took his friend's hand. "Bo, you have forgotten more than I will ever know about concrete. Somehow it just doesn't seem fair."

Willie spoke up. "Me and Bo feel pretty good that we have been able to teach you this quick. You learned real fast. You had a pretty good sized chip on yo' shoulder that first day. Me and Bo scared we gonna knock it off and we have to whup you."

"You two don't know how much I appreciate what you have done for me. You have helped me more than AA and that's not taking anything away from AA."

This brought a belly laugh all around. The three men shook hands and Tom got in his truck and went to take charge of his own crew.

*   *   *

Tom had no idea of all of the things Fredrick Overall was into. Soon he discovered a well oiled machine that ran like clockwork with each person depending on the other to do their job. Crews and businesses worked together like pistons in an engine with each one firing in proper order. He was intrigued and fascinated with Fredrick and Eva's people skills.

Christmas was five months after Tom started working in Overall enterprises. Employees received a nice bonus. Fredrick and Eva passed out the bonuses at a Christmas party for the employees.

Fredrick stood to announce the bonuses. "May I have your attention for a moment? Now don't get scared, I'm not going to make a speech."

There was a loud round of cheers and applause. Fredrick continued, "I am going to leave that for Eva."

Eva jumped up and screamed, "Say, what?"

Everyone laughed. It was a well-known fact that Eva was very shy.

Fredrick continued, "Now Overall Enterprises, thanks to you, has had a very good year. In fact we have had a tremendous year. Our bonus will reflect that this year. We are most grateful to all of you who have made this possible. As in the past, the bonus will be divided among all of our employees on an equal basis. Now I know this has not set well with some in the past, but let me explain. From one of Jesus parables we learned that a certain man with a vineyard paid all of the laborers in the field the same wage although some had worked a much shorter period of time than others. The owner knew that some workers had stood long hours in the sun waiting to be invited to work. He realized their needs must have been great to do this. The ones who worked the longest did not like it one little bit, that these men drew the same wage. What I interpret that to mean was that the vineyard owner knew that each had the same needs to support their families. Now I try my best to pay an honest and fair wage for each job. Some are simply more important and require more responsibility. You make a higher wage. That does not mean that the families of those who make less are any less important and have less need.

"It is my hope that those of you who make the highest wage will look upon this distribution as a way of you helping those who make a lower wage and share the same joy that Eva and I have by sharing this bonus with you."

Fredrick sat down. There was a standing ovation.

Although Tom had been working for Fredrick only five months, he got the full bonus. As the party broke up Bo came to Tom. "Mr. Tom, I'm glad Mr. Fredrick gave everyone the same bonus. I 'magine you needed it." Tom was overwhelmed. The bonus enabled Karen and Tom to plan and provide a great Christmas for their two sons. They would be eternally grateful. Tom and Karen began to slowly rebuild their marriage which had been at rock bottom before Fredrick and Eva intervened.

*　　*　　*

Because Overall enterprises had such a good year, Fredrick and Eva placed over one million dollars in the Mary Overall Foundation fund. Fredrick established this foundation the first year he was in college and used it as a tax shelter. It had grown to five million since Luther and Velma were both adding funds. The McDonalds had been a tremendous success, and it was funding the foundation as well.

Shortly after Christmas, Fredrick and Eva, Luther and Evelyn, and Velma and Bob met as the foundation trustees and decided under Fredrick's coaching that it was time to move on establishing The Mary Overall Memorial Library in Pressley. Fredrick decided to build it downtown across from the courthouse, right on the square. It would take up half the block with parking in the rear. In the back of his mind, Freddy planned to entice the town to build a convention center on the other half of the block, thus parking for each facility could be shared. He owned the entire block plus the property directly behind. This was property that Pressley National Bank had foreclosed on in times past. Since they were now defunct, the property had been purchased at a very reasonable rate. Many in the town had guffawed the fact that Fredrick Overall had wound up with all that old useless property.

When Fredrick announced plans to build the Library, the laughing stopped. Fredrick engaged an Architectural firm in Waco to draw the plans and build a mockup of the building. After the mockup was complete, he had a Plexiglas box made to house the model and mounted this on a concrete table just off the sidewalk at the building location. Folks flocked to the location to gaze at the proposed new building. Most in the town were elated that a new Library was going to be erected in memory of Mary Overall. Her memory had become almost legendary in the town.

Four days after the erection of the model, someone in a four wheel drive vehicle pushed over the table, and ran over the model late one night. Fredrick was called early the next morning. He drove immediately to the sight. The police were there. They appeared to be concerned. Fredrick did not say a word, he simply looked for about 30 minutes with the chief of police following on his tail. The chief was telling him how much he wanted to catch the perpetrators of the crime.

At the end of Fredrick's look, he turned to the chief and asked, "What have you done to catch the person who did this."

"Well, ah, ah we don't have any leads just yet."

"Leads. You need leads. You are chief of police in this town but don't already know who did this. I know who did it. And I just got here. Shame on you! You mark off this area with crime scene tape."

With that Fredrick left. He called Eva on his cell phone and asked her to look up a detective agency he used during the torching of his building. She gave him the number. He called and asked the agency to send a man. Fredrick told the agency, "Send someone who is good at taking tire impression and matching paint. There is a trail of clues everywhere."

Within two hours there was detective in Fredrick's office. Fredrick gave him the name of the person he suspected. There was green camouflage paint on the edge of the concrete table and a tire impression at the edge of the sidewalk. The tires on the vehicle were obviously wide mud grip knobby tires. There was only one vehicle in Pressley that met that description.

The agent took a tire impression and paint sample before he checked in with the local police department. After the evidence was gathered, he and Fredrick went to the DA's office and asked for a search warrant and asked that the vehicle in question be impounded. The four wheeled drive Chevrolet Pickup belonged to the Mayor's, 17 year old grandson and great grandson of Edwin Gipson.

The DA reluctantly issued the order, but before the truck could be impounded, it disappeared. The young man who owned the truck claimed it had been stolen.

+

The detective from the agency was livid, but Fredrick just took it all in stride. Not much missed Fredrick Overall. Fully expecting this maneuver, after they got the court order from the DA, Fredrick had called Eva and asked her to drive out to their farm and park in a spot where she could see the county road and not be seen. He instructed, "Take our Camera with the telephoto lens and get a picture of Ernie Bland's old camouflaged pickup if it passes. Hurry, I suspect they will try to hide the truck at the old Lutcher place."

Eva grabbed the camera and had just stopped her car when the pickup went by followed closely by a Pressley Police car. She got a picture of both.

Eva called Fredrick and told him what she had just seen, a few moments before Fredrick, the detective and the chief of police went to Ernie's home to look at the truck.

Again, Fredrick appeared not to be excited, anxious or disappointed to either the Chief of Police or the detective. He simply called the Texas Rangers after they left the Chief's office and explained what had transpired. The Texas Rangers came to Pressley and were armed with Eva's pictures and a search warrant within an hour of their arrival. Fredrick suggested that they look in an old barn on a forgotten farm the Gipsons had foreclosed on several years earlier. Just as he suggested was probable, they found the truck backed in the dilapidated old barn covered with a canvas tarp. Immediately the DA, Chief of police, mayor and Ernie Bland were all arrested and charged with conspiracy to obstruct justice. It was the end of a dynasty and corrupt politics in Pressley, Texas.

Fredrick had the table and display with the mock up of the library refurbished and put back in place. Within two months, Fredrick began site preparation for the library building. A new Mayor was elected and he was a man Freddy could work with. He was a retired farmer who moved to town. The Overalls and the Browns had been friends for years, and Fredrick backed Troy Brown to run for mayor. Because of his honesty and integrity, he won hands down. The old city council was slowly being replaced by a new energetic, progressive council with members who were excited about bringing in new business. They were also excited about the million dollar library being built in their town. Co-operation from the town took a 900 percent upswing.

*   *   *

Fredrick combined three concrete crews and pulled them off the chicken houses. They were to form a team to pour the foundation for the library. The library was a stretch for all of Fredrick's people. Bo and Willie certainly had not poured a job this large. Tom Williams was scared to death that he would mess up. Jim Hartman who was the other crew foreman was petrified. Fredrick hired a seasoned professional construction engineer for job oversight, and he brought materials expediter and a quality control specialist with him. They were good at their job. Fredrick balked at any more outside people being brought in. He took out an ad in the Pressley newspaper showing a drawing and outlining plans for the new library. He coined a phrase, Pressley Pride—A Pressley Project for Pressley People. Invoices were printed with that slogan on the top of the invoice. It became the trademark of the library construction project and brought out the best in all areas of the work. Every contractor in Pressley got a piece of the action and gave their very best price for their work. The town was more united than it had ever been.

The interior steel structure went up in a matter of days after the foundation was cured. It seemed that almost overnight, the structure went up and the building started taking shape. The downtown area had not been this busy in twenty years. Retirees came out of the woodwork. A drugstore on the southwest corner of the square had more business than it had ever experienced, at least coffee business. There was lots of speculation about "What that little Overall feller is doing now."

Work progressed rapidly. Within the second month, the half basement under the library was well on its way to being ready for the next floor. The walls were built using prefab stand up panels with marble inlays, but all exposed concrete in the walls was later faced with bricks from the old original buildings with a bronze plaque telling which building they came from. It was a stroke of genius on Fredrick's part to save all the old brick from the original buildings. He hired Mexican laborers for days on end to clean the bricks and stack them in separate piles. He had personally and meticulously labeled each pile. It gave the building a historic significance.

Inside work slowed the rate of construction, but one year after the beginning of construction the library was ready for dedication. The closer to the dedication came, the more reclusive Fredrick became. Eva noticed that he spent lots of time at his crying spot. She felt that not only had he withdrawn from the rest of the family, she felt isolated herself. It was a trying time. His Aunt Evelyn decided it was time to have a talk with him. She called him one day and asked if he could have lunch with her. He loved his Aunt because she reminded him so very much of his mother. They met at the Holiday Inn Restaurant in Pressley.

Evelyn had learned some things from her nephew. She did not 'beat around the bush'. "Fredrick, I know you have been busy but that is no excuse to shut your wife out of your life."

Fredrick's middle finger went to the bridge of his nose. He looked at his aunt. "But Aunt Evelyn, I haven't shut Eva out."

"Maybe not Fredrick, but she certainly feels that way."

"Well it is not my intention."

"I know Fredrick, and I think I know what is wrong with you. As the time approaches to dedicate the library, the memory of your mother has come flooding back. I know because I am feeling some of the same emotions. You should have no regrets, but you see, I have to live with the fact that I shut all of you out of my life for years. Don't do that Freddy. Let Eva in and help you through this."

Fredrick sat reflectively for a long moment. He thought back to recent days and the hurt look he had seen in Eva's face. After sorting things out in his mind, he looked squarely at his aunt and stated flatly, "Well, I'll just change then."

Evelyn looked at him studying his face for a moment and then replied, "Well, you just do that."

They each sat with their eyes locked together for a moment and a smile spread across their faces. True to his word, Fredrick walked in after he had made his daily rounds to all the businesses and hugged Eva. He hugged each of the preschool children—William Luther was at school. "Let's all go for a walk."

The kids squealed. Eva looked suspicious, but decided to go along. Fredrick took Eva's hand and they walked to a small spring fed branch behind the old Lane house where Fredrick and Eva often caught crawfish when his mother would come to visit her father and help him preserve food. Fredrick asked, "Do you remember fishing for crawfish here when we were little?"

"I remember. We even ate the dumb things after your mother cooked them for us."

David Marcus set up a howl to fish for crawfish. Eva turned around and went back to the house to retrieve a piece of bacon to use for bait. Fredrick called to her, "Bring some string and a bucket to put their catch in."

While Eva was gone, Fredrick cut three poles from a sapling. Eva brought a roll of kite twine when she returned. Fredrick tied the lines on the pole and tied a piece of bacon on each line.

For the next hour, two of the Overall kids who were still at home and not in school, sat on the banks of the branch and caught crawfish. Mary Ellen watched, but she was too little to enjoy the fun. They squealed, they got pinched, and they laughed until they rolled on the ground. Fredrick and Eva released all of the pent up anxiety they had felt all during the construction phase of the library. The burning of their office building weighed heavily on their minds.

Fredrick finally voiced their fears. "Eva, if they burn this one, I think it will break my heart."

Eva hugged him closely. "Honey, I think you have most of them behind bars now. How can they hate us so? We don't hate them."

"Well, selfishness destroys a person. They couldn't stand the thought of someone having more than they had. If we aren't careful—very careful, it will destroy us also. Please help me guard against that, sweetheart."

"It's not gonna happen to you Freddy. You care too deeply for that to happen. In spite of all its faults, you love this town. You love the people, even the unlovable. *Where love is, hate can never win*."

William Luther came in from school and he joined in the fun. The kids caught a half bucket full of crawfish. Fredrick cleaned all of the squirmy, slimy creatures and Eva and Rosa fried them for the kids. Fredrick Overall was back.

*   *   *

Dedication day for the Library finally came. The dedication and open house were held on Sunday afternoon at 2 pm. Fredrick was to bring the dedication address.

A platform had been constructed in the main foyer of the Library and the room was jam packed. Fredrick had instructed the building maintenance people to open the air-conditioning up full bore to take care of the crowd.

When Fredrick arose to speak, the audience became extremely quiet. Everyone knew that Fredrick would not speak long, and that what he had to say would be meaningful.

Fredrick adjusted the mike, attempted to push his nonexistent glasses back against his face and began, "I had my opening statement all laid out, but I ran into a problem." Pressley had just celebrated its 90th birthday. He continued, I was going to say, Four score and ten years ago our forefathers, but I discovered that line had already been taken.

The crowd erupted into laughter. Giving the crowd time to settle down, he continued, "This is a joyous and exciting occasion for me. For many years now, I have wished to do something to honor the memory of my mother. What could be more fitting than to dedicate a library in her honor? She loved reading. She loved teaching and she loved learning. She was a dynamic woman, a faithful wife and devoted mother.

"In memory of her life, I have selected three pictures of her to be hung in the foyer of this library. Number one,—he pointed to Eva as she removed the cover from the first—is a picture of my mother as a happy child." A picture of Mary as a smiling young girl about eight years old standing barefoot in the sand graced the wall of the library. She had a book in her hand.

"Now you may ask me how I know she was a happy child. Well, if you have ever stood barefoot in warm sand with a feel of the earth coursing through your body, you will not have to ask that question, and she also had a book in her hand."

There were several nods of accent and smiles among the older crowd.

"Books were always a very important part of my mother's life. She often told me that books opened horizons to explore the unknown~ allowing us to go places where we could not otherwise go. She always admonished that books brought out the Don Quixote in all of us, 'to dream the impossible dreams and reach the unreachable stars'.

"The next picture shows my mother as a happy teenager."

Eva removed the cover and a picture of Mary with a beautiful smile covering her face stood before them. Mary was decked out in a drum major's uniform complete with baton. A stack of books on the corner of a table in the picture looked as though Mary has just laid aside her books to pose for the picture.

"How do we know she was a happy teenager? Well, you will have to ask a cheerleader or another drum major about that, but somehow I feel that being a part of something important to this town brought my mother intense joy and satisfaction. I have seen that same satisfaction on the face of my father, my sister and now my brother when win, lose or draw, their team did their best to represent the town on the athletic field. But there again, please note her stack of books nearby. Mom always had her books."

The last picture that Fredrick asked Eva to unveil was a picture of Mary reading to an ugly little scrawny kid with thick glasses. "Now I can answer this one. Mom spent many happy hours reading to the Twerp, forcing me to expand my mind. It seemed an obsession with her—almost as if she knew our time together was limited. I am so grateful for Mom and this gift of an appreciation for books. I sensed the joy that she received from books even as a very small boy. This memory sparked the idea for this library.

"We, my Dad and Aunt Evelyn, Velma and Bob, and Eva and I, as trustees of the Mary Overall Foundation have chosen these pictures of my mother so that those coming into the library will recognize that reading brings happiness. It also depicts that reading is not simply for the young or the old regardless of the stage of our life.

Life happens in stages; with each stage leading up to the next. An unhappy child will more than likely be an unhappy teenager, and an unhappy teenager will more than likely be an unhappy adult. These pictures also point out that life does not stand still. It moves along like the wind. One cannot stop the wind; neither can we stop the winds of time. On that fateful day, Mom did not know that her winds were all blown away. She went to school, taught her class, prepared for the next day, and all too soon, her time on this earth ended. May these three pictures remind us all that we do not know when our wind has blown itself out, and help us all to resolve to live our lives daily without regret.

"One of Mom's greatest joys was reading. She passed that on to me, and it is our hope that the Mary Overall Memorial Library will bring that joy to all who come through its doors. I think Mom would be happy that we have remembered her in this manner.

"So, we, the Mary Lane Overall Foundation trustees, take great pleasure in dedicating this Library in memory of Mary Lane Overall; dedicated to the joy of reading and expanding young minds. This is our gift to the town of Pressley, Texas."

THE END

Edwards Brothers,Inc!
Thorofare, NJ 08086
27 July, 2010
BA2010208